Praise for Jennifer Allen's

BONE KNOWING

"Jennifer Allen's BONE KNOWING *is a powerful account of how families cope with the specter of life-threatening illness and live meaningful, even wonderful lives, under its shadow."*

Kenneth J. Doka, PhD   Professor at The Graduate School, College of New Rochelle
Senior Consultant, The Hospice Foundation of America

*"*BONE KNOWING *is about the intuitive wisdom we all have, but don't always heed. In Jennifer Allen's painfully honest account of her husband's struggle with cancer and his dying process, readers witness Jennifer's efforts to tune in and listen to her inner voice. There we find beauty and transformation, as well as selfishness, anger, old wounds, and guilt. Embracing all of those qualities allows Jennifer to be wholly present for one of the most challenging times in her young life. By viewing Jennifer exposed, 'to the bone', readers reap essential lessons on love and loss, relationship and renewal."*

Lisa Gebo
Cancer survivor and former textbook editor

"This beautifully written, vivid, and deeply satisfying memoir takes us on an intimate journey into the lives of Jennifer and Tom. Theirs is a passionate love story of two people who want to live full out, even in the face of Tom's looming death cloaking all that they do. We see the courage of both of them, as Jennifer takes us through the last days of Tom's life. Those final days are so vivid that we are right there with them.
    It is a remarkable experience to read this book."

Judy Tatelbaum, author of *The Courage to Grieve* and *You Don't Have to Suffer*

*"*BONE KNOWING *will touch those who are experiencing a loved one's serious illness as well as those who have suffered a loss. The author shows great courage by inviting us into her personal life, revealing emotional and practical aspects of caregiving.*

Vicki Nelson
Executive Director of the Compassionate Care Alliance www.CaringResources.org

"This is a "must read" for anyone working with dying patients, their families, and for anyone passionate about living."

Richard Ingle, former Bereavement Services (
Hospice of the Central Coast, Community Ho

Bone Knowing

a true story of coming to life
in the face of impending loss

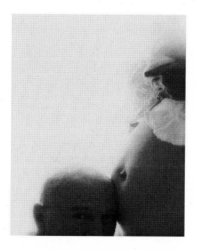

By Jennifer Allen

Library of Congress Cataloging-in-Publication Data

Allen, Jennifer Allen, jujupress

Bone Knowing: a true story of coming to life in the face of impending loss /Jennifer Allen

ISBN 978-0-578-03185-9

1. Allen, Jennifer. 2. Anticipatory grief. 3. End-of-life issues. 4. Coping with loved one's illness 5. Death and dying. 6. Personal transformation. 7. Spiritual crisis. 8. Parenting a grieving child. 9. Grief. 10. Title.

Printed in the United States of America

A note to readers

Memoir is a tricky thing, being left to the perceptions and memories of one person. If you asked other people involved in this story to tell it, this would be a different book. Because Tom isn't here for feedback, I've tried to integrate his perspective without abandoning my own. Most names have been changed to protect privacy. For the sake of organization (and keeping this from being a three-inch thick read) I've consolidated events and conversations, occasionally switching them around slightly, but always with great respect for the truth as I experienced it at the time.

This book is dedicated to the men I've been lucky to love:

Scott Prince,
Thomas Sanchez,
&
my husband.

Prologue

Mid-October 1997

Things are slipping. The most obvious being my husband as he edges into another realm, far from the one I live in.

All too often lately, our newborn's diapers go unchanged, our toddler's teeth go unbrushed, and bills go unpaid. I'm a month late for both the baby and my post-natal follow-up visits. It's okay, though. She's hearty and I'm pretty sure my stitches will disintegrate on their own.

Tom's scraggly hair is low priority. I figure anything beyond keeping his pain managed is frosting. Every time I go up to our bedroom, I can count on a ruse of guilt. It's bad enough I haven't cleaned up his mismatched hairdo after the radiation bald spots have grown back coarse and curly, but his facial hair doesn't seem to know he's dying. It's taking over his fading face, making him look Christ-like. I've convinced myself it's fitting, since he's the closest thing to Jesus in my life.

The calendar reads Monday. While others begin another predictable cycle—brewing coffee, reading the paper, and driving to work—I'm caught in a holding pattern, waiting out an undetermined amount of time in grief limbo. Patience is not one of my strong suits, so I focus on the endless task list in my head: *fill sippy-cup, call pharmacy, dog—oh my god, feed the dog!*

When I check on Tom and the baby, they are asleep on our bed, nose-to-nose. Her chubby little hand lies inside his sunken palm. She looks like a mini-Tom—eyes flaring up at the corners, dark curls, and full cupid lips. For a moment I watch, taken by the beauty of two beings so close to the place we are born from and die to. Grief starts to knock from my insides. It's too big and I'm too busy.

I bustle about, emptying the diaper pail and whisking up empty water bottles when I hear his raspy whisper: "Could you shave me?" I stop, shocked that he's actually talking to me, and not one of the many invisible characters visiting our bedroom lately. But he's looking right at me. I wait, wanting him to ask me by name, just one more time.

"Sorry, the electric razor's broken. I'm afraid I'll cut you with the real kind," I say, turning away to pick up some soiled laundry. It's true. The razor jammed on me a week ago and it made no sense to buy a new one, so I opted a beard for him on his deathbed.

"Fix it." He sounds exasperated. Taking a deep breath like he's preparing for a lap underwater, he says, "Get the shave kit, the small Phillips-head, and a tissue. Bring them here."

My pace is broken, partly because I'm taken aback that he remembers the name of the tool when he hasn't called me by name for over a week and partly because his demanding tone is unfamiliar.

I huff heavily, drop the laundry and march to the bathroom for the requested items. I'm not sure I want our last exchange to be spent fixing a damn razor, but he's insistent and there's no arguing with a dying man.

Quickly, I gather the paraphernalia of male-morning-routine and spread it along his side of the bed.

"Take your time," he says.

As if we have time! I shout in the privacy of my mind, while I search for scraps of anything to pick off the floor. Tissues that haven't made it to the trash, dust balls—anything to keep from stopping.

Jennifer Allen

He waits for my shifting eyes to return to his. "You can do this," he says with certainty. "I'll walk you through it, step by step. It isn't so bad."

This time, I hear him and I am transfixed; plucked out of a speed-grind. These are the kind of words I've been struggling to be calm enough to say to him in his final hours and he's saying them to me. It doesn't matter that it's over a razor, though I'm curious to see where this shaving thing goes. Suddenly, I'm aligned with him—caught up in his world entirely. In these moments no baby cries, no toddler needs help, and no doorbell rings. I don't give God credit for stopping time. This is pure grace; something I've learned tends to happen when hearts are in sync.

Tom lays back into his pillow, watching me as I look inside the razor. Taking a breath between every few words as he instructs me on its disassembly, Tom describes tiny pieces of the machine with accurate precision. It is as if he can see through my eyes. In front of me are about twenty parts all smaller than a dime. It's a miracle I'm not the least bit intimidated.

"Pick up smallest disc . . . lay it on top of the tissue. That's good. Now squeeze one drop of oil on it," he says. He goes on with each and every piece, guiding me methodically. I give in to each step being its own everything. I am reminded of how we used to climb hundreds of feet up rocks to have the insignificances of our lives fall away. Now, it's a razor.

A steady hum responds to the flick of a switch and I'm elated. "It works! I really did it!"

Fixing things, especially small things that require focus and patience, has always been Tom's job. Now it's mine. Carefully, and ever so slowly, I shave him, caressing his throat, rolling carefully over his chin, and gently plumbing the hollows of his cheeks until every bristle is mowed clear. When I finish, I kiss each of his eyelids. Tom smiles, his smooth skin stretches sharply over the underlying bones.

"Thank you," he says, fighting to hold his glossy eyes to mine. I don't wait for my name. It seems so irrelevant now. He knows me far beyond what I am called. Pangs of grief soften as I welcome each one into my heart, sensing that they, too, are children that need tending.

"And thank *you*," I whisper into his ear as I lay along side and watch him drift off into other realms. He has shown me how to be with each moment left until he is gone and how to be with this grief, long after. I only hope I can remember.

Jennifer Allen

Seasons

Jennifer Allen

1

Catch My Fall

Spring 1989

One thing I understand about bone knowing is it chooses me, I don't choose it. The man standing in front of me whose hand is still holding mine in a time warp of milliseconds is significant. My bones tell me so. Trouble is, I'm on hiatus from significant others until—well, until I'm myself again.

Besides, in the few minutes that have elapsed since I parked my truck and spotted this guy dragging a mess of gear through Ed's front yard, I've already determined he's a jerk. Partly, it was the eye contact that fell nine inches south of my face as I approached him, despite there being little worth gawking at.

The clincher was his introduction: "Hi, I'm Tom Sanchez. You must be my bedmate for the trip."

What the hell? His jerk-ness rendered me speechless, until this handshake. Now, an instant vibration coursing through the marrow of my bones has the same effect. *I don't need this.* Arguing with such a force is futile, equivalent to holding back a sneeze in allergy season. Drugs dull it. Been there, done that. But I'm on a clean streak now, so I let it have its way with me. *I don't have to act on it.*

In the very moment contact was made, sexist-Joe-stud with his sox pulled up to his kneecaps morphed into boy-in-a-man-suit finding his way with the female species. His smile went from game-show host to adolescent naivety, pulling to the right and revealing ruler straight teeth that glow against his Mediterranean skin. A neat crease connects his hooded eyes to each temple, like a crow with one toe on each foot. It's not like I'm attracted, in a chemistry sense, but rather fascinated—with all the sensations happening simultaneously outside and in.

Click. My bones instantly tap out a message to my photographer's eye and the moment burns into my heart, as light does to film. If I stash the sensation away quickly, like the many mystery rolls of film sitting back at my apartment in a desk drawer, I might keep it from ever developing. *Who says significance has to mean falling in love, anyway? I'm worn out. This heart stays in the dark.*

"Hi," I offer a vigorous squeeze. His hand is warm and large, though he's only a couple inches taller than me. "I'm Jennifer."

Our hands drop, but the bones and the photo-eye keep working me. His aquamarine polo shirt is exquisite against the purple and silver-green sage growing wildly over the walkway. The violet rope he carries over one shoulder plays off his deep chocolate eyes. An innocent smell of sweet peas drifts between us. Time continues in slow-mo, making it possible to take in all sensations in at once. A dull haze inside is lifting and I'm overcome by how colorful and fragrant the world is.

Ed, my boss-friend, lumbers up behind Tom with a bunch of carabineers clanking from the harness he carries, and breaks the magical moment. "Looks like you two have acquainted yourselves

Jennifer Allen

quite nicely without my help. Good, let's get on the road. It's a long trip," he says.

"Where is everyone else?" I ask. The nausea I fought on the drive over was in anticipation of being among a bunch of strangers for the weekend. One stranger—a significant one at that—might just be worse, especially if this is Ed's idea of a blind date.

"Roxanne is in the car; the others no-showed. Turns out people like to talk about climbing until it comes down to doing it. That's a special breed," he says matter-of-factly, as if he hasn't been telling me for weeks on our drives to photo shoots about the climbing brood he's forming for this trip.

I shoot Ed a suspicious glance out of Tom's view. He returns a blank expression and ducks into the car. If this really isn't a stint at playing cupid, I'm left with synchronicity and that's prime ammunition for the knowing in my bones.

"Cinco de Mayo—time to celebrate!" Tom sings, swinging the last rope into the back of the station wagon. He scoots into the backseat with me and we pull away from the curb.

"Thinko de what?" I ask, instantly sorry that I'm giving a dumb-blonde impression and more so that I even care what he might think of me.

"Oh, it's a Mexican holiday that gives Americans an excuse to overindulge on margaritas," Tom says. He's oblivious of impressions. All he hears is an invitation to talk. And he does just that, telling me about the history of Mexico, interspersing tidbits of trivia about the differences between Spaniards and Mexicans. For one, in the part of Spain his family is from, Castilliano is the dialect spoken with a lisp. His Tio Antonio, who visits occasionally from the Old Country, insists it was the purest form of the language. Tom says the story he's heard is that way back when, there was a king who had a speech impediment and no one wanted to embarrass him so they integrated a lisp into the language and it stuck. As a child, he rarely heard the language as his parents avoided speaking it in an effort to blend into the great Melting Pot. On the occasion they did speak Spanish, they were sure to use the lisp to avoid being mistaken for Mexicans.

"God forbid!" he says, rolling his eyes sarcastically. "You know, I never really got that. People are people."

I'm starting to like this guy—like a good girlfriend.

He promises to teach me how to make a Spanish tortilla, which is more like an omelet than the flat bread I associate with the Mexican version of the word. When we pass through Hollister, he names just about every other building we pass, pointing out his grammar school and the corner market that used to be his family's grocery store. The nostalgia launches him into a slue of funny stories from his childhood. He interrupts himself, and gestures to the billboard we pass. "There's Casa de Fruta—great rest stop when you're traveling with kids. They've got a little train and a zoo . . . even a few buffalo."

Kids? I glance at his hand. No ring. I'll ask later if and when there is an opening. He talks on. Normally, this kind of egocentric male behavior would have turned me inside out and I would have sighed and found a scab to entertain myself with. If he'd been a notch too unaware, I'd have taken sudden interest in Roxanne's happenings and spent the trip leaning over the front seat. Instead, he piques my curiosity. Mundane subjects come to life with his animation. Straining his eyes open for emphasis, his smooth hands choreograph a voice that rises and falls leaving exclamations of silent spaces. Places for me to fall in. The longer he speaks, the safer I feel. Like it or not, something is developing here, starting with the bones and seeping into the heart.

"This is the same route we take to Mono Hot Springs," he says. "Ever been?"

"No, I've barely left the peninsula since I got there. What's it like?" I ask.

"Oh, it's beautiful country up there. We used to fish up there when I was a kid . . . and my girls just love camp there."

"You have daughters?" I ask. Here's the opening I've been waiting for with this mystery man. *Not that it matters.*

"Yes. Jessica is seventeen and Eliza turned fifteen in February. I just can't believe how fast it's gone. It's a cliché for a good reason," he says, seemingly unaware that he hasn't mentioned this very important tidbit.

"So you're married then?" I try to make it sound casual—more a matter of collecting correct information than checking status.

Jennifer Allen

"Was. Well, technically I still am. It's in the works, I guess you'd say." He's rubbing his ring finger, as if in habit, but there's nothing there.

"Oh, sorry," I say and I am. He seems like such a nice guy, after our handshake anyway.

Reading my curiosity, he launches into an explanation of recent life events, attempting the same enthusiasm of storytelling he holds for the distant past only this is too close and not yet a story in retrospect. His voice cracks like an adolescent's and he looks out the window frequently. I'm careful not to change the subject. Sometimes I think I should have been a therapist instead of an artist.

"This must what people call a mid-life crisis or something. I'm forty-three—" he starts.

"No way!" I interrupt. I can't help myself. He doesn't look a day over 30. He smiles briefly, as if it's a familiar response that he usually enjoys, but not now. *Well that settles it: almost twice my age—we'll be great friends I bet. Nothing more,* I think, trying to shoot some reason into my bones. "Sorry, go on."

He hasn't lost his place. "There have been changes . . . too many, too fast," he says, spreading his long, column-like fingers apart as if he's got the mess all organized into five simple events that have turned his life upside-down.

Pinching his pinky he begins. Suddenly he's vague and doesn't have details like he did for impersonal data. He reiterates the separation/divorce as A #1 and I note that it would be a good idea to keep my distance. "Too vulnerable" and "disillusionment" summarize what broke his family and resulted in him returning to a rented room at the end of the day instead of his home.

Moving out must have counted as the second blow as he's cradling his middle finger now. Number three is the bankruptcy of an established dental lab business he had put his heart and soul into building up from scratch—something about getting behind on taxes. He hit the pavement with a new career as a telecommunications salesman where income is dependent on charisma. Seems to me he's got plenty to spare. Though I have to wonder how he comes up with it all when he's smack in the middle of so many losses. I glance at his hands and notice he has counted the job change as number four.

Bone Knowing

11

Then he holds up his thumb: the grand finale of change. I move in a tad too close, not wanting to miss it. "On top of it all . . ." Tom shakes his head as if buying time to figure out how he's going to convey this granddaddy life event. "Back before Christmas," he begins, "Louise and I were shopping for the girls over at Del Monte Center and I got nauseous, like someone had kicked me in the balls—really bad. Anyway, I ignored it and tried to keep on. I wanted things to be the way they were just one more time, before we were over." His voice cracks and he pauses. When he starts again, though, his thumb is folded inside his fist and he's telling me about that Christmas. Something's missing. I can't believe he's going to leave that big number five unsaid.

"What about the nausea? What happened?" The need to know outweighs my concern with being rude.

"Oh," he says looking out the window. "I think it was grief or something."

Okay, then. It's clear he's not going to tell me.

Conversation in the front seat stops and Ed glances back at Tom through the rear view mirror as if to prompt him. Tom ignores it and points out the window.

"Can you believe that giant body of water is man-made? There used to be a whole town under there before they flooded it. That's where the crop water comes from for the San Joaquin Valley." Chatting among the four of us ensues, eventually slowing to silence with the transition of the sky from baby blue, to lavender, to vermillion, to deep purple.

Tom turns to me in the dusky light, resting his back against the door and asks: "What about you? Ed tells me you're new to California. What brought you this far from home?"

"Hmph. Guess I was looking for a place where I belonged; where my art wasn't considered too personal. Graduate school is affordable here and . . ."

"Wait, wait, back up. What do you mean by your art being too personal?"

"Oh, hmm. You sure you want to know?"

He nods eagerly. "Yeah. 'Too personal' caught my interest."

"Well, you're likely the kind of person who could appreciate my work. It's not for everyone and certainly doesn't

Jennifer Allen

lend itself to making a living. Meaning, it isn't the kind of stuff you'd hang in your living room," I say. He gestures me on, like a card player requesting a hit.

"When I went abroad to art school, my priorities changed from making a beautiful product to expressing my reality and beliefs at the time. The beauty was in the common link of human experience. But," I stop myself mid-spiel and look at him to see if he's still with me, "not everyone relates to images this way."

"What if the reality or belief you expressed wasn't that of your viewer?"

I stumble over his sincere interest. "Don't get me started."

"No, really. I'm fascinated with artists. I think of myself as one, but without the paint. The world's my medium. Go ahead, it's a long drive."

"Okay, remember you asked." I explain how sharing an inner truth can be received by those ripe for it, even if they glean a different understanding. He smiles, wedging his chin between his thumb and curled index finger.

I go on: "Well, there's also the part about some of the pictures including naked people."

His eyebrows fly up. "Really?"

"Yeah, it was a series I did on dreams and memories. I painted on the developer so the image appeared liquid-like—surreal. I'll show you sometime."

"I'd love that. Working on anything now?"

"Mhmm. After hours Ed lets me use the darkroom and I've been putting together a show of portraits. I'm trying to show the aspects of each person revealed in our relationship."

"Are you in a relationship?"

"A master of clever segues, are you?"

"Sorry—just wondering."

"It's okay. So, let's see . . . my boyfriend—ex-boyfriend, I mean—Scott. Well, we moved out here together last August, hoping to start over and it didn't work out."

As if to convince myself that I had made the right decision, I list the low points of the seven-year off-and-on ride with Scott, careful to leave out the parts about prison time, suicide threats, and still loving him.

"I'm not even sure how it happened. It was like being squeezed into a reality so tiny that both of us almost disappeared. Every time we got back together, we'd start so sweetly and slip inevitably into our most ugly selves. I couldn't even recognize myself anymore," I say.

"Mhmm," he nods. "How does rock climbing fit into that?"

"I'm hoping it will help me remember who I am. High risk has always helped me edit the bullshit," I answer, surprised to be sharing such intimate reflections with a man I met only four hours ago.

"Yeah, I guess that's what this rock climbing thing is for me too," he says, leaning his head against the window. He turns and gazes out into the deepening darkness and we retreat into our individual worlds of thought.

"What's the matter—you two finally run out of things to say?" Ed teases. "Good timing. We're officially entering Yosemite Valley."

Ed announces the game plan as we wind our way to the site and unload the gear: An early rise the next morning and he and Roxanne will climb while Tom and I take lessons to come up to speed. We nod in response, both of us along for the ride.

Brilliant stars light the way to our tent cabin. The black masses of rock that encompass the valley feel like sides to a giant mixing bowl. I am in it: one ingredient of many. It's easy in this unfamiliar place to surrender to the head-chef, whether it be the creator of the diamonds overhead or the humming in my bones. Right now they feel like one in the same.

Inside the cabin, Tom asks, "Are you okay with this? I was just kidding with what I said back at the house. I'll keep to my own bag, really." He unrolls his sleeping bag along one side of the remaining bed.

"Of course," I say, trying to sound matter-of-fact, as if I always sleep platonically with older men. Nestling into my bag, I turn away from him. Sleep comes easily. *A good sign.*

Our bodies contort with slumber and morning finds us facing each other, getting the bed head and bad breath discomforts out of the way while we're just friends. Tom's arm rests on my hip.

14   Jennifer Allen

He smiles, "Woops, habit. I guess."

Call me naive, but I believe him.

We scramble to change our clothes, and while I'm struggling to uphold modesty, Tom is completely uninhibited. I glance over and see his pale olive chest scattered sparsely with black hair. I spot a large red mole, or is it a nipple? He catches the double-take and says, "It's a third nipple, want to see?"

"No, that's okay." I'm embarrassed. More so because I'm grading his body, comparing him to Scott, who is twenty-one years Tom's junior and buff by bloodline. Scott's body hair streamlined itself neatly into a sexy arrow that pointed directly into his jeans. Ah, but this time, my bones aren't concerned with attraction, age difference, or life circumstances. With Scott, potent mid-adolescent chemistry got us started and bone knowing kept us coming back together through two prison sentences and a bunch of broken dishes. It crept in steadily and was hard to track with all the blazing passion running through me. Something important needed to play out and I played it right to the edge of my being. Now that I think of it, I'm quite exhausted following these damn bone cues. Maybe this isn't a good idea. I try and focus on learning to climb.

Our class consists of the instructor, Tom, and me. Again, the four others who signed up for the class didn't show up, leaving us undiluted contact. I'm beginning to suspect a conspiracy of match making; if not by Ed, then by the Universe. The three of us stand at the base of towering granite as sunlight creeps its way down the face. My fingers are numb with cold and inept as I fumble with the rope, trying to imitate the instructor's basic figure eight knot. It's the first lesson on a steep learning curve and I'm already lost and feeling small. My throat tightens too easily. I've been postponing a good breakdown. *Not now, please!*

"Here," Tom says, empathetically, as he holds up the rope and demonstrates the knot in slow motion, "You try."

"I just don't get it!" I say, exasperated.

"Like this," he puts his hand over mine, guiding it. "Now the rabbit goes in the hole, see?" he explains.

What a great father he must be.

"There . . . you have it!" he says.

Our smiles meet and hold. "Thanks, man," I say. Tom winks and then faces the rock, where the instructor taps his toe, smiling at the two of us.

"Climbing," Tom says.

"Climb on." The instructor prompts me with the responding protocol.

"Oh yeah, sorry—climb on!" I say, giving Tom the okay to proceed up, as if I know how to catch his potential fall. Our instructor, Ted, had us practice on a boulder before the first climb. Even though it makes sense to me that the rope attached to Tom's waist harness travels up sixty feet to the top of the climb; through multiple carabineers which then connect to three separate pieces of protection wedged into cracks; and returns down the face and is squeezed through the belay device on my harness; I'm not 100% confident that the whole rig up will work if he slips. Ted reads me. He ties a knot on the side of the rope that has already passed through the belay ring a few feet ago. If Tom should fall and I panic, he'll come a few feet shy of hitting the ground.

"I want you to be comfortable with his fall," Ted says. "Always keep your right hand on the rope after the belay ring. You might want to pull the rope around behind your hip for extra friction. I'm going to give you his full weight. Are you ready?"

"I guess so." My forearms are already burning from keeping a serious grip on the rope. The last thing I need is to be responsible for anyone's death.

"It's a yes or no in this sport," Ted says.

"Okay, yes. Yes, I'm ready," I say.

"Hey, Tom." Ted calls up the rock. "Could you peel off the rock and just sit back into your harness for a minute or two so Jen, here, can get the feel of catching a fall?"

"Yes I can." Tom lets go of the rock and sits back—no hesitation. His harness is tight around each leg and waist, creating a bulging triangle at his crotch. He dangles about twenty feet above me like a kid on a backyard swing. On the other end, the rope is taut against my harness giving me a wedgie.

"Let the equipment do the work," Ted says. "He's fine, see. You don't have to hang on so tightly." Ted gives Tom a thumbs-up and cues me: "Belay is on."

"Belay is on!" I holler up, giving him the code word to continue.

"Climbing," Tom yells down.

"Climb on," I say my part without prompting.

Tom leans into the rock and continues scrambling up faster than I can feed the rope through the belay ring. "Rope!" Tom calls down, waiting for me to catch up. It's hard keeping up with the speed of fearlessness. He really believes the world is a safe place. I crook my neck back and watch his every step, hoping his secret will be evident. When he reaches the top, he hoots and then sticks his butt out over the edge and sits back into his harness, just as we've been taught. I'm ready for his weight, diluted through numerous devices, and let the rope back through the belay ring a couple inches at a time. Tom tap dances off the rock face all the way down. When his feet touch ground, he hoots again and Ted high-fives him.

"You're going to love this," he says, unclipping his harness.

I start out with the influence of Tom's bold attitude. The first thirty feet of the face are easy: smear my rubber toe against the slightest texture and get a reasonable size handhold and lift up: repeat. The stone is cold and my breath makes little white puffs that hang in the sunlight. I'm like the little engine that could, until I can't. The problem is I've looked down. Any confidence I had gained dropped out the bottom with that one glance. Suddenly, there are no handholds big enough. *This monolith is a flat as a frickin' pancake!* I look up above to where I'm going to no avail. It's too far away and means nothing if I can't get unstuck here. I've been in one place too long and my muscles are beginning to quiver in fatigue.

Petrified, I scream down to Tom, "DO YOU HAVE ME?"

Tom's voice echoes up "I got you, fall if you have to, it's okay!"

Oh, a man that I can fall into; a man who'd catch me. My tense body longs to go limp, peel off the rock and see what happens. It's enough to know that he has me.

Clinging to the rock face, so intimate with nature, I inhale the granite's vapor and hold it in, trying to pull myself back to what's in front of me—to the absolute present moment minus the "what if's" and "oh, shit's". *Life-lesson-learned-from-rock-climbing number-one: Anything but in-your-face-present time is apt to let in panic.*

Releasing a hand, I scan over pieces of lichen and find a tiny solid lump, just big enough to press against with two fingers while I free up a millisecond of balance to find a toehold. There's an indentation big enough for the point of my climbing shoe that can hold me if I keep pressure against it. I press fully onto this foot and lift upward to a new horizon, where a generous handhold awaits me. *Just take what is here and trust the next move.* The mantra drips continuously through my mind. It begins to form a groove and before long, I'm moving nimbly up the rock. Pulling myself up onto the final shelf, I smile with satisfaction. Little pieces of me are coming back into view.

Throughout the rest of the weekend there are ample opportunities to involuntarily test Tom's promise and scream "FALLING!" and feel the full sensation of the fall: stomach in throat, tickling electricity up the legs, a surrender, and then the jolt of the rope and the scrape of the rock. A little painful, but I'm saved from an untimely death by my climbing partner at the other end of the rope. Trust is coming back to me and I'm greedy, I want it solidly inside me before I leave this magical granite bowl and re-enter my life "as-is."

Roxanne's car breaks down just as we are leaving Sunday afternoon. Turns out it will take a few days to get the part delivered into the valley and we get an extension. *Thank you,* I smile to myself, unsure of whom my prayer of gratitude is directed and yet, knowing it is heard.

On Monday, the four of us climb Half Dome, ascending into thick milky fog. A flicker of doubt catches me off guard and the inner arguments ensue: *Don't you even consider getting into another relationship! What if his divorce is messy and not over? What about a future? He's older, not likely up for another batch of kids. What if he dies before you? What if you just end up doing the same dance you did with Scott?*

My bones don't often take the word form, usually they just hum along with absolute certainty, tainting my perceptions while they wait for the rest of me to catch on. Only now that they have my heart on their side, they have more pull. The mantras of the

Jennifer Allen

weekend answer doubtful questions with complete confidence: *Just take what's here and trust the next move. Hold nothing but absolute in-your-face presence.*

Tuesday, Tom and I repeat part of the hike solo, stopping to take in the beauty of a corona formed in the mist of the falls. He looks up, squinting, and then back at the wet rocks, as if to find the source of the phenomena. His skin is dewy and sweat gathers on his upper lip.

"Incredible, huh? Now we know the secret of what's at the end of the rainbow—the beginning! And to think we would have missed this."

"Mhmm," I agree, caught up in the fairy tale scenery and his very real observations.

We are standing close enough for the tiny upright hairs on my arm brush against his. He turns to me. "I don't want to miss anything."

"Me neither," I say, seeing my reflection clearly in his dark eyes. We lean into each other simultaneously and kiss. His mouth is unfamiliar, with hollows where I expect protrusions. I explore without judgment, open to something new.

Hikers stumble upon us and we part, smiling hard at the line we have crossed. In the cabin that night, Ed and Roxanne sense something is up and tease us mercilessly. We ham it up with heavy moans, while we give each other sensual foot massages, and then retreat into our own sleeping bags.

It's Wednesday night by the time we return home to the Monterey Peninsula. Under the dim humming of streetlights, we make our game plan.

"So, what do you think? Should we just do this thing?" Tom asks.

"Yup, just do it," I nod, smiling. A few days of being on the rock and we know that staying frozen in one place with searing pain in the calves and pervasive doubt in the mind is a sure fall. It's a lesson we're both ripe for and we apply it to our lives, agreeing that it would settle better with us on our deathbeds to have fallen in the midst of taking a chance. Both of us believe we're lucky people.

Jennifer Allen

2

Finger Number Five

Summer 1989–Spring 1990

We've been taking things slow and steady. On the weekends Tom doesn't have his girls, we climb at the Pinnacles with Ed and Roxanne. At least once a week, we meet for lunch. Daily, we leave sweet voicemail messages for each other. Though we tried to get physical on a makeshift bed in the back of Tom's truck after our weekend in Yosemite, it was awkward and we decided not to push things.

I request yet another extended lunch hour and head out to meet Tom for a picnic at Jack's Peak. When I get there, I find him sitting on a bench, looking out over the bay, like any other businessman taking a mid-day break to enjoy nature. The contrast turns me on: He in his pressed white collared shirt, polk-a-dot bow tie, and shiny black shoes against the Monterey pines and a soft clean breeze. I come up behind him and kiss the tip of his ear.

"Well, hello you," he says with the affection of a long-time lover. "Here, come sit. I brought us some roasted eggplant sandwiches, guava juice, and fresh figs from my parent's tree in Hollister. Ever have fresh figs?"

"Nope. Do you eat the skin?" I ask.

"Here, I'll show you." He carefully peels back the thin purple velvet, revealing an orb that looks more like a small ball of white yarn than food.

"Wait." I take the fig into my palm and straddle him. "Now show me."

As I feed him, he suggestively tongues the soft insides, slurping them up as they give way and then devours the remains. Fig juices drip down his chin and I intercept them with kisses. Warmth flutters through me. I'm taken by surprise. *Philosophical chemistry is enough—a relief in fact. But physical chemistry too? There's got to be a catch.*

When I return to the photo studio with flushed cheeks, Ed raises a disapproving eyebrow. A seed of doubt is planted. Finally, on the way to a photo shoot, Ed comes out with it: "I think you and Tom are a bad idea." When I press him, he says, "Well, you're young and coming off a rough relationship and he's old and coming off a divorce. Need I say more?"

"And . . . big brother Ed? Tell me something I don't already know," I say.

"Well . . . actually, I can't. It's not my place." He leaves it there, bound by the confidentiality of the men's group they are in together. And so do I, even though I'm sure he's referring to that mysterious fifth life event that Tom dodged talking about on the way up to Yosemite. It only takes remembering the vitality I feel when I'm around Tom to let any past baggage get in the way. *Catch or not, I'm riding this one out.*

After a scorching day of climbing at the Pinnacles, Tom and I shower together and devour a homemade vegetarian meal at his place. Richard, his housemate, is out for the evening and we pretend the humble abode is ours. Tom stands at the sink, slowly and methodically washing each dish I bring to him. I go from the

Jennifer Allen

table to the compost, into the bathroom, out to my truck for my day-planner, and back to clearing dishes—all with a toothbrush hanging from my mouth.

"Wha?" I stop mid hand-off when I notice him watching me.

He smiles, "Oh, you're just so fun to watch fluttering about here and there, touching down and taking off, so lightly . . . like a butterfly."

"And that means what?" I muddle around the toothbrush, looking for trouble out of habit.

"I enjoy watching you do your thing, simple as that. Sorry I brought your attention to it. The last thing I want to do is change you."

Some unplaced hunger inside me is satiated, with those words. "Oh," I say. *He likes me, as-is.* Immediately I feel bad for wanting to style his hair and push down his knee socks.

He wipes the last dish thoroughly and throws the dishcloth over his shoulder. "Butterfly. It's perfect," he says to himself and joins me on the couch. We nestle into the sofa with bare feet in each other's laps. The oak strewn neighborhood filters a cool, earthy breeze through the living room window. Tom strums his guitar and sings a Beetles song without reticence: "Blaaaaaaackbiiiiiiird fly." Nodding to the song list, he encourages me to choose the next number. Most of the music was popular before I was born or when I was in kindergarten and not yet cognizant of the top 40. He pauses.

"I know, here. How about Bonnie Raitt's 'Love in Nick of Time'?" he offers, recognizing the dilemma.

"Yeah, I like that one."

He sings through a smile at first, but by the time he sings the final lyrics, it looks like he's going to cry. Carefully, he places the guitar against the couch and takes my feet into both of his hands. He has a look of seriousness I haven't seen yet.

"There's something I've got to be honest with you about before we go too far here," he says.

My mind races and makes a beeline to sex: *Uh oh, an STD or maybe HIV. It's okay, we can get tested and be vigilant with condoms and . . .*

"I have cancer." He blurts it out before I can fix any of the possible problems I anticipate.

"Oh, okay," I respond, matter-of-fact. Numb and instant loyalty rises to veil the spurt of acid that has involuntary contracted my gut in alarm. Tom talks on, but I can't hear details because I'm trying to hear the gut-signal. It's saying: *No, no, no! See, I knew there'd be a catch, a bad fucking catch! Bail now, you don't need this!*

Tom's voice mixes in. "Early stage . . . bladder cancer . . . diagnosed just after Louise and I split in January." I see the optimism in his face and hear my tenacious loyalty argue its point: *Do you leave just because he's sick? It's not like he wants to die. People like him survive.*

My thoughts are affirmed by his words: "I'm going to be fine. I'm researching alternative treatments so I can maximize my chances. Doctor says I could get 20 years and I'm counting on a full recovery—bladder intact."

A flurry of figuring thoughts pull me back inside indulging themselves behind the even eye contact I offer Tom. They begin puzzling together the nausea of the fifth-finger event, Ed's raised eyebrow and Tom's over confidence on the climbs. Under all of the chatter is a heart that doesn't care about sense-making. It listens to bone knowing and the language of synchronicity. And it votes me in. *Ah, he's all about living,* it says. My shoulders soften in the relief of knowing he will live fully until he dies, no matter when that is. For far too long, I tried to sell Scott on life, while half-expecting to find him dead, by choice. Tom doesn't need a sales-pitch for life; he *is* the sales-pitch.

In my heart, the image of our initial handshake in Ed's front yard, eases its way front stage. It makes for a clear knowing and shoots strong roots from heart to bones. The voice of my wisest self comes through. *This is your ride and you know it. Get on. It's going to be a fantastic journey. Don't judge it.*

"I'm knocking it back with a local chemotherapy . . .this tube gets inserted up my penis and —"

"Just do it, right?" I interrupt him with my final consensus. "I'm still in."

Tom looks surprised. He hops up off the couch, disappears into the bedroom and returns with a joint to share in celebration of our first major hurdle overcome.

"The prognosis is good. A few rounds of local chemo and some healthy lifestyle changes and I'll be good to go." His voice takes on the tone of the suave salesman I've seen network for telecommunication contacts at restaurants where we've met for dinner.

He lights the joint and speaks on the inhale—a trick of the seasoned pot-smoker, "I really think alternatives are the way to go. I'm not into rearranging body parts with surgery." He squeaks out, holding his breath and passes me the joint, looking up to see if I'm still with him. He exhales a smooth stream of smoke and resumes with a grounded voice: "I'm planning on living, Jen."

"Mhmmm." I nod, chest puffed up with smoke. *You want to live, that's all I need to know.* Exhale.

A good high takes hold and we laugh hysterically, poking fun at our new common enemy. It surprises me that cancer's dark threat doesn't hover over me once the pot wears off. Even the next morning, when I wake to the waterbed sloshing as Tom gets up to make his signature pancakes, I feel like an eagle soaring so high, all the details of the earth become a beautiful collage. I slip into the flannel nightshirt he's left out for me and mosey up beside him in the kitchen.

"Another beautiful day," I sing.

He turns into me and kisses my forehead. "Indeed, Butterfly, let's make the most of it."

Our big coming out as a couple is Tom's 44th birthday. One night he was telling me how he had always shared a birthday with his younger sister, Monica, as a child. I convinced him to make up for lost time this year with a big bash. Partly because I've adopted his attitude of going all out now that he can't take a full life-span for granted and partly because birthday celebrations are in my blood.

In my family, birthdays serve as excuses to gather the masses. Everyone brings a dish to share and my mother always makes the cake from scratch. I'll carry on the tradition with Tom.

Together, we plan a potluck beach party and invite his old friends, men from his therapy group, his daughters, and a few people from my circle. I make him a carrot cake with real cream cheese frosting and buy party hats, knowing he'll enjoy both.

With so few hours logged in together, it's strange how easily we fall into feeling like we'd known each other forever. Stranger, I'm sure, to his daughters. I've been nervous to meet them. It's a big step. If Tom weren't serious about being together, he'd never let me meet them. When they arrive, he jogs over to them and hugs each of them long and tightly. Then he walks over to me, flanked by twin-like teen beauties, only one has golden brown ringlets to her waist and the other has chestnut brown.

Tom introduces us and the girls are polite, shaking my hand and smiling past the difficulty of assimilating Daddy with another woman—a young woman. I feel bad. Not for falling in love with their father, but for all they've been through at such tender ages. They hang together throughout the party and gravitate toward family friends who are making similar adjustments. At the very least, it looks like they've teamed up together to weather this change. That night, as we are packing up his truck, Tom marvels at their bravery.

Most of the summer passes without further contact with his daughters. Tom takes care to schedule our time around his time with them. It's okay by me; that's exactly the kind of man I'd want fathering my child down the line. The mysterious chemotherapy treatments add a gap in our time together as well. Tom told me the medicine goes in via his penis and that's enough for me to figure he's avoiding potential impotence issues. It could be that he's protecting me from the reality of his cancer, too. I wouldn't know, though, because we don't manage to get very far with this conversation without an enthusiastic subject change. Same thing happens with the talk of meeting his parents. There is always some reason it doesn't quite happen.

That is, until today. On the way home from climbing, we made our usual pass through Hollister, where Tom's parents still live in the house he grew up in. We stopped for a beer at the San Andreas Brewery. Tom swigged down the last of his brew and said: "How about we make a quick visit by my parents place?"

Jennifer Allen

"Like this?" I asked, showing off the latest scrapes on my forearms and caked dirt under my fingernails.

"Of course! We *did* just climb," he quipped.

"Yeah, but . . ." I tried another angle. "They don't know we're coming. And we have beer breath."

"Jen, you've wanted to meet them. Let's do it," he insisted.

"Yeah, but . . ." What I've wanted has been confirmation from Tom that he's not ashamed of our relationship because of my age. The dirt and dried blood is minor compared to my status as the girlfriend.

"Okay, sure," I conceded.

Now, we here: the "meeting the parents" moment is about to happen. I spit my gum into a wrapper and wedge it into my pocket as I open the car door. Ed smirks. He's having a great time as a fly on the wall to the whole shindig.

Tom's mother opens the screen door as if she's expecting us. "Tommy?" she says, shading her eyes to the afternoon sun.

"Mom, hi. We've been over at the Pinnacles climbing. Thought we'd drop by for a minute," he sounds casual and just a tad sales-pitchy.

"These are my climbing partners, Jennifer and Ed," he says turning back to us.

Well, that was handy, I think. *What happened to partner, as in girlfriend?*

She gives Tom a pressing stare as she extends her hand to each of us and says, "Mrs. Sa . . . Stella. Come inside."

We pass the wall of family photos, over the massive heating grate to the living room, where Stella points us to the couch and sits in her matching Lazy Boy, alongside Tom's dad.

"Well now, who have we got here? His dad says, hitting the remote to mute.

"Dad, this is Ed, the man responsible for getting me up on the rocks. And this is Jennifer, the woman I'm dating."

Now I know Tom means business with us.

Stella gives her husband the same hard stare. He's grinning from ear to ear.

"Well, hello Jennifer," he says looking over his glasses, "And Ed."

"Michael!" Stella glares at her husband, until a smile breaks through. "Kids," she looks to us, though I'm sure she means me. "The figs are ready. They need to be picked or they'll go to waste."

Ed and I follow Tom's lead and rise. "Here," Stella says, as she fumbles for the tray of Hershey's Minis on the coffee table. "Have some candy before you go out."

Tom scoops up a couple of Snickers acting as if he actually eats this stuff. I'm reminded of my instant regressions every time I get around family, only it usually takes me 2–3 days to fall back into old habits. Michael, Tom's dad, is still looking over his glasses when we all file out to the fig tree. Tom leads us in the routine: pick, sit, eat candy, and then leave with a grocery bag full of stuff from their fridge. As we leave, he holds my hand. Within a half an hour we've jumped another relationship hurdle. The nagging worry that I'm Tom's last-ride-plaything is quelled, for now.

With the meeting of his parents and daughters out of the way, we have a renewed our just-do-it motto. Tom is flying high with possibilities as if he's finally the captain of his own ship. When Ed tells us he's meticulously planned a 700-foot climb up West Crack in Tuolumne Meadows as the next challenge in our rock-climbing careers, Tom and I are on board before he finishes the safety angles.

Not one ounce of worry is spent pondering whether we are experienced enough for it until the day of the climb when the four of us are dispersed among a few pitches 40-160 feet off the ground. Roxanne is one pitch up from the ground and one pitch below me, the last of our party to ascend the tricky overhang, and she's dead weight on the rope. I'm anchored into the rock and standing on a pretty generously sized ledge, so holding her in place until she gets her focus back isn't a problem. Until ten minutes pass with no movement. Then, I decide to start hauling her up one squat at a time.

"I can't do this!" The wind has picked up and her scream is hardly audible. I try yelling up to the next pitch where Tom and

Jennifer Allen

Ed are perched waiting and likely wondering what the hold up is, but the wind takes my voice elsewhere. I'm in over my head, because Roxanne is in over hers. I don't know how to let her down to the ground with the equipment at hand. My thighs are burning as I cinch a foot or two of rope through the belay ring each time I squat. When she finally clears the ledge, she's shaken and wants out of this adventure. It's too late, though. Her panic easily taps into mine about being too far in to turn back with Tom, and now I'm wide awake to what I'm getting into on the rock and in the relationship.

"Keep your eyes on the rock and trust the rope," I say, sending her on up another pitch with the best advice I know, for both climbing and life. Roxanne places one trembling hand on the rock and then another; then a toe into a crack, a lift up onto a wobbly leg and then another hand. There's a fine line between trauma and excitement with this sport, and I'm hoping she crosses over to the latter before the day is done.

What's supposed to be a challenging six-hour climb and walk-off has become an almost impossible twelve-hour marathon of waiting on scrimpy ledges, 40 to 600 feet up, for three other climbing partners to face their demons, then take on my own. By evening, I'm immune to heights and as I scamper up the final crack, shoving my hands in and pulling out and up, racing against darkness and cooling temperatures. On the plateau, the stars brighten against the cool navy sky and it feels like we are more a part of that world than the one far below. And we're looking at exactly that fate if we don't come up with a game plan quickly. Our choices are to huddle close for the night and risk all of our lives with hypothermia, or risk one life by way of semi-protected down-climb to secure a rope for the other three. Ed is weighted with responsibility, trying to plan the safest option. Tom is soaring from achievement and a little too giddy for the situation at hand, "oooohing and ahhhing" over the asteroid showers overhead. As we stand together, shivering and dehydrated, we peer into the black abyss below us, backlit from the moonrise. Tom offers lightly: "I think I'm the best candidate here. I'll go."

When he says it, I know exactly what he means because I'm thinking the same thing. Not that I want his life to be at stake, but it already is. It's clear we both understand this. Tom crabwalks with his butt scraping along the granite, into the darkness. I watch him disappear over the edge with the rope trailing behind. If he falls, Ed has him on belay, only with no real anchor to the rock. They're both at risk. Ed feeds the rope steadily until there are only a couple yards left. There are a few quick tugs and then, from the sheltered side of the rock, we hear Tom shout: "Off belay!"

We take our turns down-climbing into the black void. When it's my turn, I'm surprised that I feel absolute peace. The change in temperature as I move into the shadow of the moon, the feel of every slight outcropping under my palms, the smell of cooling rock—even the subtle shades of darkness—are vivid and envelope me completely. To die, or not to die, is no longer the question. There is no question. I move slowly now, giving this peace a chance to absorb. It's a strange phenomena that the closer we get to safety, I have a growing affection for the "not to die" option. Many pitches later, when we make it to the valley floor and start joking about how well it worked out that Tom has cancer, living returns to rank number one priority. Only now I know that Tom's death, or even my own, for that matter, won't kill me.

In September my sister Amy returned home to Maine just hours before the Loma Prieta earthquake hit. I'm not sure if it would have sealed or killed her decision to move out in the spring. It was scary in the moments when nothing was predictable, not even the solid earth I've come to count on when all else is in flux. I'm certain her fear, like mine, would have melted with the way people have come together in this crisis.

For fifteen seconds of ground-buckling, window-quaking movement, I braced myself in my bedroom doorway. The phone rang just as the movement let up. It was my dad. He was watching the World Series from back East when the T.V. cameras began to shudder and he picked up the phone to check on me before the lines were overwhelmed. "I'm fine," I told him, "That was one wild ride!"

In the hours since then, Tom has come over and we've listened to the radio together by candlelight and learned about the highway and bridge collapse up north. People have died in this

Jennifer Allen

wild ride—many of them. Somberly, we walk through the pitch-black streets, down to the warf. It's the first time I've seen the stars so vividly since that night up on West Crack. The neighborhood is foreign without the humming streetlights and traffic noise. The sea lions sound excessively loud without the chronic noises blocking them. People are out mulling around in the streets, fully disguised by darkness.

As we come upon them, Tom asks: "You okay? Is your home okay? I heard they're having a big barbeque down on the pier. Can't be sure how long the power will be out so they've got to move the perishables. You ought to come check it out."

Shadowy outlines move in close. Some of the voices I recognize: like the Japanese woman who lives in the apartment building behind me and calls out the window to her daughter each evening. Most I don't recognize and I wouldn't ever, if it wasn't for Tom and his knack for bringing people together. He regularly steps over the line between trauma and excitement.

We share a glass of red wine by candlelight at a table in the middle of the pier, where a few of the restaurants have maneuvered themselves outside with makeshift barbeque pits. One grill is lined with fresh salmon, another with pork. The smoke from both mingles among the low voices of people who have gathered to make the best of a bad situation.

A tear—just one—leaks out the corner of my eye. "People died awful deaths this very evening and I feel so grateful. I don't mean because they died, but because we are alive and so are all these people around us right now."

Tom smiles. "I know what you're saying. Isn't it curious how we recognize life best when it's aligned beside death?"

"Yeah. I just wish it didn't require the juxtaposition," I say raising the glass to Tom. "Blessing on those who have passed. May we who live drink kickin' lemonade and taste every drop."

"I'll drink to that," Tom says, squeezing a lemon wedge into his water glass and taking a savored sip.

For now I feel lucky that Tom's cancer has pushed us into knowing something many couples don't: Time is limited— we all die. It's a bittersweet fact that keeps us tasting the lemonade in this relationship.

Bone Knowing   31

It's very Tom-like to want to show up on my parents' doorstep as a first meeting. We get discounted tickets just after Christmas and land in Boston where it's below zero and the snow banks are higher than any Tom has ever seen in Tahoe. Tom is elated with the white scenery as we drive up 95 and not the least bit nervous. When we get to Kittery, just a few miles short of York, he just has to stop and have me take a picture of him beneath the "Welcome to Maine" sign. We have lunch at the Quarter Deck and order a Monte-Christo to share and two clam chowders.

"Now *this* is chowdah!" Tom says, snorting up the steam over his bowl. I try and think of other tourist destinations to bring him to because I'm not sure how this is going to go over: the surprise meeting and all. I've been a challenge to my parents since back at sixteen when I begged them to let Scott live with us while he worked things out with his family, so dropping in and expecting to stay at their place with my boyfriend, who's just a few years their junior, isn't out of the realm of possibility. On the phone, they are enthusiastic for my new love, though I can hear the underlying concern about his age and health. Tom is chomping at the bit to meet my family, so we go directly there, park at the end of the driveway, and tiptoe up into the garage for the full-effect. Dad's truck and his school bus are parked outside and Mum's mail delivery car is in the garage, with chunks of ice still adhered to the yellow reflectors on top.

"Here goes!" I step in front of Tom and knock.

"Come on in!" I hear Mum call from the kitchen. She opens the door at the same time I do.

"Jennifer Lynn! What! How?" Mum pulls me in and hugs me and Dad swiftly closes the door to the frigid draft and to Tom.

"Wait, Dad," I say into his shoulder as he hugs me.

There's another knock. With a confused look, Dad opens the door. Tom stands there laughing and thrusts out his hand. "Hi, I'm Tom Sanchez."

"Mum, Dad, this is Tom," I announce, taking his bag so he can greet them.

"Leo," Dad says pumping Tom's hand. "Sorry, didn't see you there," Dad laughs along with him. *So far, so good.* Really, how could I expect anything less from my parents.

"What are you two doing? How did you . . . oh, I'm Edith," Mum shakes Tom's hand.

"We came over 2,000 miles for that moment, right there. That was great!" Tom exclaims, pleased with the door-in-the-face part. He's probably constructing a future story as we speak.

"Come on in. Here let me get your bags." Dad hauls our luggage out of the way. "Can I get either of you a beer?"

"I'll have one, thanks Dad." I feel like a genuine grown-up whenever he includes me in the liquor call and this is a particularly good time to be perceived as an adult who makes her own decisions. Joyce and Larry come down from their studio apartment over the garage when they hear the commotion. They've met Tom while contemplating a move out West and have fed Mum and Dad nothing but praise for him ever since, so we aren't starting from scratch. We all sit around the bar in the kitchen for hours, while Tom sweeps them up into his charismatic storytelling. Even I'm glued, listening to him retell the West Crack adventure. Amy comes home and hugs Tom like he's a long-lost relative. Come New Year's Eve he's an integral part of the family, dealing out cards for the blackjack game with his party hat and white suspenders. When we leave, he makes the rounds with hugs and my parents seem to understand why I take such wild rides.

With the exception of Tom's ex-wife-in-progress, Louise, who is too angry to consider ever meeting his *young* girlfriend, we've met each other's key players. Tom has salvaged a handful of friends from his own circle after their separation and has blended seamlessly into my eclectic group of friends from art school who independently moved out West after graduation. We reunite for beach parties on a regular basis. It's unbelievable to me that Scott came down for Thanksgiving with a bunch of our common friends last fall. As crazy as it makes him to see me with someone else, he admits Tom is okay. Since then, he gave up his spying trips and started planning a move back East. It's clear, even to him, that Tom and I are committed for the long haul.

Our first anniversary is upon us and it seems only natural to make plans for a future together. The problem is: We have an unsaid rule in our relationship of not planning too far ahead, as if neither of us wants to jinx the cancer. But I'm young, with a full life ahead, and I want to know where things are going. I tell him this when I call and make a date to climb the wall down at Lover's Point and talk.

Tom pecks me on the cheek when we meet and averts eye contact. Something is up. Scaling the wall, we talk climbing shop all around the topic we came here to discuss. It's the first time I've felt nervous and dread around Tom. I can't tell if it's me waiting for him to drop a bomb or if it's him feeling pressure to make a plan. Eventually he says: "I'm taking six months to travel Europe and write—two things I've always wanted to do."

I drop off the rock wall into the sand, feeling his words like a blow to the solar plexus. In his conflict-avoiding ways, this is as close as saying it's over as I imagine he'll get.

"Oh."

Our first awkward silence comes to be.

He continues to climb, keeping his focus on the next hold. When he comes to the end of the wall, he hops off and walks toward me, digging the chalk out of his nails.

"I'll go in August, when the lease for my room at Richard's is up. I've just got to do this, Jen."

I nod, "Mhhhm," and turn away. Now I'm certain I've been just been a filler in his crisis. *Shit.*

"Jen, listen . . ." he pleads, following behind me as I gather my gear.

"I've got to go," I squeak out, briskly walking away. *I* don't get dropped. Especially by an *older, sickly* man who has already promised to catch my fall. Back in the safe-haven of the tiny room I rent in the house I share with two wild and sweet men, I swear bone knowing is all a bunch of crap. For days, I feel lonely and rejected, until the cancer implications start to flood in, if only to salve my bruised heart.

I'm off the hook. *He knows he's not getting through this cancer alive.* I consider the possibility that he's trying to spare both

Jennifer Allen

of us a loss and gather evidence: The promise of survival swiftly shifting from twenty years to twenty minutes last summer on the West Crack climb; and the way he treated chemo like having a period. He'd come up with excuses not to see me until his body regained pace with his libido, thereby keeping his cancer to a convenient theoretical idea that had us living in the now and not something that had real, physical consequences that might scare me away.

When I've worried, he has pacified me with the promise: "I'll get at least twenty years, Butterfly; full to the brim."

Instead of realizing there would be an illness dragged out over the horizon of my bright future, I thought: *Twenty years, hmmm. I'll be forty-four. That's old enough to raise our kids and handle the loss of a spouse. He'll be sixty-five and that's old enough to die.* It was all so far off.

But now, lying alone in crisp cotton sheets night-after-night and reveling in the simplicity of my life, I begin to peel back the blinders of the potential mess I'm getting myself into. Maybe his plans that don't include me are my ticket out. All of my best arguments for bailing fall on deaf bones that know better. *It's as simple as this: It's your ride—get on.*

Knowledge that comes by way of bones doesn't waste its time trying to convince head-thoughts that this is a no-brainer. None-the-less, reasoning must have its say and it opts for a desperate elimination of the barrier to our future: the cancer. I resort to the God of my youth with prayers that I'd have scoffed at from the safety of my latest theories. The "Universe" that had taken *his* place in my late adolescence is too big for personal accountability. My pleading needs a force with a bearded face. *All right, I get it. I'm supposed to be with him. So I'll respect the cues you shoot through my bones if you do your part and let him be healthy. Let him live. Please? I'll be your best fan. I'll convert, repent, and praise you on street corners—whatever it takes . . .*

Negotiations with the Daddy-God are ongoing. Meanwhile, I miss Tom. I realize how much enthusiasm for the simplest of life pleasures he ignites in me. A giant spider crawls up the windowsill and I'm not terrified. I want to answer one of his many calls and tell him that he cured me of my phobia by introducing me to his pet tarantula. Instead, I leave a voicemail for him asking if he wants to try a re-do of the scene we had last week at Lover's Point, keeping any lilt of need out of my voice. He calls back immediately and I let the machine take it.

"I'll be there," he says.

I'm scaling the wall when he arrives so as to avoid the awkwardness of a hug if we are not "us" anymore as I've suspected. He reads me and begins a traverse climb. "Hey, you," he says affectionately when I look his way.

"Hey. How are the Europe plans coming?" I ask between strenuous moves.

"Great. Actually I'm glad you're talking to me again, I've got a bunch of questions for you about Florence, seeing that you're practically a native there."

I laugh and remember how much I like this guy.

He covers a litany of subjective questions, engaging my memory and love of the place. "Florence sounds like an artist's haven. Wouldn't it be something to go back there?" he asks.

"Yeah—on both counts. Maybe I could overlap with you for the Italy part and be your tour guide."

"Really?" He sounds genuinely enthusiastic.

"God, I'd love to. But I don't want to edge in on your quest," I say.

"You of all people understand the needs of the artist to have space to create," he says.

"Of course. Look, if this is something that is important to do alone, I understand. It's just I thought when you first brought it up, you wanted maximum space; as in an end to what we have going here."

"No, no, Jen. It's more that I don't want to forget my dreams of traveling and writing. It's all too easy when I'm here wrapped up in you. And you've been talking about going to grad school. I don't want you compromising your dreams either."

I'm getting the picture. I wasn't too far off with my first hit, only this time bones prevail over pride. "Tom, you're the one who is always saying it's possible to have it all. Why can't we fulfill both our dreams together?"

"Good point," he says. I never get sick of hearing his cliché response. "Okay, let's have it all, but I call first," he says, grinning and then turns his gaze to the lavender and gold sunset. "I can lend you a little money if you want to come for the full trip. The house sold and I'll have my half by then."

"Nope, I'm good," I insist. "I've got the money put aside for school and I can replenish it later. Waitress jobs and colleges aren't going anywhere. Besides, I know how to do Europe on a shoestring budget." A hopeful smile pushes through as I look down, wiping the coarse sand from my hands. The distance between us closes as we sit together on the beach, sweaty and spent from our games.

"It's not that I didn't want you to come in the first place, really Jen. I just don't know if this whole thing is fair to you," he says smoothing the sand between us. It's obviously more than a trip to Europe he's referring to.

"Why don't you let me decide that? I'm not a child." I turn to him and smirk, "Close though!"

He laughs and presses my hand to his mouth, kissing it. "You're more of an adult than most people I know. It's just . . . this could get sticky."

"Yeah, I know." I hear myself gloss over the "sticky" implications. "When I said I was in, I meant it."

"God, you're amazing," he looks to me with wet eyes.

I feel amazing—even Goddess-like, in that moment. The best part is that he sees it.

"So, you'll have me along?" I ask.

"I'd love nothing more than to take this adventure with you, Butterfly." He leans over to hug me and we end up lying in the sand, making out like teenagers. "We" are back and ready to head into unknown territory.

Jennifer Allen

3

New Territory

Summer 1990–Winter 1991

For the next month we eat together at my place nightly, spreading maps over the dinner table and plotting a full circuit road-trip around Europe. We agree to do it freeform. The only reservations we make are the flight and rental car. As we close down our separate lives and prepare to leave, it sinks in that we are entering a trial marriage of sorts, as in 24/7 togetherness. No escape hatches for six months. I'm eager to see what our relationship is made of. I double take the scene of Tom's antique furniture contrasting with my eclectic yard sale bargains in the storage unit before I pull down the door. If this is any sign, it looks like things will be interesting with us, though they might require a tweak in our perspectives to appreciate. I'm hopeful as we drive to the airport and launch into new territory together.

The second leg of our flight is delayed overnight, leaving the passengers to bunk down together amidst luggage and rows of divided chairs in the waiting area of the J.F.K. International Airport. Tom is like a kid in a candy store—so many people to talk to and not enough time to make the rounds. He tries anyhow, going about comparing itineraries and listening to any pointers world travelers might offer. Well into the night, I wake to reposition myself and hear him talking religion with an older Jewish gentleman. In the morning, Tom brings me into their fold and introduces me as his partner. It's not just a P.C. term; it's literally the way we have operated. Everything is 50/50.

Thanks to Tom's social graces, however, I owe a word to every aisle passenger on the way to the bathroom. It makes for a full bladder and a longing for the return to the privacy of a window seat. By the time we make an approach to Paris, Tom is on first-name basis with the crew and a third of the passengers. Everyone applauds as we circle over Charles de Gaulle Airport, preparing to land. The flight attendant announces that we're catching the culmination of Bastille Day. Tom points out the window at a spray of colors illuminating the dark sky just above the city lights.

"Look, Jen! Fireworks! What a welcome, huh?" He says, curling in his bottom lip to hoot a whistle. Everyplace is a potential party and he's invited. I marvel at how easy it is for him to engage in life. Meanwhile, I shuffle through our documents meticulously and tuck the traveler's checks into a purse under my blouse.

From France to Sweden, my dimples cramp from smiling so hard at the sight of Tom's never-ending awe of everything new. He brings out a forgotten imaginative enthusiasm in me that, as a child, wasn't always convenient to getting five little girls to church on time. We sit on benches, swigging good wine from the bottle and ripping bread from warm baguettes, while we make up elaborate dramas about each passerby.

I want only to live from this place with you, I think, watching him and feeling the delirium of the wine and seduction of a romantic life.

Jennifer Allen

The next day comes and the one after that, and slowly but steadily, his quixotic nature leaves me holding the maps and planning our next move. Tension begins to vacillate between dimples and brow as I weave between idyllic trust and skeptical logic. It feels like a battle of heart and head and he has the former well covered. Eventually, I make a neat niche for myself 18 inches north of the heart and become the relationship's designated worrier. I figure that I have years to be in the heart place and he may not.

When we arrived in Sweden a month later, there's respite. We stay with Johanna's family. She and Sonja were my art school roommates a few years back in Florence. Being with them breaks the pattern Tom and I have established and he's unusually pre-occupied with making a game plan for his treatment. I suspect he's hiding symptoms. When I ask he answers, "Nah, never felt better!"

He stays behind to contact a well-known Italian oncologist who specializes in bladder cancer while Johanna, Sonja, and I take a drive out to the southeast coast, where Sonja's family has a cabin. The wind whips our cheeks a bright pink as we walk the beach and talk. The afternoon sun is low, and as we drive back to Lund, I realize how much I miss friends and time to myself. As much as I love being with Tom, 24/7 is too much. In a few weeks we'll stay in Florence for a month. Then we'll both have space to be the artists we've dreamed of being. Until then, I'll take time to go for runs alone and sketch.

Tom greets us at the door of Johanna's family home as we climb the stone stairs. "Hey, good news! I contacted Dr. Tancredi." He grabs the basket of apples from Johanna. "We got by between his English and my Spanish—close enough to Italian I guess. Anyway, he'll see me!"

"Oh, that's great, Button." I peck him on the lips.

He's eager to give details.

"Yeah, he concurred with my ideas, Jen. He's got a lot of patients in the same boat and, get this, he says many of the men who get the surgery in the early stages regret it."

"So they *live* to regret it?" I say, smiling at Johanna and Sonja. Their faces break into ease, but Tom's becomes serious.

"We didn't talk longterm outcome," he says.

Of course not, I think. Tiny resentments are catching up with me, though I thought I was completely supportive of his decision to forgo bladder surgery before we became "us."

He goes on, "The *point* is that he understands my plan and he's willing to assist me with chemo for the road." My women friends duck out of the kitchen.

"Good. Really, I mean it." I try to speak from the part of me that knows the significance of this success for him. I hug him. The solidness of his chest feels affirming.

"I told him I'd check in a few weeks after Czechoslovakia. He's in Aviano at the base of the Alps, not too far off course from Florence. We've got a plan." He pats my back, as if it was his own.

In Czechoslovakia, we stand in line for hours waiting for our turn with the healer. Danielle and Tom whisper back and forth, getting straight what she is to tell the man. It's a crisp afternoon with fall leaves blowing around like confetti against the dull grey buildings of Brno. If nothing else, Tom deserves some major brownie points for even showing up.

It started when Danielle visited her aunt, Tom's co-worker, back in the States the previous spring and Tom readily invited them both to dinner, always eager to learn about other cultures. Danielle had told us about a renowned healer who would be passing through her hometown in late October and Tom nodded affirmatively saying: "I'll be there."

Yeah, right. I thought, smiling in agreement as if it were one of those let's-do-lunch-sometime pseudo promises. But by God, he has pulled it off! For a moment, I see the rock-solid will behind his dancing jester façade and I dare to believe anything is possible with him, even a full-on cure.

The assistant motions us into a small, rust colored room, where we sit in three of the five metal chairs opposite the healer, who sits in trance. Other than his eyes being at half-mast, he's ordinary: just another sixty-something, heavy-set man with an untucked shirt, baggy pants, and silver hair creeping out of every skin surface except his head. Danielle begins to tell the assistant about Tom's condition when the healer raises his hand flat toward

Jennifer Allen

us. He lowers his head and takes a low, guttural breath. A clipboard and pen arrive on his lap by way of his intuitive helper and he sets off into a frenetic scribble, his hand and breath perfectly choreographed. The three of us lean in, mesmerized by his motions.

"Tick!" We jump in unison when he strikes the board with the pen to mark completion. The assistant exchanges a glass of water for the clipboard and motions us into the hallway.

"What does it mean?" Tom asks anxiously when the assistant comes out of the tiny room and hands over the drawing. I look over his shoulder at a tangle of lines and make out a vague human figure with concentrated circles around the abdomen and stray scribbles wandering around the body.

The assistant begins in English: "You have illness. Whole body—in blood."

"No," I say automatically "it's in the bladder only." He cocks his head to my comment, shocked that I question the healer.

"Sorry, you go now."

"Danielle, talk to him! I don't think he understands." I urge her to find a different answer. Tom stands, silent, staring at the picture. Danielle offers the home-language to petition for a better outcome. The man speaks hurriedly as he ushers us out into the street where the line is long and people look hopeful in their desperation.

I look to Danielle for a hint and her wide young face contorts in disbelieving wrinkles.

Danielle turns to Tom: "I'm sorry. He's what in your country is called a medical intuitive. He gives diagnosis, not treatment" Her eyes well up. "He thinks the cancer has spread. I'm sorry Tom."

Tom snaps out of a daze. "Doesn't matter, he's wrong. He doesn't know *me*. I can handle the healing part." He folds the paper and slips it into the back of his journal. Tension is high, with Tom clinging to hope and Danielle and I trying to shake the big "D" word out of our thoughts.

Tom claps his hands then rubs them together briskly.

"Got any casinos around here?" he asks.

All three of us know he needs an affirmation of his good luck, something to prove he can beat the odds. Danielle walks us through narrow alleys and points to a small brown door, hardly discernable from the building around it. She leaves us there and goes on to the church for prayer. Tom's odds need all the help they can get.

The door opens into a room full of noise and color muted by cigarette smoke. Tom cashes in a week's worth of his half the hotel money for more chips than he can carry. He joins a blackjack table as if he belongs there and places a hefty bet. I stand behind him with my fingers crossed. He wins big. *He'll live. Healer, schmealer.* And then he loses big. *He'll die. The healer man has a knack for knowing.* It goes back and forth all night and I'm exhausted by the roller coaster of hope and fear. In the end, he breaks even and I'm glad he knows when to walk.

"Well, consider that free entertainment!" he says, tossing up a Czech poker chip and swiping it from the darkness as we walk back to our room. *Good enough*, I think. Maybe this means he'll live *with* the cancer. The healer hadn't said he'd die.

We leave Czechoslovakia, just as the cold catches up with us and Tom's chemo vials run low. From an Austrian hostel, Tom calls Dr. Tancredi to cash in on his offer. The doctor speaks to him as if he were an old friend: "Tom, you come. We'll see whatta we can do. Okay for you?"

The next morning we laugh easily as we pack up the car, unaware until then how strained things had become with us during the time in Czechoslovakia.

"Forget the healer, bring on the meds!" Tom jokes as he pushes our tiny Peugeot Jr. to 150 kilometers per hour, in hopes of making it to Aviano by nightfall. We'll stop for a day or two, get his medicine and head to Florence, where I'll take Tom around my old 'hood and show him the best kept secrets of Firenze.

I close my eyes to the blur of dead grey trees lining the highway. Nostalgic memories from three years ago, when I was last in Italy, come to life behind my lids.

It seems like a lifetime ago since I left Scott at the Rome airport and launched into the transformation I was ripening toward. At twenty-one, I realized that if I didn't blossom the bud pushing forth, driving me out of my skin, I knew it would die and take part of me with it. I'd end up bitter, holding everyone around me hostage in resentment. It was my last year of art school and I needed to escape the influence of everyone around me: my instructors, my friends, my family, and even Scott, so that I could birth the artist and the woman I was to be.

A flyer posted on the college bulletin board had caught my eye. There was a woman on it, standing on a hillside in front of a blank canvas, poised to paint the first stroke. She looked out over the red-sepia city of Florence in the valley below.

That's where I need to be. In no time, I had the exchange program worked out. My parents knew it was important, otherwise I never would have asked for a loan. Dad didn't understand *why* and tested my determination.

"Now, Jeff (short for Jennifer when you're expecting a son), why does it matter where you are if they're the same classes?" he asked.

In the end, it was probably a combination of Mum's unslaked wanderlust and my unwavering resolve that convinced him to dole out money that was likely earmarked for other important things; like the weddings and educations of their four other daughters.

The leap scared Scott, so I invited him to come along with me before the semester began for a *practice* honeymoon. It was his first time out of the country, and probably his third out of New England. He was pushed up against his edges in foreign territory, which made for irritation and indulgences in wine to obscure the fear into something comfortable.

We got drunk together in Salerno and took pictures of ourselves naked. I set my camera on the sink, unraveled the thirty feet of cord and placed the rubber bulb into his palm so he could control the shutter. We wrestled playfully. *Click . . . Click . . . Click.* He captured the last of "us" before inevitable change took its course. When the honeymoon was over and we kissed goodbye at the Rome airport, I knew the pictures would serve as reassurance for him during our months apart. I feared they would be sweet nostalgia for me. Once in Florence, I developed the photographs. Blurs of merged bodies caught in motion surfaced under the red light of the darkroom. There was no telling whose body was whose. That was both the delight and the problem.

In the company of my new housemates, I began to extricate the "me" that had been lost in the blur between Scott and I. Johanna and Sonja were my Swedish housemates. They spoke perfect English, knew their heritage and called women, women (and not girls). Fast bonds were established. We met at bars after class and took to the backrooms for quiet where we discussed politics, art, and men over cappuccino. The bud inside began to open. When I picked up my camera and took to the streets, I shot from this budding place. If something from the unfamiliar outside culture resonated with the internal landscape I explored simultaneously—I pressed the shutter. My pictures showed the impact places and experiences had on me. Seeing graffiti on every unsupervised landmark helped me define my goal: To be marked by the place and return home changed vs. marking the place and return as the same woman I arrived as. It wasn't until the cathedral shoot that I understood it was a two-way street.

During an art history class field trip, I scoped out the Cathedral of Santa Maria del Fiori for possibilities. Jesus pointed down at the bible from a huge painting behind an altar and looked out at me. Compassion emanated from his expression. It was permission enough. After class, I returned to the silent nave with camera gear, waited until the coast was clear, and moved behind the velvet ropes to the altar. I lay my journal atop the bible and opened it to blank pages. Jesus' eyes seemed to follow me, consistent with consent—even encouragement—on my path of discovery. A five-second exposure at the candle-lit altar was all I got before a guard spotted me and demanded I leave.

"Mi dispiace," I apologized, folded up the tripod and skulked out, before a scene could be made.

I wasn't very different from the graffiti artists, really. I mixed myself up with the place and made a personal dialog with it through the images, only I took the evidence with me. It occurred to me then, that the ideals I had for returning home and finally loving Scott "as is," mood swings and all, had been a one-way street: me being impacted by him without considering myself in the mix. Just like with the images, I realized it had to be a mutual

Jennifer Allen

process, otherwise it would be empty. Whether it was art or relationships, I knew I must cop to my part of the exchange.

The thesis I returned to the states with at the end of the semester was a collection of hand-painted black and white photos with personal items: a bra, a toothbrush, bed sheets and the like, strewn among cultural symbols; the two coming together to create a new meaning. Once the reflection of my young soul's blossoming was etched into me through the art expression, I cleaned up my personal affects and moved on.

It was the same with Scott. At the summer's end, we packed up whatever personal belongings we could fit into a roof-rack U-haul and headed to California. From the moment we got there, he teased me whenever I wanted to try something new: go to a poetry reading, sign up for a dream-work group, or buy a conga drum. Anything different from what he grew up with back East was coined *"Californian,"* a.k.a. hokey. Meanwhile, he sat on the couch in front of the T.V. with a bong on his lap all afternoon, determined not change. To tell the truth, he looked a bit more the Californian stereotype than I did and my pointing this out only infuriated him. Other than our walks down to Gianni's Pizza and our yard-sale scouting on the moped, good times between us were dwindling. Our record skipped more often over the same dust balls and I found myself beginning to fade with each hopeless cycle. When I rallied up the last of my voice and called for change, he threw things. *Time to clean up and head out.* I swept up the broken glass, drove him four hours north and left him with his only acquaintance.

It was my blossoming that killed us—and that's exactly why we had to end. I remind myself that this round, I have a chance to grow in the fertile atmosphere of Florence with the encouragement of a mate. This isn't just Tom's dream we're living; it's mine.

"Hey, Jen. Wake up, we're here!" Tom rouses me out of thought. As we make our way into the small city, I direct him to the art school, pointing and reminiscing as we go.

"See that hole in the wall place over there . . . that's Mario's—the best trattoria in the city if you ask me. And cheap." We rumble through narrow cobblestone streets lined with hues of yellow-umber buildings.

"Medici Palace at three o'clock. School's just up ahead."
Tom pulls into a side-street and we get out, taking full breaths of
Vespa exhaust and fresh baked bread—a scent so uniquely
Florentine.

Being alumni pays off as the school's director readily
hooks us up with a villa on the upside of the bowl that the ancient
city sits in. It's the cozy basement of an old Signora's home, with a
fireplace, white stucco walls and French doors that opened to a
view of the city beyond an orchard of persimmon trees. Tom sets
up his writing corner and I unpack our luggage into the dresser and
our toiletries in a bathroom we share with two German women
who rent the first floor.

Just four days of walkabouts and we are completely
oriented with a routine: espresso, fresh chewy Tuscan bread and
jam; followed by a few solid hours of touring on foot, a visit to the
open market to get our meal fixings, window shopping over the
Ponte Vecchio and back up the hill, with a pit-stop at the corner
Tabac for our daily purchase of Kinder Eggs. We cook up late
lunches, open our eggs, savor the chocolate, assemble and add the
intricate toys to our collection, take siestas, and wake fresh for our
creative endeavors: Tom's writing and my painting.

And then it's Wednesday: the dreaded treatment day. Tom
is back on a regular schedule with the chemo now that we've got a
hearty supply and a predictable place to administer it.

Our neat little routine is broken by the undeniable evidence
of Tom's cancer pushing to the foreground, yet again, reminding
us why we we've been living all-out and treasuring every sweet
moment. We end our walk through the lush Boboli Gardens early
and proceed through our routine, only it feels mechanical. In the
kitchen, we unwrap our eggs, savor the chocolate and occupy
ourselves with the clever little toys inside, as if to postpone the
next part.

"Well, time to glove up, I guess. You ready?" I finally say,
the sweet chocolate taste fading.

"Yup." Tom goes to the bathroom and washes his hands for
a long time. He returns naked from the waist down and opens his
chemotherapy paraphernalia box. I watch him methodically unfold
the cloth, lift out a long tube and lay down on the bed.
Painstakingly, he catheterizes himself, snaking the rubber tube

carefully up through his penis and into his bladder, expertly stopping as he meets each sphincter, breathing deeply and whispering: "That's it now, release . . . good . . . thank you."

I strain to keep my attention on my nurse job of preparing the potent brew of chemotherapy. Ever since Paris, when he let me in on this very real part of his cancer, I have felt entirely taken by his exposure. It is the closest I have felt to him yet. I re-read the directions for the twelfth time and simultaneously feel my heart well up with love. I've risen to the occasion for the task he has assigned me and it's about the only area of my life where I am meticulous.

"I'm in," he says.

I hold up the vile of vermillion hope: "Here's to your health!" I say, carefully pouring every last drop into the tiny funnel. I watch it move into his body. When the tube clears, he waits, then gently backs it out, and hands it to me. As I receive the weaponry on a wad of paper towels, I deliver it to the bathroom where I rinse them thoroughly and then pop them into a boiling pot on the kitchen stove. I've got the whole routine down to thirteen minutes. Pulling the gloves off inside out and tying them up in a plastic bag, I join Tom.

He lies still with his eyes closed, talking the medicine into his body and telling it to feast on any cancer it finds. The afternoon's peach-pink light flows in over him. Sitting alongside his body, my hands hover over his abdomen. My gaze softens looking out the French doors to the muted orange rooftops of the city just beyond the persimmon trees, bright with ripe fruit. There is beauty and, at the same time, the ugly reality of Tom's cancer. A bridge begins to build between the contradictions as I imagine the colored light from the outside enter through the top of my head, rush through my heart, pick up the love I'm feeling so strongly for Tom in this moment, stream down both arms with it, and send it all out through my palms—where it radiates into his body, healing wherever I direct it.

In no time, the palpable energy between my palms and his body is humming, confirming there is more to prayer than pleading. I am not asking for anything; rather I'm opening myself as a delivery service, like the rubber tube is for the chemotherapy.

We stay together, eyes closed and breathing synchronized, lost in time as we know it, until the clock goes off 45 minutes later.

"I could feel you in there," he says. "Thanks." He gets up to release hoards of dead cancer cells into the toilet. At least that's how I imagine it works.

We spend the evening exercising our creative juices. I feel an unusual ease; a clean emptiness that comes when something dreaded is realized and it's nothing like the monster it was imagined to be. Cancer is a condition, fleeting or not, that lives in the man I love. That's it.

Somehow the simplicity of this frees me up to see the blue spaces between the persimmon tree branches so vividly as shapes of their own. Painting them, I'm pleased by the contrast and compliment of the orange fruit that defines them. Each has its place. I delight in this little wisdom dropped onto me. I am not seeking to make meaning in my art as I had three years earlier in this same place. Interestingly enough, meaning reveals itself as I follow simple pleasures of blue and orange.

Frequently now, as I paint, meditate and practice laying on of hands with Tom, rushes of peaceful elation come over me. All this and more, without the assistance of good weed! Surely I'm becoming a poster child for natural highs.

Surprisingly, Tom's enthusiasm for my self-discovery chills when he realizes I've found a replacement for our shared ritual of pot smoking. A tiny, invisible wedge forms between us because, not only am I sold on au-natural peak experiences, I now have a towering soapbox to view him from. What I see is Tom slowly killing himself by continuing to smoke. This contradiction isn't sitting well, like the blue sky and orange persimmon had.

"Life's too short," he casually replies when I try selling him on the longer route to his destination of life highs.

"Hmph. Well that sure makes sense. May as well make it a little shorter," I say, rupturing our comfort bubble. The comment slides off Mr. Easy Going. Again, I'm up against the irony or being bugged the hell out of by the same quality that I admire about him.

"Anyway, it's about the quality. It's about enjoying the time I have," he finally adds.

A wall of silence stands between us. I feel the tension of a tightly held paradox that neither of us wants to grapple with. Tom

Jennifer Allen

breaks its hold, saving himself from having to face the implications in choosing quality of life over quantity.

"You know, Jen, I need this for my pain and nausea from the chemo. It's *medical* marijuana for me."

I bite the inside of my mouth and nod numbly. "Yeah, okay."

That's it. We have hit our ceiling. I am angry that he isn't the life-lover I thought he was and now I want to know whom it is I'm really dealing with. I want to see all of him—his doubt, his fear, and his rage at the invader in his body; not just the quality-of-lifer who never breaks form.

Fear has the better of me. A month of settled life in Italy and another in Spain over the holidays makes this spontaneous side trip across the Straight of Gibraltar to Morocco feel like a tight corkscrew on a roller coaster. Foreign was exciting in Europe. Here in Morocco, it's downright scary. It's been over an hour and still I haven't scored any pain relief for Tom. All of the signs are posted in Arabic and I haven't seen anything that looks remotely like a pharmacy symbol.

Children in the street pretend they have machine guns and shout "Keel Juj Busha," as I pass. Men sitting around small tables at outside bars follow me with their eyes. There are reasons. One: I'm a woman out with no male accompaniment in the evening (in Capri stretch pants I might add). Two: I'm one of the few Americans I've spotted since we arrived a couple days ago. Three: As of yesterday, President Bush has pushed his ultimatum and Operation Desert Shield is now Operation Desert Storm. To top it off, Tom is writhing in a bout of unexpected pain back at the hotel room. I can't tell if it's the cancer or bad water. It's getting dark and I don't dare go further into the Medina to find ibuprofen. At least I've landed a couple liters of bottled water.

Back at the room, I find Tom curled up screaming into space: "You're trying to kill me! Get away from me!"

I freeze, scanning the room without moving my head. Adrenaline is pumping through me full-bore now. I'm sure someone is going to jump out with a gun. But the room is empty. Rushing to Tom, I'm confused. Then I see the pipe and the bag of dense charcoal-like blocks on the sink. The resin smell suddenly stands out from all of the street aromas I've come in from. He's tripping on something—probably hashish.

"Tom, it's me, Jen. I'm here with you. No one is trying to kill you. You're safe." I force my trembling voice into a soothing tone. His body quakes and his eyes shift about wildly. It's as if all the fear that had rolled off him up until this point had been stored in a compartment that only this drug had the key to. He lets me hold him, though he doesn't seem to recognize me. Visions of hauling a strung-out Tom to our car in search of a hospital in a country full of American-despising folk run through my head. I'll give him until morning to snap out of this paranoia.

He heaves as I pull him up over the toilet. The Special Moroccan pancakes we had for lunch make an *especially* big mess on the lid before I can get it open. We spend the night in the bathroom with me holding his head up over the lip of the toilet and wiping puke off his mouth. Doubt rises, yet again. *What the hell have I got myself into?*

When he wakes late into the next day and recognizes me, relief prevails. Not without harbored anger. Tom taught me by example how to let the small stuff wash over me without leaving a residue, but this one is sticking like tar. Paying the last of our unhidden cash to exit, we promptly leave Morocco by evening, moving on from the "event" with a minimal explanation. Nonchalantly, he mentions his desperate effort to kill the pain in his back resulted in a street corner purchase of hashish.

Tom has always told me to be careful what I wish for. I'm getting just that: a glimpse of his underbelly. It's becoming apparent that it's not only his physical pain he medicates; it's his emotional pain. Still, we haven't talked about what the healer said in Czechoslovakia, though I've seen him open his journal multiple times and unfold the drawing with scribbles running through a figure like veins. The last time it happened I caught his eye and said, "Does it worry you?"

"No." he said, folding the paper back up as if I'd caught him in the wrong. I should have known better than to ask a yes or no question. I'm really the only one he has to talk to for these six

Jennifer Allen

months and I'm only hearing roses. Something is getting stuffed. Neither of us can afford it leaking out through episodes like the one at the hotel room the other night.

For moments at a time, my heart and bones rule with gentle reminders: *Remember what you know. You love this man. Is there anything else more important?*

Reason cuts in abruptly: "Yes! A future to love him in. That means coming clean, dealing with his demons, consideration for my future, planning . . . blah, blah, blah." It's the same old speech.

Bones steer clear of rational thought. Instead, they, like my heart, wait patiently for the tiniest of openings, to be heard and remembered, once again.

Jennifer Allen

4

Anticipating

Spring 1991–Spring 1992

Six months abroad is enough. We return to the states and settle
into a new house on a postage stamp sized lot in Seaside,
California. The crime rate is intimidating, but Tom insists that he's
been watching it improve dramatically over the past few years
from the neighboring white bread town of Monterey. It's what he
can afford with half the proceeds from his family house and one
grand European trip later. And he's sure this house will double in
value over the next decade. That's the longest span of time I've
heard from him, outside the placating twenty-year promise, and
I'm off and running with it.

Our life as a live-in couple is beginning and I feel hopeful. A new house, without history is the perfect place to begin. Chemical smells of freshly laid carpet still linger and there are no oil stains tarnishing the concrete driveway. Our first day, we walk the neighborhood and Tom introduces himself to everyone in earshot. The door of the tiny box of a house next to us opens and out walks a thirty-something year-old guy, his hand extended as he intercepts us.

"Nice place you have there. I'm Carl. Welcome to the neighborhood." He's got the Beach Boy look, with his grown out sandy-brown hair and flip-flops. The three of us stand on the sidewalk and chat for almost an hour. Three school-aged girls skate in the street and whiz by Carl giving him high-fives as they pass. "You go girls!" he hollers to their backs. "Great kids," he says looking back to us.

The girls make a second round and the tallest one stops on the heal of her rollerblade and says: "Hi new people, I'm Zoe!"

"Well hello Zoe! I'm Tom and this is Jen . . . and, hey, you are quite a skater!"

"Thanks," she says zipping off to join her friends.

Tom smiles and says, "She reminds me of my daughter, Eliza, so outgoing."

That night, we begin what I hope will be a regular ritual of evening star gazing talks in the hot tub. "This neighborhood is so alive," I say. "And isn't it great that there are other kids on the block? You know, potential playmates. More like babysitters, I guess," I say, veering dangerously close to the slippery subject of children.

"Yeah, I love having kids around. Makes me miss my girls so much, though," he answers, transfixed on the sky. "It goes so fast. Jessica, gosh, it seemed like just a minute ago she was whinnying around the yard pretending to be a horse . . . and now she's almost a grown woman! Hmph," he laughs to himself. "I used to love braiding their hair in the morning before school and listening to their girl-talk . . . and then I'd drive them to school . . ." He fades off, lost in memory.

The kid cue never even penetrates his thick history-in-the-making. *First things first*, I console myself, *he's still raising teen-*

Jennifer Allen

agers and he's still got cancer. I decide to hold off on the kid issue, at least until his cancer leaves the spotlight.

While we are on a roll, setting up our lives together, getting jobs, car insurance and the like, Tom makes a doctor's appointment before he can talk himself out of it. When he gets home, I can tell by the skip in his step and his beaming smile that the cancer is gone.

"Cancer-free man in da house!" he shouts. I rush over to him and cover him with kisses. We make love in celebration. It seems so fitting. No cancer means no risk to the vital sex organ nerves, no impotence from the chemo, no sabotage to future babies. It also means we might grow old together.

The weight from anticipating losing Tom and the unconscious bracing my heart has contorted into is evident by its sudden release. Our bodies are lighter and move into each other with a new ease. No protective barriers; however subtle. Afterwards, I fall asleep in the cocoon of his body spooned around me. He's even safer when death isn't threatening to take him.

Every morning since the big news I rise to a loud vibration of foot-long carrots being shoved down the juicer and I swear I love Tom a few degrees more. His commitment to a strict preventative diet feels like an investment in our future together. I'm more than happy to drop the nag-role and get on with dreams of my own.

Time passes as if there is an endless amount of it. Days float into weeks and then months as I busy myself with forming a master plan. There is comforting normalcy in taking it for granted. We slip into the day-to-day living with an assumed future, postponing visits and "I love you"s. The beach bonfires we used to have with our friends and my two sisters, who moved out last year, are sparse now.

My nose is to the grindstone manifesting dreams. Evenings, I wait tables at fancy restaurants to replenish my college fund. Days are divided between working just enough hours at a center for adults with developmental disabilities to get on their dental plan, and get my wisdom teeth pulled; and taking pre-requisite courses at the community college. Lunch hours are spent filling out applications to graduate schools. If all goes well, phase-one of my ten-year plan starts next fall.

Now that Tom doesn't have cancer, Tuesday nights are sketchy. He was looking forward to rejoining the cancer support group he was in before our trip, but he doesn't feel like he belongs there anymore. Mostly, he spends that evening and most others, keeping himself out of the group with a strict adherence to the Gerson Treatment.

His research and his gut tell him this is the best alternative to what he calls the "poison and butchering" of Western medicine. Instead of the preventative surgery his doctor has pushed from the start, he has taken on a rigorous schedule of juicing every vegetable known to humankind, coffee enemas twice a day and handfuls of supplements. The flax bread he makes from scratch could double as a weapon if need be. Ugly roots are transformed into smooth soups between his Renaissance-man jobs.

Health is priority. Work gets woven into the routine. Mornings are spent at the computer alternating between Tom's love of writing short stories and formulating a marketing plan for a friend's invention. And then it's: juice, take enema, bake bread, juice. By afternoon, he is out in the fresh air at baseball games, standing behind the plate barking his trademark calls: "Riiiiiike three." The money is minimal. If he wasn't saving up to bring his daughters to Europe for the '92 Barcelona Olympics, he'd have gladly umpired gratis.

We still climb with Ed occasionally, always making promises of getting back into it the way we had before Europe, always knowing it isn't likely to happen. Though both of us are in the mode of planning for a future, Tom's plans go no more than two years out. This doesn't go unnoticed. Subtle things—like a change in the sound of his urine stream, the life insurance envelope going out in the mail and slinking off the subject of children—start to build and gather over time, culminating in a hard pea of fear, hidden deep beneath the layers of comfort I have relaxed into since his remission. At least now that his faith in doctors and himself is at an all-time high, he's been going to follow-up appointments. There is still no evidence of the cancer. Despite his reassurance, I can't stop myself from viewing every potential sign as a bright red flag.

Candlelight, silk sheets, a thick comforter, and Tom's warm, cancer-free body against me: The coziness of our lives

Jennifer Allen

invites trust in God, fate, the doctors, Tom—whatever is keeping the cancer at bay.

Then I feel it. A tiny grating in the back of my mind distracts me. It's telling me get ready for what is to come. I try and talk the pea away: *Relax and focus on what is, not "what if."* Paying it any mind at all only seems to give it more substance.

"We're going to have nights like this for a long, long time, you know." Tom reads my mind.

"Hmmm…" I agree superficially until that nagging little pea demands a voice. "Don't you worry that it will come back?" I ask, propping myself up on his chest so I can check his eyes for twitches of doubt.

"We know what to do if it does. All that soul feeding with the writing, adventuring, laying on of hands . . . it worked, right? And, okay, maybe the chemo made a contribution. You know I'm doing everything I can to keep it away, right?" He answers the question indirectly with his usual confidence. At least he's not lying.

"Yeah, you're working hard at it, man." I decide to overlook any minor differences in our cancer battle plans, reminding myself that it's *he* who is in the ring—not me.

Outside our tight little world of two, I come up against the same resistance to the hard little pea I have learned the formal name for. I pour over books in search of more about the phenomena of anticipatory grief. It's the elephant-in-the-room-grief that happens before the subject of grief is even dead. Nobody dares name it aloud, lest they kill hope.

On our weekly run up Jack's Peak, I try calling it with Amy: "You know, the strange thing about remission? I want so badly to forget about the cancer thing and I can't."

"*What* are you talking about?" she asks as if she had already forgotten Tom had cancer just three months earlier.

The hill incline keeps my words to the point: "I'm afraid. It will come back. We . . . won't be ready."

"Oh, the cancer you mean," she says.

Just as I thought, we were supposed to be acting blind of such life threats.

"Yes—the cancer. It's just that . . ."

"Jen," she cuts in, not even out of breath, "It's gone—the doctor said remission, right?"

"Yeah, but . . ."

"Don't waste the time worrying, then," she says impatiently.

I get it. People don't want to hear this stuff, especially when death isn't in plain view. Okay then, I'll just keep that pea under the mattress and hope the weight of comfort squishes it.

What Amy doesn't know and what Tom hides so well, is that once death has become a real possibility—an untimely one—there's no going back to the naïve notion of immortality. I have seen that elephant and felt that hard pea for a long time and I'm just coming to realize that it started long before Tom.

The low-grade angst of anticipating a loved one's death and pulling all stops to try and prevent it was my dance with Scott; only his death threat was not from cancer. He had already been there as a child, when he had escaped death to cancer. It cost him one of his eyes. In his rebellious spirit, he would show death it couldn't ever mess with him again. He would beat it at its own game. Suicide was the ace up his sleeve.

Tap dancing to keep him in the lead of life so that he wouldn't ever have to contemplate using that ace wore me down. At sixteen, the dances took the form of whispering love promises before hanging up the phone, rolling the family car over the crunchy snow to the road, driving to his house across town, sneaking into his cellar, and finding him in a slump on the floor—rope in hand. I had held him for hours and had made it home before sun-up.

At twenty-two, it was different. I pounded on the bathroom door with only the sound of breaking glass and running bathwater in response. After an hour of tears, guilt trips, and starts and stops of dialing 911, the door opened. Scott stepped over me, unscathed. I had become a hostage to his threats. The constant dread of losing the love of my life had soured even our closest moments. I had stayed with him until the fact sunk in: Ultimately, my love couldn't make him choose life. Those tendencies were beyond me.

Adrenaline pierces me, synchronizing with the harsh ring at 6:30 a.m., one foggy Sunday morning in July. I grab the phone quickly before the second ring pulls Tom completely out of sleep.

"Hello?" I whisper.

"Jen, its Mum." Her usual singsong is absent. The tone is vaguely familiar. I place it to the time when I was fourteen and she roused me from sleep on a Saturday morning to tell me that a friend, who had been a boyfriend a few weeks earlier, had been killed by a drunk driver. It had been my first official visit with grief.

Oh no. I hold my breath.

"I am so sorry," Her voice catches. "Scott's mom just called. Scott hung himself last night. He's dead, Jen."

"Oh my God . . . oh my God!" I'm on autopilot drawing out time to comprehend. "Where? Who found him? Was he drunk? High?" I feel numb at the abruptness of the news and then a strange relief. "He did it. I can't believe he finally did it. I knew this was coming someday —just not when. Now it's here."

There is a well-worn path to my heart that this long, slow grief has made. It allows the shock to subside quickly once I hang up the phone.

Rolling over toward Tom, I say it: "Scott's dead." There's nothing left to feel helpless about, it's a clear surrender.

Tom strokes my cheeks, wiping tears as they fall. "Oh sweetie," he says, pulling me to him and enveloping me. As he rocks, I feel the irony of him comforting me through the loss of a loved-one. He's getting it all in up front, just in case it's him the next round. Once my stuttering inhales smooth out, he slips out of bed, tucks the bedcovers lovingly around my body and goes downstairs to make some breakfast, leaving me space to be with my grief.

I fall into it completely, my heart twisting inside out with the finality. It's no less painful than other times with Scott, only different because now I know I'll be okay.

Grief has me remembering both the bitter and sweet. Once, after our relationship was over and we were just bed-buddies trying to break our strongest bond, Scott told me: "Sorry Jen, but I need you to hate me. It will make it so much easier when the time comes, trust me."

"That's fucked-up." It was as articulate as I could be at the time, with a heart in knots of futile fury. He had stolen the hope out of our relationship prematurely in pursuit of his death-mission, claiming it was in my best interest.

But it *did* work. In the beginning his innocence made our love binding. Separation from him was unfathomable and I contemplated a mutual suicide. Over time, though, his angst built, his moods swung and we broke up and reunified repeatedly. I watched the intelligent and affectionate emerging man slowly drown in the relief of drugs, declining any life-rings tossed to him. I had been grieving the loss of "us" even before we ended. What remains now is the tragedy of Scott's lost potential: dead at 24.

Tom encourages me to do whatever I need to do. And I need to see Scott dead. I need to be in the middle of the chaos his choice has created, to feel the implications of it completely so that I can believe it. Otherwise it's just a story and I'll forever see him on street corners just out of the corner of my eye.

When I fly back East for the funeral service, I'm launched into a heavy drama so sudden and immediate, time takes to warping and only the grieving exists. The rest of the world is on a different channel, speaking a foreign language.

It's hot and muggy; standard fare for Maine in July. The afternoon air smells of salt and it matches the taste of my lips, wet from tears. The wake is at Lucas-Eaton funeral home. It's pretty much the only place in town. Scott and I attended our friend's Dad's wake here back in high school. Afterwards in the car, Scott leaned into me and cried without end.

"His dad is gone . . . gone forever." He had sobbed.

When I remember this, I know Scott knew the trail of pain he'd leave behind and I know how much that fact tormented him. I'm saddened and angry as I enter the building and follow the red carpet to the viewing room. A blast of death's perfume carried on a draft of air conditioning causes me to look up. Florist's shops will never be the same. There he is, at the front of the room—his

Jennifer Allen

familiar profile peeking out just above the lip of his casket and a jungle of flowers cascades down either side. It's all I can do to restrain myself from walking straight up the aisle and screaming into the box: "WHAT HAVE YOU DONE?"

Instead I glare at him and practically see him sit upright and laugh: "Gotcha!" Either way, I want to ring his neck, but he's beat me to it.

I'm raging at him one minute and then I'm breathless with sorrow that he is gone—never to be again. I can barely look at his parents. A chair meets the back of my knees as I take a dizzy step back and I drop into it. A mix of shock, lack of food, and exhaustion from crying overcomes me. Any grief stashed away in a some-other-day pile over the course of my life, is hauled up for an overdue release. With each liberation, watery snot sprays onto my dress. I half expect my head to turn a three-sixty.

A hand arrives in front of me with a tissue and present time returns like an arrow to the forehead. Surreal becomes real again. Once I've secured any inappropriate impulses, I walk up to the casket and look in at Scott. He still looks himself, though his mohawk has been shaved off in favor of a buzz-cut, leaving him with a proud soldier look. His usual cupid lips strain flat against the threads holding them together. There is no sign of rope burn on his neck.

How many times have I watched him sleep? I touch his cheek. All the sensual memories of it are jolted out by the stone coldness of death. Brain signals run amuck. I have touched this face thousands of times before and it was smooth, warm, and responsive. Now it is a hard cold nothing. *Not right.* Too real. Too dead.

The harshness of this reality ties a knot of irreversibility for me. I'll never flounder in disbelief of his death. I make a quick mental note to never use flowery words or shelter my future children from their father's death, if that should be the scenario. Truth makes for better access to the heart.

The funeral follows a day later. I wear a bright, tie-dyed dress and walk up the church aisle with his parents and younger brother, looking out of place like Scott would have with his mohawk and leather jacket. Though we've been apart for well over two years, I represent his adult history to his family. They include me in their circle as if to keep a piece of him alive through me. They've asked me to speak at the service. My tribute is to the spicy, passionate man who thought for himself and mended birds' wings; all the while knowing the other side of him, including his secret.

Back at their house after the service, I recognize the heaviness of guilt in his parents' faces and I feel it in myself. Why? The unanswered "why" hangs in the air oppressively. The promise I had made to Scott must be broken and probably should have been before it came to this. He has broken the rules, so all is fair game now.

"I don't know if you know this and I'm not sure it helps at all now. Scott was diagnosed with cirrhosis of the liver just before he moved back here. He didn't want me to tell. Maybe he saw this as the best option . . . " *His time to pull the ace.* Even as I speak, his parents' faces move through comprehension and just the slightest degree of relief is evident.

"Thank you, my Jen," his mom says into my ear as I bend to hug her goodbye.

I'm not sure how the implications will sit over the long haul with them, after immediate relief wears off. It has already been too heavy for me knowing something that could have made the difference. It will take a long time to talk myself out of this guilt trip.

It's a long few days before I return to my cool, foggy home out West. On the plane, a black widow thought persists. *Maybe I'm not the best candidate to be fighting off cancer with. Strike two in the boyfriend department.* I feel cursed. The truth is, in the back corners of my mind, I saw a split-second of death when Tom told me he had cancer. I figured it was because I'd been steeped in the possibility with Scott for so long: death-on-the-brain kind of thing. Tom provides me with an easy opportunity for redemption in my moments of weakness, when I am sure it is my fault Scott is dead. There's relief in Tom *wanting* to live. It's a gruelingly slow lesson to understand I have nothing to do with either of them dying or living. Meanwhile, I keep the curse idea to myself, especially when I realize Tom is oblivious to it.

Jennifer Allen

At the airport, Tom sweeps me away from the deplaning crowd and into his arms. I know then he'll never blame me, no matter what happens. *If only I could be so pure.*

We drive home to an ease that has grown between us in our little world of carrot juice, eucalyptus soap and body contortions that press as much warm skin against each other as humanly possible. I want to know "live is live" just as "dead is dead" and remember that cancer or not, Tom is alive until he's dead.

In a quiet gesture of support, Tom helps me convert our garage space into a darkroom. My sobs are audible through the black visquine walls as I try to recreate Scott, printing life-size images of his face that I had taken while we were together. I look into his good eye and he is almost there. I curse him to his face for what he's done and then kiss the paper tenderly—so sorry for his pain. For months, I come to bed in the late hours, after printing up endless old negatives of Scott, and Tom looks to me, inviting me to tell all. His open ears make me fall deeper in love with him for how well he loves me.

On a whim, I had signed up for swimming at the community college while I was knocking off prerequisites for graduate school. It's turned out to be great grief therapy. Throughout the fall and into the spring, I rise each weekday morning, kiss that sweet man of mine goodbye and bike to class, where I ease into the cool water and begin rhythmic strokes in sync with my breathing. As my body takes over, my mind relaxes its controlling grip. Feelings bubble to the surface. Occasionally I must break rhythm to empty my goggles of tears. The pool is about the only place I can pull off red-puffy eyes without being questioned as to what is wrong. There's something about swimming—the breathing, the cadence, the floating, the wetness— that makes memories and feelings flow, weaving the loss into my being and history. Part of me is acutely aware of needing to become familiar with grief and healing. Although it's unsaid, both Tom and I are watching to see how I do with this. Even though he's still on a roll of remission, I think we both suspect I'll be revisiting grief somewhere down the line—*way* down the line.

Bone Knowing 65

Scott's death has cracked open a thick, crusted layer over my heart that has held so many feelings at bay. The Velveteen Rabbit, from one of my favorite childhood books, keeps coming to mind. My heart, like that inanimate toy, comes alive as I listen and attend to it. As it awakens, my love for Tom becomes more vivid. I let myself fall deeper into him with faith that I'll make it through the loss if and when it comes to that.

Jennifer Allen

5

Certain Uncertainty

Summer 1992–Summer 1993

Paris in July is more than any travel poster can express. All senses are stimulated and indulged. Pastries and espresso permeate the warm flowery air that catches under my sundress with each step, caressing my thighs. Amy and I talk incessantly while we scan the masses of colorful people we walk among, stopping occasionally to look up in awe at the architecture. Just ahead of us, Tom walks with his beloved daughters, one on each arm. He's laughing and pointing to the Eiffel tower, his "Just Do It" t-shirt glowing in the light of high noon. His pencil thin braid swings at the back of his neck, keeping time to his step. Joy radiates from him.

Click. I press the shutter without looking through the viewfinder. It's a mental marker more than anything. Like many other moments, I want to store this one for later.

Tom is high on life. He has worked hard over the last year to manifest another dream: Bringing his daughters to Europe and the '92 Olympics in Barcelona. This is his opportunity to show his children a world beyond the one they know and to teach them, by example, how to embrace it. It's the best thing he can offer them, when he knows time isn't a given. Throughout the trip, Tom-style adventures abound. Everything feels poignant—as if this is actually a memory-making trip while the going is good, *just in case* the cancer comes knocking. Occasionally, Tom winces and then tweaks it into a smile when he sees me looking. He doesn't want to hear the knock in the midst of living, so I say nothing.

Neither of us shifts from Europe-mode back into health-mode once we return to the States and relocate to Sacramento where I've begun grad school. Instead of the daily carrot and wheatgrass juices we'd been religious about for the past year, we have espresso in the morning and a glass or three of wine in the evening with some exotic cheeses and chewy breads; followed by fine chocolate. With a Trader Joe's market en-route to my new job, we can afford to feel like we're still touring Europe.

The glitches are growing in this fantasy of ours, though. For one, marijuana indulgencies on the weekend don't carry the feel of Europe as a pack of cigarettes might. The stress building each day Tom doesn't find a job, in addition to the mounting evidence that our nice home is affordable because it sits in a high crime neighborhood, is really blowing the feel of an ongoing vacation. Tom is well off the wagon with smoking and drinking and I'm midway, trying to keep at least a base number of brain cells alive for graduate school. In Europe, it was living. In Sacramento, it wreaks of addiction.

On a hot afternoon in mid-September, I drop my bike outside our ranch-style rental and rush in to the bathroom before I pee in my pants. It's a four-mile ride from the college and there aren't many safe pit stops along the way. Just as I sit down on the

Jennifer Allen

toilet, a swatch of red along the inside rim catches my eye. *I don't have my period.* "Tom!" I yell over the loud stream of urine hitting water.

He comes to the door. "What?"

"There's blood!" I part my legs and point at the stained porcelain between them and then look to him. He looks away. "How long has it been?"

"It started on the trip. I didn't want to alarm anyone. I was hoping it would let up once we settled. It hasn't yet," he says.

"Why didn't you tell me?"

"I wanted to find a doctor here and have some tests run first. No need for un-do worry."

"Well, did you find someone? Have you gone yet?" Here I go, slipping right back into the nagging-parent I resent being.

"No, I'm working on it. I did find a support group at Sutter and its manageable; about the same size as the one I used to go to in Monterey. They even meet on Tuesdays." He sounds like a teenager trying to make things right.

"Man, Tom, how long has it been since your last check anyway?" He shrugs. It's clear he's not to getting into the blame game with me.

"Can't you at least call Dr. Stinson and have him order a blood panel so you know where you stand?" What I want to say is where *we* stand. *Has he forgotten I'm on board for this ride too?*

"I'll see who the people in the support group recommend. I'm not taking on another butcher-happy doc who'll only shame me for the choices I make about *my* body," he says, with a whiff of irritation in his voice.

Two birds are down with that comment and I'm one of them. Really, I don't want to be his parent, it just that I'm so scared his rebel spirit will cost him his life. "Yeah, it's a much bigger city here. More choices. You'll find a good match," I say, trying to find optimism that can hold water, before he throws me some that can't. If he dares make his twenty-year promise right now, I'm going to scream.

"Yeah," he says and that's it. No big claims, no denying something might be wrong. Tom is unusually quiet for the next few weeks, with the exception of the phone calls he's logging on for hours at a time. The juicer is back in operation and Tom passes on the wine at dinner. He looks scared the evening he tells me that he's finally found the right doctor and I brace myself for the next swoop of this roller coaster ride.

"When's your appointment?" I ask.

"Next Monday."

"Should I take off work? Do you want me to come?"

"No. It'll just be some tests. It'll take a week to get the results."

"Are you worried, Button?"

He leans back on two legs of the chair and bites his lip. "Yeah, I am."

I don't know whether to blame him for hiding his symptoms and then dragging his feet to get help or thank him for letting me in. It's hard to be mad when he looks like a frightened little boy.

"Whatever happens, we'll be okay," I say, surprising us both that it's me coming up with the cliché of confidence.

Just as we suspected, the cancer is back. In response, we torment ourselves with "if-only"s. *If-only* he had stuck to the Gerson Treatment. *If-only* we hadn't taken on the stress of relocating. *If-only* I hadn't gone astray from our positive thinking stream and felt that damn pea grating in the tender bowels of my mind. *If-only* we hadn't started smoking again. *If-only* we'd lightened up on the wine once we returned from Europe. I'm exhausted from this "if-only" game and, still, I can't seem to convince myself it will never change the fact Tom's cancer has returned.

Once again, Tom's warning to "be careful what you wish for" resounds in my head. Certainty was what I've been wishing for and it is for certain that Tom's invisible opponent is back in the ring with him.

But wait, what I meant was . . . Once again, I bargain irrationally with the powers that be. They're accustomed to it. I start over: *What I really wish for is to have a quality life with Tom and our children until old age. If that's asking too much, then at least until the kids are grown.*

Intentionally, I leave out the part about cancer for fear some other dreadful disease or accident will take its place as a cruel joke on my greedy wishes. It's easy to become superstitious when I'm not sure who or what is in charge and how he/she/it works.

Prayers, hopes, and wishes spew out in a flurry over the winter months since recurrence has made the passing of time palpable. It's painstaking to avoid any concrete conversations about our future together, now that we're at a level ten on the uncertainty scale. The bittersweet is back, only this time it feels more bitter than sweet. We need to talk.

Me: What is your biggest concern about us, Tom?

Tom: Would you stay with me if I had no sexual capacity and couldn't have children?

Me: I can't promise a forever on that. It's been an adventure, no doubt, but I'm growing up and I want to start a family at some point. With the sex, we'd have to think outside the box, literally. Wink. What about you? What if cancer-free meant no orgasms for you, no kids together, and maybe blow our relationship?

Tom: Not worth it. My sexuality brings me to life and I want this relationship. God knows I love fathering too, if only I knew I'd be well long enough to raise them. It's overwhelming to consider right now, but I want to reserve the possibility. Will you blame me if I die doing the treatment that I think is best?

Me: I have so much respect for the courage it must take to do what you think is the right thing. And, I've got to admit, when things don't go well and our future is at risk, I do blame you. What if your treatment is aimed at 'quality of life' and we need 'quantity' to raise children?"

Tom: It's a catch-22. If I choose 'quantity' with the surgery now, children are a moot point. I've got to go the 'quality' route for me and hope that I get good time, if not a cure, out of it. If we end up having children, it'll be a hell of a dilemma. By then, it might be too late for the big guns. You know, Jen, I'm not interested in suffering so that I can stay alive and be a burden.

Me: So what exactly is too much suffering?

Tom: If I'm in pain constantly. I'll become another person—not likely a good spouse or parent. And, frankly, I'm scared I'll lose you or the possibility of any future relationship, if I lose my sexuality. I don't want to be a pathetic bitter old man. If I can't be wrapped up in life, why live?

Me: Are you saying you'd kill yourself?

Tom: No . . .well, I meant that the treatment choices that let me live fully, might rob me of time down the line and I'm good with that. And, if things get too bad and if I know death is impending, I might request a mega dose of morphine. I'd prefer to make the journey naturally after coming into the world on the fast track of of a C-section and all. You think you could deal with that?

Me: Being with you for your death? Yes, definitely. Helping with your suicide, no can do. I could understand it, but I couldn't be a part of it."

Tom: Yeah, okay—makes sense. Jen, I know you'll be fine however things turn out. That's what makes it possible for me to even consider marriage and children with you. If this is my last chapter, and I hope it isn't, I want to be free, especially of guilt. I'm going to trust that you can make your own decisions and live with them. Just remember, it might mean taking care of me down the line.

Me: Yup, I think I'm superhuman sometimes too. Don't be fooled. Just under this Wonder Woman façade, I want you to take care of me. I know it completely defies my whole feminist thing, but it's the truth. And I'm loyal to a fault. I worry marriage will keep me tied to a situation I'll grow to resent. What if you're sick for a long time, we never have children, and I put off my career and give up my prime years? I might hate both of us for it.

Stop. Breathe. Look at the cards on the table. What rules here, knowing in my head or knowing in my bones?

Tom: Anything is possible. We either peel off here, with a few cuts and bruises, or keep climbing and risk heavier damage for the adventure and the view. What do you say climbing partner, are you in?

Me: Hmmph. Yeah, I'm in.

Tom: Do you, Jennifer Allen, agree to take on me, Thomas Sanchez, in sickness and impending death, knowing that you might end up a caregiver for an unknown period of time and that you're likely to become a young widow and single parent, raising bereaved children.

Me: I do.

Do you, Thomas Sanchez, agree to take on me, Jennifer Allen, knowing that I want children and you may leave them early and be up against more guilt and grief than you ever bargained for? Are you willing to be challenged to find 'quality' in your loving instead of your adventures?

Tom: I do.

Together: Let it be known that we both believe it would be better to be together and bring children into the world and love well for as long as possible, rather than not. Let it be known that we vow to listen to our bones and live from our hearts.

If only we weren't so frightened of scaring each other off, this conversation could happen. Instead, though, it lives in my imagination as an ideal summary of all that we desperately need to talk about. Mistakenly, I figure the communication skills I'm learning in graduate school will spill over into our relationship. The problem is maintaining the skills once I cross the threshold of our house. What could be a tidy ten-minute dialog, or a one-page disclaimer and contract, ends up being many small snippets of conversations, both aloud and assumed through our actions, over the course of months since Tom's recurrence in October. Slow going but by Valentines Day our indirect tactics have us casually agreeing over dinner to one of the most serious commitments either of us will ever make.

In the months that follow, we move ahead in the face of uncertainty and plan our July weddings—one on each coast. At last, a common goal that doesn't include cancer! We have fun with it, playing off each other with ideas for vows, the reception, and the rings. At least twice a month now, we take trips down to the Monterey Peninsula to plan the West Coast version on site. The ulterior motive is to leave behind the crazy scene that goes on in our neighborhood when the weekend hits and paychecks are cashed in for booze and drugs. The trips also give us a chance to pass through Hollister and check in on Tom's parents. His dad's health has been failing for a while and Tom recognizes time is short.

This weekend when we stop, Stella tells us her hip is bad and she'll need to be in rehab for at least a week after the replacement. She's frantic about who will take care of Michael while she's out of commission. Tom signs on as caregiver for a week or two, knowing he can easily get coverage from fellow umps looking to pick up more games and his latest job serving subpoenas is flexible. "Now I'll find out what it's like for you being with a sick old man 24/7," he says in the car after we leave.

"You are *not* old!" I squeeze his leg teasingly. "Sick—yes," I take my eyes from the road to look at him briefly, "It's easy to forget with no hospitals, no chemo, and no bedpans to remind me. And there ain't nothin' like a strong libido to have me forgetting!"

He laughs. "I'm doing okay. I think getting back to the Gerson treatment has helped. Or maybe it's the Chinese herbs. At least the bleeding has stopped. I'm so lucky that this hasn't been constant misery. Look at what my father goes through. If it was me, I'd ditch the dialysis. What's the point?"

"He wants to live, that's the point," I say, feeling an unusual push to defend life at all costs now that I'm investing in Tom as a long-term partner.

"You call that living? He can't do any of the things he loves doing, except watching the game on television and even that is irritating to him lately. I think he's afraid of dying," Tom says.

"Like everyone else," I say, matter-of-factly.

"I'm not. What I'm afraid of is being kept alive in a miserable state. If I get like he is, promise you won't bring me for treatment," he says.

"Okay. As long as you promise me to do everything not to get to that point," I say, half-kidding, half-serious.

"What do you think I'm doing now?" He's edging toward the defensive side.

It's tempting to bring up his pot-smoking instead of congratulating him on all the research and follow through he's made with alternative therapies, but we're down here to pick out stones for our wedding rings. No need to blow the whole weekend.

"You've been doing all you can, I know," I say reaching over to caress the side of his face.

"Oh, there's the place," he says pointing to right. The tires squeal on my hard turn and brake.

Jennifer Allen

"You go ahead and scope our options and I'll get some homework done. Come get me if you find anything interesting," I say, pecking him on the ear. He scoots off to the gem store in search of stones he'll use to make rings for the full wedding party: His daughters, my sisters, and us.

I'm plowing through chapters on family therapy when he comes skipping over to the car. It's so hard to stay upset with a man that can skip.

"You won't believe this, Jen!" He's talking through the glass as I unroll the window.

"Tell me, Button-lovely, what?"

"Well, there is only one stone in nature that contains two birthstones simultaneously. And, get this, they are complimentary colors: purple and yellow side-by-side in one stone. Guess which birthstones those happen to be?"

"Ours, really?"

"Yup. Amethyst for you and citrine for me—together in a stone called amytrine. Meant to be or what, Butterfly?"

"Meant to be," I say and join him in choosing the stones he will craft into symbolic reminders of divine order.

Any onlooker wouldn't have picked up evidence of doubt, unless they read signs like we do. Then, the dense fog on our wedding day would have told them this couples' future wasn't going to be clear sailing.

With my final vow, I too, become vulnerable to the sign of the fog cloaking the ocean landscape in a dull grey. It's bad timing to worry about marriage robbing our colorfully lit relationship and exchange it with a chronic monochromatic, resentful one. Tom takes me in and I rush to soothe myself before he can pick up any traces of second thoughts in my kiss. I remind myself that no couple really knows their future, no matter how sure they are of their health, relating skills, common beliefs, financial security, loyalty, or life plan. *Life happens and we find our ground.*

A narrow path, meandering through ice plant, leads the wedding guests down to the isolated beach, where our homemade reception awaits us. We sit down with fifty guests to white linens, red wine, and lukewarm lasagna Tom has made from scratch at Amy's apartment. The sunset we planned on as backdrop to our celebration goes unseen behind the darkening curtain of fog. Despite the bone-gnawing cold, we're determined to make it work.

My friend, Jeff, lights the beach fire and Amy and Joyce help us pour champagne for the toast. Surrounded by loving people wishing us well, hope emerges from the flame-lit warmth. Sade's *Kiss of Life* plays on the boom box and we kick off our shoes and take to the coarse sand for dancing. As we sway, the lyrics sink into me and I feel a connection to Tom beyond any condition. Firelight illuminates our wedding rings, reminding me of the perfection they represent and the sureness I feel in my bones when I'm not flustered with controlling outcome.

The next morning, though, we wake in each other's arms and take each other's rings off. One day out and my finger already feels naked without it. We've agreed to hold off official marriage for a week until the East Coast sunrise version of the West Coast sunset ceremony takes place with the witness of our other circle of family and friends.

There is only dense blackness in the early morning of our East Coast ceremony. Torches light the flat hard beach, until the sun rises and glows the fog lighter shades of grey. My four sisters take turns reading from Kahlil Gibran and voice our vows back to us in question form. Only this time, they sink deeply into my heart, without the doubt trailer. When it is my turn to answer, I scan the circle around us and see smiling faces through the bubbles hovering among us. Love emanates from every person. Even Grandma Allen's mouth is cusped with an unusually tender smile. Taking it in, I look to the sand below, the sky above, to Tom's ring and, finally, settle into his eyes.

"I do."

The fog can't touch my certainty in this moment.

6

Making Way for New Life

Fall 1993–Late Winter 1994

Garlic rides the current of Indian summer air as I haul in a heavy bag of books from my car. After a long day teach art to adults with developmental disabilities, followed by evening classes at the university, I'm spent. Thank God Tom has an updated view of gender roles in marriage or we'd be living on cereal and yogurt. He's made dinner again. It's easiest for him, working from home with volunteer hours covering the suicide crisis line, umpiring fall ball games on the weekends, and putting in time at his desk with his cancer research packets and short stories. Besides, he loves cooking and he's good at it.

Candlelight shows through the screened windows from the backyard. *I'm home.*

Tom hears me come in and calls: "I'm back here, come on out. Dinner's hot."

Joining him, I pour a generous glass of wine and melt into the chair, looking up to where he's pointing.

"Wow, I can actually see Orion's belt tonight!" he says.

Our nights of relaxed conversation from the hot tub of our Seaside home have been replaced by hurried outside dinners in the warm climate of Sacramento. There's always homework to be done and city lights to blow stargazing. We do our best to make special moments.

Tom twirls steaming pasta around a fork and bends in to feed me. The thudding of a distant helicopter builds sound momentum. I wait for it to veer off into another direction. It doesn't. In no time it's deafening, the way it chops the air and sucks it out of my ears. A searchlight streams over the neighbors' homes and then ours, stripping away any illusion of safety. In hopes of countering the sharp hit of adrenalin already pulsing through my body, I chase the pasta down with a long swig of wine.

Gathering dishes off the table Tom says: "Let's go in. Looks like another bad guy is on the loose,"

Damn, just when it starts to feel safe in our little world.

While we were back East for our wedding a few months ago, rats moved in and took over our kitchen and have been here ever since. They raid the fruit bowl nightly, being sure to steal at least one bite out of every piece. It's starting to feel like a personal vendetta. We both take out our cancer-rage on the invaders and devised torturous ways to kill them. The bastards just keep coming back. I scream at them from the bedroom when I hear them rustling around at night. Anger is a little better than fear, anyway.

If it were only the rats, we might battle it out with them for another year, but there's also the unnerving cacophony of domestic violence that breaks out every weekend, the woman across the street who was murdered with a frying pan, the violation of Tom's truck being stolen and burnt to a charcoal skeleton and the auto accident in our front yard that ended with a car-jacking getaway. And let's not forget the guy we heard moaning inside a chunk of metal way too small for a body to fit in, after a train hit his car below the overpass we chose to take that day instead of a jog across the tracks. Nightmare material is abundant. Fear creeps in

Jennifer Allen

from the outside and merges with the scare that Tom's symptoms give us when they pop up unexpectedly. Who knows which comes first: the fear or the symptoms. A vicious cycle of stress about being stressed is well underway.

Tom can't afford such things and fights back with intense research into alternative medicines. Kombucha mushrooms multiply daily in giant pickle jars under the sink, while masses of pungent smelling sticks stew in a Chinese clay pot on the stove. Simultaneously, he nurses away the immediate stress with a little pot smoke before he gets caught up in the cycle. Instead of being relieved he isn't shooting his immune system full of adrenalin, I come down sharply on his coping device, partly because I'm not using my own.

"So that must be what—medical marijuana you've got going in there?" I shoot through the wall at him as the sage-like smoke drifts out to the living room where I'm stretching after a run. He walks out of the bedroom, eyes red, and sits down on the floor with me. All the sarcasm in the world isn't going to get him to stop, I realize.

Finally he says, "If it works, it works. Look Jen, I could let the stress take me down first. Which is worse?" His reasoning stumps me. I want to buy in, badly. *Good point*, I think.

Just then, a car skids around the corner outside. It startles me, but Tom talks over it as if it were the refrigerator coming on: "Anyway, I'm quitting next month so I can train for the marathon. I'm finishing off my stash."

Hmmm, a quick fix. That works for now. I'm desperate, I'm tired and I want to be on his team. "You want help depleting your stash?" I offer.

His face warms into a smooth smile, "Sure." He gets his pipe and I pull off my sneakers and lay back, ready for relief.

And it comes. We are the old us again, with our bottomless bag o' weed, swinging on the hammock in the hot evenings, talking of the stars and not cancer or the latest neighborhood crime. Weekend smokes quickly lead to weekday tokes and I'm back to calculating when I can squeeze in a little reprieve amidst the heavy load of work and school.

Mid-November my cousin Theo calls and says he's got a two-hour layover in Sacramento. Coming clean can be postponed to a New Year's resolution because right now I've got a smokin' bud coming to town. I meet him at the bus station and set about picking up where we left off seven years earlier, when he lived with our family for a summer while his parents ironed out divorce details. I'd been home from art school and we worked together at a Pizza joint in the tourist haven of York Beach, Maine. Scott and I were on pause during his jail sentence for robbery. Meaning I was free to be a bad influence. After our shifts, Theo and I would drive around Nubble Light Point, smoke a joint and stop at Brown's for homemade ice cream.

Sitting in the parking lot with tapes of Boston and Aerosmith playing, we'd contemplate new flavors of ice cream.

"They ought to make lemon meringue pie flavor, with the crust and all," Theo would say.

"Oh man, what about Indian pudding with Grape Nuts?" I'd throw back.

"For cryin' out loud, that would be genius, Jen!" He'd scream.

"How did they come up with the name Grape Nuts anyway? No grapes, no nuts. What's up with that?"

On we'd go until neither of us could remember where we started.

Now, I look to Theo and see he isn't the teenager anymore, but a full-on man. I'm not the big-sister-like cousin, showing him the ropes, either. I'm not sure how to be with him until he pulls out a joint and looks to me for an okay.

"Sure," I say and we pass it back and forth as we comb the streets of Sacramento looking for an ice cream place I swear is just around the next corner.

Eventually, we happen upon it. A giant neon ice cream cone sits cock-eyed over the roof, flashing pink and green into the evening air.

"Hey, check this place out. They rank up there with Brown's," I say.

"Bet they don't have Indian pudding!"

They don't, so we order larges in a sampling of California flavors like cookies and cream and mocha java. We eat them in the car just like old times.

Jennifer Allen

Theo rolls a second joint. "Jen-Benjin?" He hands it to me and offers a light.

"Bring it on." I inhale deeply, letting myself forget my age, my plans—my reality.

"Got any Boston?" He asks, thumbing through the cassettes in the center console.

"Nope, I packed light when I came out. How about some Indigo Girls?"

"You got to be shittin' me, Jen?" Theo twangs playfully.

Pop— the balloon of the past disappears in an instant. There's no salty air, no Indian pudding ice cream, no Nubble Lighthouse in the distance. It's Sacramento and I'm a graduate student in pursuit of becoming a therapist. We are sitting in the Volvo wagon I purchased from a co-worker with the intention of starting a family, not the pea-green smoke-mobile we got for summer cruising after Grandpa Allen died. I look at my watch. "Oh my God! It's already nine-thirty! Doesn't your bus leave in twenty minutes?"

"For cryin' out loud, your right!" He mocks my sudden seriousness. On the drive to the bus station, I drive too slow, leaning into the wheel with shoulders crunched up to my ears.

"Am I going the right way? Isn't this a one way? Theo, look for a sign, quick, quick!" I'm panicked.

"You're good, you're good. Settle down," he says, bobbing his head to the music.

"That's it, right there—hold on!" I cut across two lanes, making a semi-u-turn in the middle of a four-lane one-way.

Just when I'm sure I've made it, "WhoooKUNCH!" An oncoming truck nabs my side of the car, just missing the door I sit behind. It drags us into the turn, pinning us up against a curb catty-corner to the police station. Flashing blue lights are immediate.

"Shit, shit, shit!" I blink hard, pressing all four window buttons down and grabbed for the gum.

Theo is instantly straight. "Listen, Jen. I'll clear the weed and bail. I can find the bus from here. I'll call you later if I miss it. I've got to hurry before he sees me. Are you good with that?"

"Yeah, yeah. Go!" I watch him push a full bag of pot through the flap of a garbage can on the corner. He runs into the shadows. I'm on my own. The officer's flashlight is already blinding me.

"License and registration, Miss." He's a white, middle-aged cop with a donut waist. His wrist expertly rotates the light and scans every square inch of the car. "Where's your friend?"

"What friend?" If there was ever a time the dumb-blonde thing could work for me, I want this to be it.

"Come on, Miss," he says, lowering his voice to a growl. "I don't have time for this bullshit. Where is your friend? Did he take the marijuana with him?"

"He had to catch a bus. What do you mean, mari—what?" I can't remember if I've already admitted to smoking. Nerves are much worse than drugs for tricking the mind.

We set about a frustrating ping-pong match of Q&A, with me dropping the ball to each question and him being distracted by the other driver who is calling me a "drunk bitch" and the constant crackling of his radio. The cop backs off, looks away and casually says: "Looks like you're going to get yourself a little visit to jail tonight, Miss-Zero-Cooperation-Pot-Head."

The lump in my throat is too thick to talk around. I think: *but I can't, you don't understand. That'll end my career path. I don't have time to start at something else, my husband is sick . . .*

Just then, a woman officer shows up and relieves Big Scary Cop so he can get on with some *real* crimes.

"Look, Ma'am, we got a busy night tonight. I'm going to give this guy your insurance information and we'll see if you need a tow." Her tone is matter-of-fact. Even in my stoned paranoid state, I don't read threat into it. She copies the information on to the back of a card and hands it to the guy who's still cussing at me from his truck.

"Start it up and pull ahead," she yells over.

The car screeches, metal on metal, when I edge forward. Though she's petite and middle-aged, that policewoman walks herself right on over to my fender and gives it a solid tug, bending the contorted metal away from the wheel well. The whole car rocks a little. This woman is my new hero.

"Now try." The gears grind and the car jerks forward.

"Good. Can you get out and walk a line for me?"

The driver door is crunched closed. "It won't open," I say.

Her radio scratches the air with urgency. "Forget it. Could you be a little more careful?"

"Um, yeah. Sure," I answer.

"Drive slow and get some coffee close by. I don't want to see you again," she says, waving me off. In my rearview mirror, I notice her tossing a bunch of papers into the same garbage can that holds the incriminating evidence that could kill my future. Up until now, I believed only Tom's health could take it away.

My hands tremble on the steering wheel as I limp home with the metal fender dragging along the pavement. *Thank You.* Suddenly there's a God who gives second chances by way of angels dressed as policewomen.

The clock on our bed stand reads 11:46 when I slip between the sheets. Tom is snoring. He's so cocksure I can handle anything that he never waits up in worry for me. It's part of his attraction to me. I lay awake, starring up at the constellation of glow-in-the-dark stars we'd stuck to our ceiling, longing for his comfort, but not ready to wake him for it and break his illusion. *Maybe this 'independent woman' thing has gone a little too far.*

The next morning I tell him, in full composure, about the close call. At the end of my story I announce I'm back on the wagon. The conversation I've started with God continues. *You just watch. I'm coming clean for good. No need to up the ante.*

Tom is fascinated with the story, as if it's a clever sales pitch for quitting pot. With an index finger curled over his chin, he looks over the proof: The crumpled left quarter of our Volvo.

"Lucky you weren't hurt," he says. Funny, getting hurt never crossed my mind.

Perhaps he's giving my pitch credit for the risk involved or maybe it's convenient timing. All that matters is that he quits too. Whenever he wants to smoke, he runs instead. It's part of the training for a marathon he committed to run with my sister, Joyce. A challenging short-term goal, that isn't *my* idea, is just what he needs to distract him from years of habit.

The best I can do is pray the AA Serenity Prayer that I've learned in substance abuse class last semester, never imagining that it would apply to me. I ask for the courage to change what I can, the acceptance of what I can't change, and the wisdom to know the difference. With that, I return to a meditation practice, work hard in therapy and find us a tiny house to rent in Folsom: home to the state prison. At least there, we'll know where the bad guys are.

Between semesters, we made our move into a tiny cottage on Scott Street, just blocks from the quaint historic downtown of Folsom, California. Every time I write our return address, I smile at the synchronicity of adding "Scott" just under our names. He was a clever man in life, so it doesn't surprise me that he's maintained it in spirit. A white adobe funeral home with a manicured lawn sits across the street from us. I wondered if it, too, is some kind of sign or reminder.

Strangely, I'm comforted watching a black hearse pull up as I wash the Saturday morning dishes. Sometimes I can catch this scene three times in one day. It affirms for me that death is frequent and seemingly objective. *Nothing personal, it happens to us all.*

In the evening, we set out on our walk and take the route Tom has deemed the most prolific upon moving in two months ago. Bouquets of citrus fruits dangle from branches that overhang the street.

"Fair game," Tom claims, twist-pulling a few lemons off and adds them to our basket. Oranges, lemons, loquats and fennel are plentiful as we make our way down to the musky trail along the majestic American River.

Tom whistles, calling Kizma to us. She's the shepherd puppy we rescued from the pound at Thanksgiving in hopes of channeling my maternal urges at least until graduation. He throws her a stick and turns to me like a proud papa: "What a sweet pup, huh? We did good with her."

"We did." I smile back, reveling in the common delight of our dog/baby. Visions of diapers and infant seats flash in my eyes. To parent with this man is all I can think of lately. It makes concentrating on classes a challenge. Reaching for his hand, I squeeze it.

He pulls me close and kisses my forehead. "It's a good life, huh?"

"Mmmhmm," I agree, guilty for wanting more.

It's dark when we make it back to our tiny safe haven. A warm rosemary aroma of soup in the Crock-Pot, welcomes us in. No helicopter lights. Just candlelight. I feel myself exhale, finally.

Jennifer Allen

In February, we head to Wilbur Hot Springs way out in the sticks of wine country, courtesy of my sister, Joyce. She has found herself amidst a divorce and doesn't want to waste the romantic getaway fighting. Any remnants of fear left over from living in a bad neighborhood and anticipating cancer's next move melt away in the burning sulfur tubs. Tom and I cook ourselves until we are sure we've boiled out every last drop. When we can take no more, we lift ourselves slowly into the unseasonably crisp air; our steaming bodies shone silver in the moonlight. Dizzying lightness overtakes me, as if I've just dropped a hundred pounds of luggage. I can almost fly.

Tom walks ahead into an open field of virgin snow. I watch him and feel the sweetness again; the sure love that hides under the seemingly important stuff of getting by. He motions for me and I join him in the surreal scene.

"C'mon, lets make snow angels for the stars," he whispers. Lying beside each other, we move our arms and legs back and forth like simple marionettes. A dusting of snow begins to fall. The muffled silence reminds me of being out on a winter's night in Maine, when I was a child. All except for the naked part, that is. Heat from my body melts through the thin white blanket, down to the disintegrating leaves. I can feel them wet and spongy under my back and the thought of becoming soil again one day seems completely natural—even pleasurable.

"I'll never be cold again," I say.

"It's a full moon, and you're a hot woman, that can only mean one thing," he says, nudging my shoulder. We rise up carefully leaving behind two perfect imprints of dark angels merged together and wrap ourselves in thick robes as we head back to our room. As we tiptoe through the lantern-lit corridors, Tom rips one of his trumpet farts. He looks accusingly at me. My laugh catches in a snort and I fumble with the room key. Inside our room, we tumble onto the bed giggling. The last of the armor I've held in place to protect me from all the worst-case scenarios I've scared myself silly with, drops, clearing a path straight to my heart and womb.

What cancer?

Over the next few weeks, I dream of kittens and puppies and figure it's because my birthday is approaching—likely a message for me to nurture this inner child I'm learning about in class and in my own therapy. I bring a drawing I've made to session. It's an image that came in a meditation of me sitting cross-legged with colorful chakras aligned and a huge ball of light in my lap. It seems obvious to both Anastasia and me that my second chakra, the one that is all about creativity and sexuality, is waking up in the absence of substances and chronic fear. Something inside me is coming to life.

It dawns on me later that maybe the *something* isn't me. Though I'm only a couple days late, I pick up a pregnancy test at Raley's and stash it in the cupboard until morning, when my urine will be most concentrated with hormones. All night I am buzzing in anticipation, unbeknownst to Tom. As soon as it's light enough to read the directions without turning on the light, I go to the toilet and piss all over my hand trying to capture urine into a tiny tube. The indicator ring at the base is instant and unbroken. Life is officially already growing inside me! No more pondering the decision, it's a done deal, albeit a little earlier than planned. I run into our room and jump on the bed, waking Tom with my elation.

"Button! We're having a baby!"

"Hmmmm?" He rubs his eyes and comes-to. "A baby . . . a baby!" He conjures up a smile. It's too late, though. I saw the wince first.

My heart drops from the heavens with a thud. Apparently, he felt the loss of leaving his child within a millisecond of the theoretical becoming reality.

"I thought we decided that you're alive until you're dead?" I remind him.

"Oh, Butterfly," he says lovingly as runs his fingers along my scalp and down to the ends of my hair. He's definitely trying to make things right. "It's great, I can't wait to watch you become a Mamma." He intends reassurance, but I read it as "bail." Whether it's by emotional means or physical means, bail is not part of our deal.

"Tom, this is a *we* thing. I can't wait to watch *you* be a Daddy alongside me," I counter; fear strangling my elation. *Don't think you're going anywhere. You promised twenty years and I'm cashing in, starting now.*

Jennifer Allen

The response I hoped for comes from each of my sisters as I call them. Problem is, I'm not married to them and they won't be parenting this child with me. Tom says all the right things, but I can feel that he is torn. He wants this and he knows it will hurt— and not just him. Meanwhile, all I can think about is what *is*: I'm pregnant.

As I plug on through the literal throws of morning sickness, I realize my adolescent fantasies of being home baking bread, my husband calling from work three times a day to see if the baby has kicked; are just that: fantasies. They get bagged up and pushed to the back, like outgrown clothes. *It's okay; morning sickness would have ruined the smell of freshly baked bread. And, anyway, they need me at work.*

Pretending I don't need anything is familiar protocol. It works until I see how easily Tom buys it. My part of our unspoken deal is about being a low-maintenance cheerleader. His plate is too full with the responsibility of curing his own cancer for any other kind of arrangement.

But then it happens. Somewhere amongst the fatigue, nausea, and foggy headedness, I need—*God damn it!* Mother bear rage comes over me, wreaking havoc with the comfort zone we have so carefully constructed. I demand Tom step up to the plate and make responsible choices for *our* future. The last thing he wants is the restraint of a parent policing his every move and the last thing I want is to be my husband's parent.

I'm sick of avoiding the bitter part of our relationship for the sake of maintaining comfort. Any attempts to placate me only ignite frustration. Not only do I want to recognize the bitter—I want to taste it, digest it, and feel the strength of letting it run though me as I confront its threat. And I want this for *us*.

Resentment has been growing each time I come home to Tom typing away at some story or project that isn't going to pay this month's bills. Most of the time, a heavy "hmph" goes over his head. This time, I sink my teeth into the bitter.

"Well, lucky you, home all day, while some of us have to work for a living." The words, said with a non-so-subtle sarcastic tone, roll out like marbles from a jar. They've got away from me and I sound like a martyr with an attitude. Not pretty.

"Actually, I'm researching alternative medicines specific to breast cancer for a friend in the support group," he says in monotone without looking up.

Touché

"Is that a problem?" he adds.

I try to soften the rough edges of the challenge. "Nope. It's not that. I think it's great that you're providing this service to people, really. Maybe you should get paid for it."

"You know how it is with illness, you can't always work and you don't always have money," he says, typing away.

"You *can* work. In fact, why don't you try a lab job instead of officiating? It's more reliable and not as physically demanding."

"Jen, I *meant* the people I make these packets for. They're under the same stress we are," he says, his voice tight with the threat of losing patience. "I do the work I love, there's no reason to do anything else."

"Well, you know how much I hate waiting tables, but if it's what I have to do, then I do it," I say, hauling him up to the plate, knowing full well the only waitressing I plan on doing is in nightmares. It's not like me to push this hard on him and I can see his shame surfacing.

"It's always more with women. I thought you were different," he says under his breath as he brushes by me.

"*What?*" I'm pissed. "Don't think you can drop something like that and walk away!" He busies himself in the kitchen putting away dishes and avoids looking at me. "Look, Tom, all I'm asking for is some back-up here, not a big house or a new car—that's not me and you know it. You might be bringing in enough to maintain your half of things now, but what happens if I can't do my part when this baby comes? We can't just fly by the seat of our pants anymore, it's irresponsible."

"Jesus, Jen, give me some credit. Why do you think I've been busting myself to get the dental software program off the ground?" He still won't look at me. "It's never enough, is it?"

"Oh, stop. I know you work hard on all your projects. The software is a great idea but it's a pie-in-the-sky payoff. This isn't the time to start a whole new business. Why can't you just do what you know—go back to the lab business. Just pick up something part-time."

Jennifer Allen

"It's not as simple as that. Besides, I could work for years and not come close to what's possible with this software. I'm not willing to grind out years in a lab, when I've come this far."

"I'm not asking you to give up of your dreams. I'm asking you to re-prioritize them; that is if me and this baby are part of them," I say, going straight for the beef of the issue.

"Hmph," he wags his head in disbelief as if I've thrown a punch below the waist. "I'm going out for a walk."

While he's gone, I cry in helpless frustration. I've never needed like I do now. Whether it's pregnancy hormones making me into a crazy-woman or I'm finally coming to my senses, I'm not sure. All I know is that life is ratcheting up its seriousness.

Jennifer Allen

7

Joy and Pain Coin

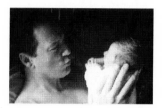

Spring 1994–Fall 1995

Dwindling finances and pregnancy don't mix. I am pushed to push Tom, beyond the Band-Aid protecting the festering wound of the past: the culprit behind his resistance to dental lab work. When we met, polka-dot bow ties and pressed shirts were all I saw. In reality, he was struggling to hold on to the scraps of his professional identity with a telecommunications job after losing his business. We both took part in the illusion—Tom being a master at feigning confidence and me wanting only to see someone sure of himself.

It's not just us anymore. This fact must be sinking in for Tom too, as I notice the Sunday paper beside his computer, folded open to the classifieds. A lab job is circled. I say nothing, tiptoeing around progress, for fear of blowing it. It's been over a week of superficial niceties since I dropped the ball in his court and it looks like he's at least considering picking it up.

On Wednesday, we take our evening walk along the American River and do our usual gathering of fruit and pondering of names. Between blackberry picking and fig plucking, we hold hands and watch the pink light glow off the huge slabs of granite that shuttle the water from Folsom Lake to Lake Natoma.

"God, this river is beautiful." Tom says. He pauses, curling his index finger around his chin the way he does just before an epiphany hits.

"What is it?" I ask.

"It could work for a girl, but I'm sure it's a boy. What do you think of River—River Mariano?" he asks.

"Button, it's gorgeous! I love it!" I press the back of his hand to my lips.

I'm easy. Any investment from him has me flying high. This moment is better than any pregnancy fantasies I've imagined to date. I wish I could make this feeling last, but so far life has taught me repeatedly that it's not possible. The coin will eventually flip back to some struggle I could do without, making this joy all the sweeter. At dinner, we toast with sparkling apple cider to one mission accomplished in the baby department.

Tom lifts his glass a second time, "And here's to the dental lab job I just landed!"

"*What?* Tell me!"

He gives me the blow-by-blow of how he's gone about picking up part-time work in a small lab run by a couple in the El Dorado Hills. He's their dream employee: overqualified but humble and an interesting third wheel to spice up long days hovering over dental crowns. From what I can tell, it's mutual. Tom gets a steady income, a wife off his back, people to chat with and a chance to air out his old wound, giving it a chance to heal.

Over the next month, Tom settles into a work routine. The familiar territory of lab work has brought him back in time, like a déjà vu, reviving stories from his *other* life—the one before me. Memories string out, bringing others to the surface. Each one gets soaked up readily, filling in the missing pieces of the man I want to know.

Jennifer Allen

I listen intently.

Yes, he made mistakes that resulted in losing the lab. Out of that mistake came one of his greatest regrets: the joy of working with his hands. Creating tiny abstract sculptures that would serve as teeth in the mouths of loved ones and strangers fascinated him. He immortalized himself in many a mouth, including his sister's full smile; restored after her mule bucked her off face first into a boulder. Jessica has a molar with a rose inscribed onto it—a forever reminder of her dad.

It all began with a high school football accident. Tom's full front grill was claimed just five yards shy of a touchdown. When he tells me this, it feels like a big secret. Hard to believe I fell for a fake smile back in Ed's front yard five years ago. Quickly, though, he redeems himself with the explanation of the picture-perfect smile that replaced the subtle character of his slightly overlapping front tooth and extra-fangy bicuspids being what drew him to the field. Not for the perfection, but to make *his* trademark the craft of keeping character. *Now that's my man.* Really, it was the ideal field for someone with impeccable craftsmanship, a flare for style and a fascination with the miniature. The side benefit was the ticket out of ag-town Hollister.

Years of hungering for a bigger world were fed when he had indulged himself in the city life of San Francisco. Everything had captured his attention: venturing into neighborhoods in search of new places and people, learning how to make teeth, playing guitar in small bands and, especially, being in the company of women.

Louise was a nursing student he was introduced to by his brother's girlfriend at a party. He found in her a freedom to explore all that he had been raised to be ashamed of. Her mother had died soon after they met and they easily became each other's home. With school, the wedding, boot camp, and a close call with the draft cleared, they headed south. Eventually, they settled on the Monterey Peninsula in a modern 70's style glass house that looked into a forest of tangled coastal oaks. For well over a decade, Tom and Louise raised their two daughters, a dog, a pony, and some chickens on the rural cul-de-sac. It was just a few miles from the lab Tom opened and the hospital where Louise worked as a nurse. The racquetball club was only five minutes away. Tom would pop over regularly for pickup games and end up seeing the same faces at the monthly Jaycees meeting, where he was residing president.

Though I've heard bits and pieces from this part of his life before, this telling is not for the story. It's for his healing. As he follows threads back in time, into the full fabric they were part of, I begin to understand just how devastating the loss of his picturesque life was once the house of cards began to collapse, one undermining at a time.

"White lies," he tells me. "Honestly," he laughs at himself, "I thought they were in everybody's best interest."

It started when he couldn't pay the quarterly taxes on his business on time. Keeping it to himself until he could catch up with the next big order, seemed like the best plan, especially since Louise had been battling the blues for over a year. Neither of them knew what was wrong. At the time his best guess was early menopause. In retrospect, he votes it was a midlife crisis. Either way, he didn't want to add to the problem with a financial stress. After all, they had a big bash planned for their 20th wedding anniversary and he wanted everything to be perfect; indicative of the two decades they'd shared already. Even before the big party, the bottom had begun to drop out and his lies had grown exponentially along with the penalties. The pattern he describes reminds me of how he handled his recurrence symptoms—keeping them to himself so as not to bother me with worry. Only now I'm worried all the more.

"Anyway," he says, "the lab began sinking and the only way to save it was to fire a couple employees. You've got to understand, Jen. They were like family. I felt so responsible for them." He frowns, describing how he'd go to work each day, resolved to drop the bomb, but couldn't bring himself to say the words. On days he was overwhelmed, he'd shove his mail into a desk drawer to save for a day when he could deal with it. The problem was—a speeding ticket and a fine for having his dog running free in their rural neighborhood were among the unopened envelopes. Unpaid fines and missed court dates equated to a warrant for his arrest. *That* envelope came on a day he was up for opening mail.

I stop him there. "Does that mean you still have a warrant—as in you get stopped now and go to jail?"

Jennifer Allen

"I guess it could go that way," he says looking at the floor.

It's all I can do not to jump down his throat on this one with a baby coming and all.

"I've been trying to clean it up on my visits down to the peninsula. I've got the dog one cleared. What a complete pain in the ass, I tell you. Shouldn't have been a ticket in the first place. Laddy was only doing what nature intended."

Again, I'm shocked with this other life he has going on unbeknownst to me until now. I don't want to give him any reason to keep secrets, so I keep my mouth closed and ears open. It's good therapist practice, anyway.

He goes on, "The irony is that the lies began over money, but over the course of a few years they bled into other areas, killing the marriage I had been faithful to for twenty years. By the time the lab went belly-up, all those well-meaning little lies weren't looking so innocent. I think Louise felt like she'd been had and started a life of her own secrets," he says pausing as if to absorb the realization. "Strange . . . at first we got closer. A couple secrets were exposed and I think it made both of us realize there was more to the other than we knew. Kind of a spark thing, but then it felt almost like we started to compete with secrets and it tore apart what we had. Like every marriage, I suppose, partners want out at times. Never in my wildest imagination would I have guessed Lo and I would end in divorce. Over the course of a couple years things just spiraled out of control." His index finger wraps around his chin while, unconsciously, he kneads at the flesh underneath with his thumb. His eyes shift as if he's reading some script off his own forehead.

Finally, as if he's found the common denominator, he reels himself in from the past and looks at me. "Trust. We couldn't rewind and get it back."

He takes both of my hands in his. "You know, Jen, Lo and I had a good thing for a long time."

"Yeah, I know you did."

"It's important to me that you know I take marriage seriously," he says, contorting his forehead into a rare furrow.

"I'm glad you do because I don't want any stupid little lies blowing this," I say.

"I've learned the hard way."

Bone Knowing

I hope so.

"The cancer was the ultimate bottom dropping out and I can't help but think sometimes *it* started when the lies did and grew along with them." His hand moves back to his chin indicating a new stream is coming up. "Pinocchio Syndrome," he says and smiles to himself. "When it hit me, all of my focus shifted to saving myself. That meant getting on with a new life free of lies and all the emotional binds they cause." The furrow returns, "If my life was going to be cut short by an unknown measure, I didn't want to waste time ruminating on the pain of the past, but it's catching up with me . . . and the lies have slipped back in too. They're so small and automatic. I can barely tell when I make one. I'm trying, that's all I can give you."

"It's enough," I say squeezing the hand that still holds mine. When he's this honest, any marks on his slate get wiped clean with me.

As the days get longer, Tom rises up with them. Either he heads to work or to the side yard, where he's plotting out a garden on his off days. Baseball season is underway and I walk to the fields in late afternoon to see my Blue behind the plate, totally enthralled by being in the game. He shines. Something is different—no Band-Aid masking his full self.

Early on Saturday I'm combing the neighborhood yard sales for baby-finds, when I come across this ugly brown crib. I'm into the challenge of transformation these days and the price tag will let me brag that I've set up the cutest nursery for under fifty-bucks. Tom helps me unload it onto the front porch where I set up a full spectrum of paint colors and a stool. All morning I paint, while he works the crabgrass into a garden.

Both of us lose track of time, caught up our respective nesting instincts. It's three o'clock before we break for lunch. Tom makes roasted eggplant sandwiches and brings them out. He sits back in the hammock chair and smiles, his face is lit with victory and beads of sweat gather at the end of his nose. He lets them linger and fall where they will, taking pride in his own hard work.

"Garden's planted," he says, with hands linked behind his head and legs spread in that manly kind of way.

I put down my paintbrush. "Really? You transformed that dead patch of grass already?"

"Yup. Chili peppers, arugula, cukes, mint, and summer squash." He hands me a glass of homemade lemonade. "Wow, what a make-over you have there. Looks great, Butterfly. Got to love the rainbow theme," he says raising his glass.

"Yup. Here's to a non-gender-stereotyped nursery!" I say toasting him.

"Hey, let me come see your garden." I extend a free hand and he hauls me up. A protruding belly keeps me from the quick, agile movements I'm accustomed to.

Tom gives me a tour of his future expectations: "When the first round of lettuce passes, I'll plant pumpkins. They'll be ready for Halloween and the baby."

"Wait, right there. I want to capture this." I waddle in to get my camera.

Tom stands tall for the picture, a shovel in one hand, a bucket of weeds in the other and a stain of dirt across his forehead, just one shade darker than his skin. His yellow t-shirt reads "Peace" in twenty different languages. In the background are lines of tiny green plants among freshly overturned soil. The moment emanated hopes. *Click.* I capture it for reference down the line, in case there are days when hope is sparse.

The summer is hot and Tom's garden thrives. There's enough lettuce for salads every night. Not a leaf goes wasted. By the time it shoots to seed, we're ready for something else. Tom plants the pumpkin patch and hooks up with a programmer to help manifest the software he has designed for tracking orders in dental labs. Both are signs of a sure future.

On weekends, I continue to score almost-new baby clothes as an early bird at garage sales in the fancy housing developments just outside the historic district. During the week, I make it through the workday by napping for the entire lunch hour under a tree at a neighboring park and spending breaks talking baby to my co-worker, Lillia. She's early on in her pregnancy. It's so nice to talk about morning sickness in retrospect. Even at the college pool, where I swim two days a week before evening classes, I'm literally over-the-hump of suspicious glances across my growing tan belly and onto the official pregnancy turf, where the regulars ask when I'm due.

At home, Tom and I are on the same page. Every conversation ends up on baby and, yet, we are vigilant not to miss what *is* before it changes. We take all opportunities to be a couple before we are a family. Monday evening walks along the river often lead us into the water, adrift on inner tubes, our puppy swimming circles around us. Wednesdays are dollar movie nights at the Birdcage cinema and we go, regardless of the show, just because we can. Friday is Island Night at the local Sheraton, where a reggae band plays poolside and we get our entire dinner compliments of their Caribbean happy-hour spread. Lately the crowd is mobbed around the bar to watch the ongoing O.J. Simpson fiasco, leaving the pool area vacant to the few of us immune to vicarious drama. We order no-alcohol beers, put on our bathing suits and dance around the water's edge until we're too hot to stand it and then jump in. Tom carries me around in the shallow end, my tightly stretched belly rising like a sand dune out of the water. I rest into his arms, building a reserve of holding before I become the "holder."

Often, in my final trimester, and usually commuting to work with a cup of tea in hand, windows down and Paul Simon's *Rhythm of the Saints* cranked to maximum volume, I cry joy. The nectar of my life overwhelms me at times. There is something about birth, with the awareness of death that is so beautiful I can't contain it. Both my body and my heart brim over. For moments at a time, I find myself in the place just between joy and pain, where the two become indiscernible. As the birth gets closer, these moments stretch out. I'm feeling completely honed into this little person about to enter our world, from whence it comes.

At week 38, I can hear this baby and my mamma instincts loud and clear. They tell me to make some changes before I leave for the hospital. Between contractions, while waiting for Tom to come home from work, I disassemble the crib and move it from the nursery to our tiny bedroom, leaving only a narrow path of floor

Jennifer Allen

space. We have to be together. The next instruction is to set a round of mousetraps, guilt-free. Though we've been cohabitating quite nicely; meaning the mice crowd behind the refrigerator when I enter the kitchen and they don't touch the fruit (unlike those rude rats from the last place); babies and mice don't mix and our house is now deemed for "humans only." Even our trial baby has to relocate to her doghouse. By the time Tom shows up, my clothes are damp with perspiration, even though there is a cool cloud-cover outside. I'm ready.

At the hospital, the first storm of the season begins as sheets of water pelt the window with irregular gusts propelling them. Inside the warmly lit room, I fall into Tom, again and again, surrendering to the excruciating pain. Just like on the rope, when I need to peel off, he has me. It's safe to go inside myself and access all resources.

Hours of mustard-yellow pain pass through me until a new sensation comes: red-hot fire. Veins spring out of unexpected places as I bare down hard, joining the squeezing wave of age-old body knowledge. "Faaaaaahhhhhhhhhhhhhhhhh!" I keyia on a thorough exhale harder than I ever had in my judo career. With Joyce holding up one knee, Amy holding up the other and Tom ready to catch, our baby burns its way through the last boundary and slides into the world.

The coin flips and with it goes the pain. Ecstatic joy fills me as I feel the mass of steaming, slippery baby on my chest and meet those piercing black eyes for the first time.

"Welcome, baby," I say, in utter awe.

"We've got ourselves a little River!" Tom announces, hardly able to contain his glee. He snips the umbilical cord and wraps us both in warm blankets. I'd forgotten to care about gender, but I'm glad inside, knowing what it means to Tom to leave no stone unturned. He had raised daughters. A son is an experience unlived. His piqued curiosity is insurance that he'll invest himself fully into parenting, no matter how long he'll be around to do it.

"So I can have it all," he says, reaching for my hand later that night as we drop off to sleep together in our side-by-side hospital beds. River is between us, latched on to my breast, elevating their status from sex toys to life sustainers. *Ditto,* I think. *Got the man and the baby. Life is good.* Elation permeates the room and my love for our child is met and matched by Tom's. It's all that I've hoped for. I send hearty thanks out into the ether.

We are up at six a.m. waiting to decline all the needle sticks and eye drops so we can simply leave and bring our joy-boy home to meet the family members who have come to welcome him in. It's hard to believe this tiny baby, with his brown hair looking like he just came from the barbers, has been out breathing air for less than eight hours by the time we are home with him. He feels natural in my arms and I can barely stop staring at him long enough to share him with others. Joyce and Amy have baked eggplant parmesan and apple crisp for lunch and Eliza has made the drive up to meet her new baby brother. The aromas coupled with the presence of loving company, warm our home against the cold rain outside. By evening everyone goes separate ways, leaving me to settle into mothering. I can't wait just to stare our son without interruption and smell the creases of his neck.

Awkwardly, I rig up the baby bathtub on the dining room table, in preparation for River's first bath. Tom goes out for groceries and to buy me a few good nursing shirts as the implications of breastfeeding every hour-on-the-hour no matter where I am, have already hit home. I'm reveling in our miracle when Tom returns.

"Button, come-come! Our little River just loves the water! No surprise there, huh? Button-Lovely, Hurry, look! He's all wide-eyed. You won't believe how alert he is."

I smell Tom even before my eyes met his red, spacey ones. He has checked out, just as his son checks in. *Shit.* Mamma-bear rage sets in: "WHAT ARE YOU *DOING*? You just went out to get stoned didn't you? How long has *that* been going on?" I shoot bullets at him, giving him no time to lie in response. "I can't believe you! We've got this little miracle here and you're escaping reality. *This* little guy right here is the greatest high ever and you're missing it, just one day out! What's wrong with this reality? Aren't we enough?"

I begin crying and bundle River up, as if to protect him from taking any of this personally because I sure can't. Tom brushes past me and puts the groceries away in silence, offering no explanations. The coin flips and with it goes the fleeting joy of our cozy home. The rest of the evening I cuddle River in bed and tell

Jennifer Allen

him he is the best thing that has ever happened to me, until we both doze off into sleep.

I wouldn't have believed that my entire orientation would shift to baby growing, but it has. *Everything* else is second to that, including Tom. Mother nature has ways of protecting new life and her medicine is strong. I'm drunk on it and tangled in a string of hurts and anger. It's taking me days of unraveling to feel even a pinch of compassion for Tom, in his plight to mask the pain of eventually leaving his son.

The rain breaks on Saturday morning and we go out for our first walk as a family. River nestles into the sling of soft cloth I wear across my chest. I pull the blankets away from his nose, checking continuously to make sure I'm not smothering him in the new contraption. He begins to cry.

"What is it baby boy?" I coo to him. His cry turns into a shriek. "What Sweetie? What is it?"

I look up at Tom and clear the new-mom checklist: "He can breathe, he's not wet and I just fed and burped him before we left."

"You want me to take him?" Tom offers.

"No, it's okay. I've got him." River continues bellowing. My lips tremble and I turn to walk down the trail. *He's only got me and I can't help him.*

"Let me take him, Jen," Tom insists from behind me.

I stop, the quiver tugging the corners of my mouth down.

"Why is he crying? I've done everything I know!"

"My Jessica used to cry like this. We tried everything under the sun and finally discovered the car. We'd drive around the neighborhood for hours on end to settle her down," Tom consoles.

"Yeah, well you weren't leaving Jessica, were you?" I throw him a shot from left field—shrapnel left from the blowout just a few nights before. Little does he know that I haven't been able to shake the anticipation of this precious child's eventual abandonment since he gave me that sneak preview with the pot-smoking homecoming.

"I just didn't know it then and now it's a possibility." He catches the shot in mid-air, with straightforward acknowledgement of his potential abandonment by death.

"So, you bail with your heart, just in case?" I yell over River's howls. He knows I'm talking about his pot checkout.

He put his hand up, dismissing my accusation, and walks past me.

You bastard. The dance is looking all too familiar.

He turns and looks me square on as if he hears my thoughts. "I want this so badly, you can't even know! Why do you think I was so hesitant to have children at this point in the game? Jesus, Jen," he whisper-shouts, so as not to make matters worse with River. "It wasn't because I don't love fathering and all that comes with it. It was because it's unfair. Unfair to him, unfair to you, unfair to me! You've got the luxury of knowing you'll be here for him. I don't."

Mamma-bear ammo is at the tip of my tongue, ready to defend, until I see his eyes well up. "This fucking cancer!" he spits out. His nostrils flare, catching a tear that has spilled over his lower lid.

I move in close and put my hand on the side of his face. Our heads drop to center in unison, propped up on each other's foreheads. Baby River is wedged between us. All three of us are crying now. In our huddle, we strategize against our common enemy. The game plan is to love anyway. Illness can threaten to take away many things, but not the capacity to love.

Tom makes the choice. The crack in his heart is palpable, and so is the little opening it makes. We give a silent *"Go team!"* and break huddle.

River stops crying: mission accomplished. I duck awkwardly out of the sling and offer it to Tom: "He wants his Daddy."

Tom tenderly gathers River and his heap of blankets out of the sling and holds him at eye level. "And his Daddy wants him," he says pressing River's tiny body against his chest. "More than he'll ever know."

We walk on into our future, committed to never taking it for granted, regardless of which side of the coin we are on.

Just a week into being a new mom, resentment has already begun to quietly seed itself under my skin. It's not the baby but the education. Winter break is still a month away and I have projects to turn in and classes to show up for—in order to pass, in order to graduate sooner, in order to get a career up and rolling, in order to keep our family afloat if and when Tom gets sicker. Each time I pack River snugly into his carrier, stuff thick breast pads into my bra, load up a backpack with diapers and textbooks and head to class, I must remind myself of how this very move is connected to caring for our child. I sit through Statistics and Methodology every week, trying not to gaze at the beloved baby sleeping in his carseat at my feet, but my brain is jelly for anything else. It's all I can do to ask a question every class to prove I'm still on board. Inevitably, River whimpers and my breasts tingle heavily and a surge of milk floods the pads, making dark bulls-eyes on my shirt. As usual, my body knows what we both need. I fight it tooth and nail in the name of a bigger picture of survival.

Winter break finally arrives providing respite, or rather a tease of what it's like to be an at-home mother. Nothing to date has been as consistently challenging as switching gears out of mother mode and into teacher mode at work or student mode at school. Laurie, the boss I've made a terrible habit of complaining about to co-workers, takes mercy on me and tweaks my job description, putting me on chart duty and out of the classroom so River can come to work with me while he's still in his infant slumber phase. No more Laurie dissin' for me.

By February, River is wide-awake and needs more attention than a Mamma cooing to him while typing out reports. When I tell Laurie I need to switch to part-time, she offers a job share set up to Tom and me that will maintain our medical benefits. She had met Tom at a work party and, like so many people, took an instant liking to him and invited him to sub for other teachers according to his availability. Back then, I had rolled my eyes and told my co-worker it was because he was eye-candy for her. Now I'm feeling guilty for undermining her generosity. She's officially a saint and I tell her so, repeatedly. Tom comes on board two days a week and works at the lab two days a week, leaving two seven-hour windows a week for River to be in day-care. Not bad.

"See, it all works out," he tells me, for the thousand-something time in our six years together. One day I hope to have the vision of retrospect like that.

On the days Tom or the babysitter have River I must supply the milk. Dairy cow is added to my many roles. The generous breaks at work I used to spend keeping my life as an artist alive are now spent pumping milk. Retreats into the darkroom produce baggies of milk instead of developed negatives. The cow routine goes like this: After locking myself in the darkroom, I methodically lay out a towel, bottles and bags on the counter opposite the chemical trays; then I rig up the mess of tubes that connect the pump to the cups; assemble the bladder that keeps milk from flushing back into the motor; screw it to the bottles and the bottles to the cups; roll up my shirt and tuck it under my chin; unlatch the flaps of my nursing bra, center the suction cups over each nipple and hit the power switch on the shoe-box size pump. The machine pulls each breast rhythmically through the cone and into the column of the cup, contorting them into long cow-teets as the milk shoots against the tiny rubber bladder and drains into the bottle. Closing my eyes, I picture myself at home, rocking and nursing River and pray no one blows the flow by knocking on the door.

Once in awhile one of the autistic students, Sean, talks incessantly through the wall at me, obsessing on the intrigue of the mystery machine I pack in and out of the classroom. If I'm lucky and uninterrupted, I'll get about three ounces before the break is up. That's just enough to keep up with River's feeding cycles. Before the next bell rings, I've got my breasts tucked back in for respite, the paraphernalia cleaned and packed up and a baggy of mamma's milk ready to stash in the lounge fridge next to my co-workers' Diet Cokes and Starbuck mochas. Nothing short of maximum efficiency is what's required to pull off the work, school, and mamma thing.

Over the winter and into the spring, our son grows into his own little person. Like a magnet, my attention keeps coming back to him, no matter how interesting I thought the subject of my thesis was or how invested I've been in the study and practice of art as a healing modality. In bed at night, Tom shares his delight in every miniscule advance of River's development I missed while I was at evening classes.

"You should see our little man in the Johnny-Jumper. Man-o-man, he's so funny! He just figured out how to bounce today and already he's a little Mexican jumping bean. He gets all worked up yelping and drooling and pounding his little fists on the tray each time he springs up," Tom says laughing.

"Tell me more," I say patting Tom's chest in the dark. Like most parents, I don't want to miss a moment of the miracle of a child growing at the most rapid pace of it's life outside the womb. At the same time, I'm comforted Tom is taking in every drop I'm missing, while he can.

During the summer, I sign up for classes and plug away at my thesis in order to graduate by December. Fantasies of what it will be like once I finish this marathon education begin dancing around my head during lectures. In them, I imagine being home with my toddler, playing pat-a-cake, finger painting, taking walks to the park, and even getting back to my art when he's down for naps. Working an internship doesn't factor into the fantasy, nor does Tom getting sicker. It's been easy to bypass the latter, as there haven't been any indicators that the cancer is progressing. Tom jumps to his feet behind the plate at the ball field. Good. He comes home from weekly cancer support groups at Sutter with enthusiastic stories of alignment with the doctor who facilitates the group. Great.

Back in June, we celebrated Tom's 50th and invited the doc, along with family and friends from all over. Tom and a dozen or so others rafted down the American River. Our son crawled among the sour grass and Kizma ran circles around him, while I set up a massive tent in the backyard for overnight guests. Late into the afternoon Tom returned, brown from a day in the sun and ready to celebrate. We all ate dinner on the back lawn, toasting to Tom's milestone and convinced we'd someday be celebrating his 60th in similar form.

It's hard to believe it's been a whole year since this precious son of ours came into the world. River is cute beyond cute and I don't think its because I'm partial. He's sinewy, like a little muscle man and has his daddy's olive skin, almond shaped eyes and hefty bottom lip that reminds me of Kris Kringle from the Christmas special that was on when I was a kid. At the back of his head a bald-spot, worn through since the early days of too much sitting in car seats at Mamma's feet while she worked, is growing in with the same curly blonde hair that cradles his face. His eyes range the spectrum from grey to brown depending on the day and his smile reveals six bright Chicklet teeth—four on top, two on bottom. Like Tom, and Mum would say like me too, he's curious about everything. A pinecone or a washcloth can be made into elaborate play experiences, entertaining him for long stretches of time.

In early November we hold a party in the backyard to celebrate his first birthday with a mix of friends and family from multiple circles. I look across the lawn at Tom, sitting in a beach chair, running a hand through his thinning brown hair and offering River a sip of his alcohol-free beer. River wobbles upright, hanging on to his daddy's leg, and grabs for the bottle with his free hand. Tom laughs and talks on with the other adults who sit in a circle watching the babies crawl around the grass in the middle. His eyes never leave River.

I walk over and squat behind his chair and whisper into his ear: "We've done good, huh?"

He reaches for my hand and presses it to his heart. "Yeah, it's been a good year, Butterfly. We're so lucky." His pulse is strong under my palm. *Yes, so lucky.*

We watch our son with button-popping pride and joy as he falls to all fours, scrambles to the next chair and pulls himself up for a bottle scan. *Click.* Francisco takes our picture.

"You two look love struck!" he teases and Tom and I look to each other knowingly. *Absolutely.*

Frankie—Francisco, as he's insisted on being called since his move out West, was like a little brother to me in art school; annoying and yet, lovable. Occasionally we still banter like siblings and get caught up in rivalry around being artists. He's making a living as a graphic designer in San Francisco and drops subtle innuendos about how I've sold out going back to school for art therapy—as if it isn't really art. Actually, it's a sore spot for me and I can't tell how much of it is him teasing and how much is me,

Jennifer Allen

ripe for such interpretations. It's not that I wish it any different. I simply miss the time to fully indulge in creativity. Right now it's Frankie behind the camera. I remind myself that I gave up photography because, ironically, it kept me one step removed from the moment.

When it's time for the cake, Tom encourages River to do what he wasn't allowed to as a child: "Go ahead, little man, put your hands in . . . that's it. Tastes good, huh? Oh, I guess it makes a good hair mousse too." Tom opens his mouth and River feeds him whipped cream and squeals when Tom pretends to eat his tiny fingers. Both of them have white beards of cream. *Click.* Another shot from Frankie. He's reading the moments like I would have, leaving me free to be directly in them.

As the sun gets lower, the babies get crankier; ours included. Guests start to leave and I feel a growing angst. What I want is to be a normal family: clean up, bathe River and fall asleep nursing him, with Tom in bed beside us. But, there is schoolwork to be done—a thesis project to complete before I can be free of it.

Again, the coin flips. I'm sucked out of the sweet joy of our child's first birthday and into educational obligations that had once held my enthusiasm. I'm limping through the homestretch of six weeks until graduation. One minute I'm full of regret that I've overridden what I wanted most in favor of a future survival plan. The next minute, I'm confident that I'm taking care of my family in the best possible way.

So here I sit, in front of the blue screen, wanting to blame the man I felt immensely grateful to just hours before.

"I'm going to bed," Tom announces and pecks the top of my head. "It was a great party, Jen."

"Mmmhmm." The sweetness from earlier in the day is out of reach. When he leaves the room, I let the tears trickle out. *Why don't you support us more so I don't have to crank out a career so fast? Why are you going to sleep when I'm the one who's exhausted? Why am I wasting my fucking time on this thesis when you don't even care?* I stop myself after a good solid five minutes of getting nowhere in the blame game. All I really want is for Tom to catch my fall, like he promised way back when. Only he doesn't know I'm slipping.

Back to the screen and the stack of books. Minutes turn into hours and everything I write strays off topic. *I can't do this.* I'm reminded of the ultimate fatigue I've felt hundreds of feet off the ground when down-climbing wasn't an option and remember the mantra that renewed me many-a-time: *Just go with what's in front of you and trust the next move.* I sit up straight and try to remember why I'm writing.

Graduation is the carrot that lures me by notching me a step closer to a secure future and the illusion that I'll be free to mother. Somehow I've forgotten that the point of the education was a career. The subject of the thesis is where my words fall flat. I'm deflated by the unappreciated effort of fighting my husband's enemy for him and somehow feeling like I'm missing the point.

Being a queen of efficiency, I chose a subject that would support our real-world experience. "Art Psychotherapy Support Groups for Cancer Patients" was the title. Early on, every article or book I read resonated with the mind-body connection and the synergistic nature of group support I experienced vicariously through Tom. Our discussions over dinner were lively with hope as our passions overlapped—his of alternative medicine and the power of support groups and mine of using art for healing. Psychoneuroimmunology was a budding field and I quickly realized the implications for the creative process on the immune system. The art interventions I designed for the groups had slowly moved from emotional support to healing—as in *cure.* Secretly, I had been out to save Tom.

Priorities have changed. Getting through his illness, wherever it goes, without finding ourselves out on the street with a baby in tow, has become number one. It means I *must* hang my hope on a stronger hook, for all of us. Emotional and spiritual healing for everyone involved becomes my new hook. Pecking away at the keys, I focus on the carrot, instead of a rescue mission.

"Cure" as a concept is released, again. Renegotiatons with God follow. *Got it. Quality time—you decide how much. And hey, could you maybe keep a roof over our heads?*

Jennifer Allen

8

Walking Dark Valleys

Winter 1995–Spring 1996

Graduation finally comes mid-December and I'm surprised that
it's over without event. At least in art school I had the satisfaction
of walking across the stage and shaking hands with professors who
knew my name. Sac State is too big for such personal attention. It
seems like I've jumped through a million and one hoops, including
the purchase of a cap and gown when we can barely make rent, to
get this diploma. As it turns out, hundreds—if not thousands, of us
line the floor and stands of the Arco Sports Arena, only to hear our
names listed and the diplomas mailed to us later. Afterwards, we
have a small celebration at home and Tom presents me with a ring
he's been secretly working on for months. It's a gold yin-yang
symbol with my name and credentials in itty-bitty raised letters
along its edge.

"Let this mark the integration of all the opposing forces that you've grown from in order to complete your dream. You're going to make a great therapist, Jen," he says slipping it onto my right ring finger. Now I have two rings, from this dear husband of mine, to remind me that the choices I've made have been perfect.

Even weeks later, Tom spontaneously smiles proud, shakes his head and says, "You really did it Jen."

I'm filled to the brim with his strokes of appreciation and reveling in motherhood now that I am free when I return home from work. My only extra-curricular item has been sending out resumes so that when we move back to the Monterey Peninsula over the summer I'll have a paid internship lined up. Everything is humming along, with only minor health glitches for Tom, resulting in a day of laying low every other week or so. He passed kidney stones a couple of years ago so he theorizes they're building up again. Not enough to warrant a visit to the doctor. *Yet.*

Tom sold his prized Fiat convertible for a second-hand family car out of my insistence last week and all hell has broken loose ever since.

"Psycho-man just left another message. Actually it's the eleventh one today," I say, in place of a greeting, when Tom returns from work. He bends over to kiss my head while I nurse River.

"And how was *your* day?" he asks.

I ignore the niceties and muster a casual tone: "He's says the car's a piece of shit and we're going to pay for ripping him off. The last call was a bit graphic . . . had to cover River's ears."

"Yeah, something's off with him. I gave him the mechanic's number, but he insisted Kenny was lying when he gave the thumb's up before the sale. I'd give him his frickin' money back if I hadn't already bought the kid-mobile."

Tom heads to the kitchen muttering: "Knew I shouldn't have let that car go." With his back to me, he reaches up to a high shelf, pulls down his switchblade and slips it into his back pocket.

Fear gets the better of me. "I'm calling the cops," I say.

Jennifer Allen

"Already did," he calls from the behind the refrigerator door. "Sure enough, he's got a record but they can't do anything until he does something first."

"Oh great, so we need to wait until he sneaks in at night and slits our throats?"

Tom looks over the door, contracts his brow and puts a finger to his lips. "Jen, we'll be fine. He's all talk."

Yeah, right—and you've got thirteen years left too, huh?

"We'll be moving in a couple months anyway," he says and comes back into the living room, scoops up River and nuzzles his belly. "Right little man? Nobody's going to mess with us, huh?" River giggles and I fume.

I'm not good with splashing foolishly around in the water while the music quickens and the fin surfaces, so I take a stand. "Well, I'm going to start packing us up."

"Good plan. I'll take Rio out for a grapefruit raid," he says in breaths between raspberries.

That's about the closest thing I'm going to get for validation of the danger we are in. Though I doubt it'll ever be said aloud, I can hear his argument now: *Fear is like wildfire—it gets out of control all too easily. I'll cover mine so that you and the baby don't catch it . . . and just maybe, I can even hide it from the cancer.* A few pounds down and a shade paler have me worried the cancer is well aware of his fear and thriving on it. Tom claims it's the extra hours he's putting in trying to get the software program up and running before we move.

Meanwhile, I collude, pretending not to notice the baseball bat hidden under his coat by the front door or him slipping out of bed each night to peek through the blinds for long periods of time.

Working at a teen prison isn't helping matters. I've got two more weekend gigs at the California Youth Authority, where I teach art classes to sex offending boys who keep one hand under the table at all times. Only since a staff-member clued me in, after watching last week's class from the security monitor, do I realize just how naïve I am. The boys have been literally getting off on it. Another hit of violation on good intention primes the slope into victimhood. Between chronic cancer worries and psycho-man, I'm already halfway there.

At the next class, I fight back: "All hands on deck. Everyone . . . or you're out of here! In fact, why don't you leave now if you can't respect me or what I'm teaching you," I say, feeling the heat in my ears. I'm pissed. The room is silent and twelve sets of hands are on the table except for Victor, who slouches with his arms crossed and legs spread eagle. He puckers his mouth, scrunching his sparse black mustache into a Hitler fashion and forces a cocky laugh out his nose.

"You, Sir, can leave!" I point at the door and flash him the security alarm that hangs from my belt.

"Whatever." He gets up and saunters to the door. The class continues with me on red-alert to every gesture, making damn sure I won't be had again.

The vigilance follows me home to what was once our safe-haven and I add violence to the growing list of things I resent. Having a baby to protect only ups the ante and I've got our lives packed up in two weeks flat. I forewarn my employer and reserve a moving van. All the while, Tom and I keep our smiles up, loyal to the unsaid pact against fear, counting down the days and counting up the threats. At a last minute's notice, Joyce and an old housemate of ours from college, show up to help load the U-haul. We slip away all at once one day, leaving no forwarding information for Psycho-man to track us down with.

Our caravan arrives at two a.m. to the Seaside home we left behind four years ago. A recurrence, a marriage, a baby and a Master's degree have happened in the interim. The vision I hold of our little family starting up a new chapter in the safety of the community we call home evaporates when we open the door and are greeted by a stench of shit. Tom hits the light switch. Only the florescent bulb lights up, creating a vibrating green haze in the entrance. It's so far off from my vision that I consider giving such nonsense up. Other than both toilets being at maximum capacity and a few Burger King wrappers on the living room floor, the evidence of disaster is primarily in the wear. The baseboards are scuffed up, the carpets are matted and the walls have stains. Actually it feels dirtier than it looks. Not the kind of place one wants to have a toddler wandering around in. And not a place that feels like a fresh start.

Jennifer Allen

"Shit, shit and shit!" I say, looking to Tom for an explanation. I knew there was a messy eviction going on, but he assured me it was handled—well, except for the six months of rent that we had to compensate for.

"Yeah, like I told you a few months ago when I came down and checked in, it looked like they had about ten people living here. Probably some kind of drug scheme," he offers nonchalantly.

"Tom," I say, feeling at the edge of a breakdown. "You said it would be ready for us."

"And it should have been if the renters had kept their word. Look Jen, we're lucky enough to have them out of here. Remember we weren't planning to move for another month or so. It's easier to do the clean-up from here anyway."

None of his reasoning matters to me at this point and I want to blame him for everything. *Why didn't you tell me what to expect? Why didn't you get better renters? Why didn't you make sure the car was fixed before you sold it to Psycho-Man? Why didn't you do what the doctor's said? Why did you have to get cancer in the first place?*

"I know, babe, I know," he says, trying to invoke some stability to catch my fall.

No, you don't know. My heart bumps up against another ceiling in our relationship. It doesn't matter that he's trying hard to make things right. They aren't. The sooner we acknowledge that, the sooner we can move on with life "as is."

Joyce nudges Tom to the side and slips in with River asleep in her arms. "Where should I put him?" she asks.

"Can you hold him until I get the air mattress inflated?" I ask her. I'm in no position to hold anyone.

"Sure," she says and finds a place on the floor that looks relatively clean. I drag the air mattress up stairs to what was our bedroom, four years earlier. It smells like cigarettes and there are unfilled nail holes spotting every wall. The ceiling light has become the local fly cemetery and it barely illuminates the room. I open the slider to the balcony and step out into the cool salty air, staring out across the bay to the glowing lights of the peninsula. Humming from the streetlights and a dog barking in the distance are the only sounds. The neighbors are packed in tightly, though all seem to have come to a consensus about quiet time.

Just breathe. A tight knot loosens in my throat, releasing weeks of postponed tears. For a long while I watch Tom from above, unload the cab of the truck and the back of my car. And then I notice that Carl's place next door is abandoned. Yellow caution tape seems to be the only thing holding it together. The last time Tom spoke to him, he was depressed and having no luck finding work. I wonder about him, but I don't worry. Steadily, my perspective changes to that of the timeless night sky and it's as if I am the universe hovering over the world with no attachment to the outcome of even the most tragic events. Everything is in its place at exactly the right time. Even the plastic bag dancing up the street in the breeze has its role in this grand symphony. Acceptance drifts into the mix of fading anger and overwhelm causing an alchemic reaction inside of me: home. It's not the house either. It's our life—as is—and I'm ready to reclaim it. In silence, I nod to the stars a gesture of understanding. A zephyr of ocean air washes me clean of any cling-on doubts and I return inside and start over.

In the morning Ed and Roxanne come by to welcome us back and end up helping unload furniture and endless boxes from the truck. We spend the day scouring bathrooms, unclogging toilets, cleaning out the refrigerator, unpacking boxes of kitchenware and picking up dog poop from the mini-yard. Daylight makes a world of difference. So does the smell of Mr. Clean. Joyce and Katy stay for the weekend and take River for walks to neighborhood parks while I go out to rent a steam-cleaner and pick up groceries and Easter basket fixings. By Saturday night, Tom has the toilets in working order, our basic furniture assembled in place and all the light bulbs replaced. Easter is tomorrow and it feels fitting to celebrate a holiday that represents new beginnings.

Sunday afternoon we drive down the coast to a meadow in Big Sur where a bunch of Tom's friends gather for the annual picnic and egg-hunt. He has attended this picnic every year, since his girls were small. It was a family tradition that went through an awkward stage when Tom and I got together. His friends were welcoming and kept their skepticism well hidden as they adjusted to us as a couple. At least they didn't have to choose allegiances since Louise stopped coming after the divorce. It's been made clear to Tom that she and I are never to cross paths. I'm hoping she has a change of heart before some life-event, say Tom's funeral or one of their daughter's weddings, is upon us. It would be crazy and awkward, but so much easier for the girls in the long run.

Jessica and Eliza join us again this year, after brunch with their mom. With them, their respective boyfriends, River, Joyce, and Katy along, we are a family of sorts, and people relate to us as such. The adult egg-hunt frantically ensues. Many a hot and cold clue later, I end up finding the coveted golden egg and it feels like I've made my final rite of passage into the group. Later in the day, after bellies are full of potato salad, ham, and boiled eggs and the small children are groggy from chocolate-egg hangovers, the whole group poses for a photo. I'm reminded of big family get-togethers growing up back East and the sense of belonging that has always been so important to me. *Home again, home again, jiggedy, jig.*

When we left the Peninsula four years ago I was waiting tables, photographing weddings, and assisting Ed on photo shoots. Now I'm pursuing professional work as an intern therapist and feeling like my own boss. I'm quite proud, if not a little cocky, until I realize that interns are considered cheap labor by non-profits who can't offer their services without them. Waiting tables was clearly a better venue for making ends meet. No matter, though, I figure I'll emphasize my degree, avoid the word "intern" and imagine myself working with people in the trenches of their lives, where things are vividly real.

Within a month, I've followed up on all the leads I made from Folsom and have landed multiple jobs of interest. Thanks to that *goddamn* thesis of mine, I get on at Hospice doing social work and find myself in the role of speaking the big "D" word. What I can't talk about at home, I practice daily at work. Coming up to speed with medical terminology, local resources, and learning the area for home visits is daunting, though nothing compared to lending emotional support to dying patients and their families. Like I've done many times in my life, I gravitate to what scares me the most in hope of annihilating the fear with intimate familiarity. It takes time, though. At first, I'm detached and not sure this work isn't going to put me over some kind of edge.

Part of the job includes visiting the local hospital and talking to potential hospice candidates: a.k.a. those who have "lost the battle." I check with medical records and then zip up to the fifth floor and squeeze into a tiny office shared by Michelle, the discharge planner, and Barbara, the oncology program director. We sigh heavily for the unfortunate cases: young parents, children and those who don't look ready; and nod in agreement for the cases that seemed acceptable: the elderly, the homeless alcoholic and the patient whose body has been kept alive after the spirit was long gone. Though I know Tom might be on such a list in the future, it's comforting to be on the objective side of things. I'm only the messenger offering services that could, hopefully, result in a *good death*.

As I become a regular on the cancer floor, I see those who come back again and again, each time getting weaker, but not ready (or their doctors aren't) to call off the chemo troops. It isn't that people *never* get better, only I wouldn't know it because I have no reason to visit them. Somehow, seeing those nearing death's doorstep after having been through the ravages of conventional treatments helps convince me that the subtle increasing signs of Tom's au-natural decline—the pants bagging off his thinning waist, the empty bottles of ibuprofen and the hours of cat-naps—are just a phase. On one hand, he doesn't look like them—like he's dying from this disease. On the other, it's getting hard not to assume everyone with cancer dies, when that's all I see happening.

During one of my routine check-ins at the hospital, Barbara gives me a lead on an opening for the position of Director of the Healing Arts. The job is a ticket to see all the patients: the full spectrum of cancer possibilities and experience proof that people do recover—at least for long stretches of time. Hope is crucial to me now as Tom and I start up another chapter of our lives. Money is the other factor. Every last drop goes toward keeping up with the mortgage. The hours sync perfectly with my hospice work and both jobs benefit my working at the other. Medical art therapists are sparse in this area and I'm an in-house choice.

Barbara welcomes me on board and I begin the following week pushing my well-stocked cart of art supplies through the halls of oncology and pediatrics free to work with anyone who's interested. Quickly, I find, with the exception of children, art is the last thing many patients want to do. So I listen.

An older man sits up in bed and tells me in great detail about his financial success. He's unaccustomed to having his playing field leveled by a hospital johnny and no special treatment.

Though Javier speaks little English and I speak even less Spanish, we relate easily. He tells me enthusiastically about his plans for life. He is still young and considers leukemia God's message to him that it's time to break through the ceiling of farm-work.

And then there is Anna, who, at sixteen, is the eldest of five children. Until her cancer diagnosis, she watched her younger siblings after school while her parents worked. She feels guilty for getting sick and for even caring about losing her long brown hair.

Each person has their own story in response to their illness. If they choose to share it, I get to hear it. That's beginning to feel like a privilege instead of a burden. Barbara invites me to facilitate a breast cancer support group for women, a caregiver's group, and the Candle Lighter group for kids with cancer and their families. Cancer is all around me and, strangely, I love it. Listening to people with cancer, I feel like I get an inside scoop on what might be going on with Tom, without the immediate threat I feel when he says it.

The difference between pity and empathy has become pronounced for me, making it easy to offer caregivers the kind of compassion I wish I could give myself. Feeling for another and hearing the supportive words come from my mouth is at least one step closer.

When I run into an acquaintance in the line at Safeway, she asks me what I'm up to since the move back. When I tell her about my work she asks, incredulously: "Why?" She doesn't see a gain for me in the deal beyond the steady income.

I try and explain, "Believe me, if it wasn't mutual, I wouldn't be doing it. Martyrdom is highly overrated."

She shakes her head, "I'm missing something here."

Yup. You sure are. I agree with a smile, grab my cart and head out.

It's the first Friday of the month and I'm attending my first-ever professional luncheon as a therapist. I feel like a genuine grown-up until I sit and scan the room. From the looks of the local therapist population, I'm not going to get that kind of credit. This is one of the few occupations where it's hip to be older. What I do revel in, however, is the satisfaction of a past fantasy realized. It wasn't too long ago that I waited tables at similar events and imagined someday I'd be an attendee instead of a food server. It makes no difference to me what menu choice they bring or what the speaker is saying. Simply being here is enough.

After the applause there is time to mingle. A woman introduces herself and asks if I'm the intern with the ad.

She says, "I wasn't looking to take on an intern, but I saw your last name was Allen-Sanchez and it caught my attention. Are you bilingual?"

"No—well, I used to speak Italian. I'm rusty, though, and my Spanish is even worse. No worries, my plate's been filling up lately, anyway," I say.

We walk out to the parking garage together and discuss the possibility of my interning in her private practice one day a week. Simultaneously, we stop at two silver Volvo wagons parked side by side. Only difference is the year.

"That's me," I say, pointing to the older one on the left.

"And that's me!" She gestures to the one on the right. "Well, look at that!" Janice says laughing. "Must be a sign. Think on the internship and let's talk next week."

A woman who reads signs – I'm in. I call her on Tuesday and start advertising for private clients. It's a long haul to licensure via private practice, but I'll need the know-how if I'm ever to be my own boss. Besides, there's something about Janice. She seems important to the bigger picture and, occasionally, my curiosity outranks practical matters.

The world of work is unfolding beautifully for me, leaving me two days during the week to be one-hundred-percent mother to River while Tom rekindles his ties in the dental lab business on a part-time basis. Despite the fatigue he suffers afterwards, he

Jennifer Allen

spends evenings on the diamond, officiating for the spring baseball season and reviving his local reputation as the cool Blue with the braid who never loses his head. His off days are "on" trying to simultaneously parent a toddler, keep up a moderate version of the Gerson treatment, and complete the software program he began in Sacramento. If the project hadn't held the significance of righting finances, he would have dropped it in a heartbeat, resting himself into being with his son for every possible moment. It occurs to me that he, too, gives up some of his present for the sake of a future, even if he may not be in it. In our own ways we are both preparing for the big "D" without calling it such.

Tom gets life insurance: good. I get copies of advanced directives from my work and we fill them out: good. Tom reconnects with his cancer support group: good. Tom is writing again: good.

I don't think *I* needed a support group, yet: not good. Tom becomes obsessed with outsmarting the lottery: not good. A year past-due property tax bill sits in the paper recycle: not good.

With the rising sunshine of our new lives, shadows are cast. This time, I'm not going to God to negotiate ridding life of this shadow-factor. Somewhere along the way, I think it was after Psycho-man, I gave up on making deals with Him. Anyhow, I've known since adolescence, when I begged Him to inspire a love of life in Scott, that the paternal God who grants personal favors was a big fat hoax. Why I've bothered to rekindle my belief puzzles me. The only reason I even returned to using the three-letter word was that I was frequenting the source so often I had resorted to a nickname. And, perhaps the childhood beliefs tagged along with the namesake as a familiar fix in desperate times. The pleading that permeates my prayers is bordering on pathetic. *Enough, already!*

My final conversation with the Daddy-God goes like this: "You want him? Well, just take him and stop the teasing, already! You are one cruel fucker, you know that?"

Nothing.

"And I don't need any *Goddamn* favors from you anyway!"

No signs. I half expect a bolt of lightning for such blasphemy. The curtain's been pulled, the gig is up: no personal

God. All the things that have happened that I'm tempted to classify as either sunshine or shadow: He loves me, he loves me not—well, they are all just life in its grand complexity doing its thing. Nothing personal. The love in my very own heart gives me more of what I expect from God than any return on prayers—the pleading ones anyhow. I've decided there's nothing like a good crisis of faith to bring one into one's own humanity. *And maybe this is where the God-mystery has been hiding out all along.*

Meanwhile, Tom is having a crisis of his own. It's hard to believe he's depressed when he and River tumble through the door. They are laughing after a walk around the block to pick the last of the sour grass before the summer drought begins. There's a sparkle is in his eye and he's wearing vibrant colors, like always. I'm floored by how well he pulls off being fine, when he had handed me a plea for help only an hour earlier.

In an unusual gesture, he asked me to read one of the stories he'd been working on before he left on their walk. "I'd like to hear what you think," he said.

"Sure."

As soon as the door closed behind them, I sat down and read. It didn't take rocket science to uncover his suicide wishes under those of his character. All of his writing is about him, disguised in myriad different characters. *Did he think I wasn't on to that? Or did he give it to me because he knew I was?* Suicide is a touchy subject with me after Scott. This story was probably the only way he dared tell me. And then there's the contradiction of him having been a suicide crisis counselor during our four years in Sacramento. Everyone who knows him buys into his drive to live. *How could he even think of cutting out on purpose?*

It's all I can do not to pin him against a wall and demand explanation when he gets back with River. Good thing there are hours until we'll be alone to talk, because right now, I'd only call him a liar and a deal-breaker. Later in the evening, after River is tucked into his big-boy bed, I've settled down enough to tread lightly into Tom's darkest valley.

"So Tom, I read your stuff. Interesting," I say, using his catch-all response. "Your character, Jacob . . . you know, when he rigs up the accident on the rock, before it goes awry and he ends up killing his friend instead of himself. Maybe he dies too, does he?"

"That is left to you to wonder. What was your point with Jacob?" he asks, clearly wanting to go there.

"It's bugging me that his incentive to pull off such an accident was because he thought he would burden his family. He wasn't even disabled by his illness yet. Why would he make such assumptions so early in the game?" A sticky black ball of tar lodges itself in my gut. It reeks of earlier days with Scott. *How had it come to this?*

"He had to do it, don't you see? One: because he could still pull it off and two: if he was too sick already, the life insurance wouldn't have bought that it was an accident." He answers matter-of-factly.

"So it's all about the money?" My voice holds evidence that I've bridged the scenario over to him, but we aren't naming names.

"For his *family*. He would have taken them all down if he let it drag out. It was better for everyone that it was quick and accidental."

My face is burning hot now. "Oh, I see. Better for his kids, who would have no chance to say goodbye, better for his wife and friends who were robbed of showing their love by caring for him, or was it just better for him because it was an easy way out?" Barely shielded by the character, I can get away with such accusations.

"It was a selfless act, you're missing the point," he defends.

"Well, just for the record, don't do me any favors by jumping off any rocks. We both signed on for the long haul, here," I say unable to weed harsh tones. No more suicide for me. That's not our deal.

"Jen, this could get really messy. I'm in way over my head," he says. I can't believe he isn't trying to convince me that I've concocted this whole thing up from a simple story.

"What do you mean?" The ball of tar grows heavier.

He starts to cry. It scares me because it's so out of character for him and, simultaneously, I feel a perverse excitement at witnessing his exposure. I hope it means we might bust through our glass ceiling. He's letting me in, like he had with his history awhile back. Now it pertains to us.

"I'm getting sicker . . . I can feel it." He breaks into a sob.

Relief at hearing the truth overrides my panic. "I know, Tom," I say, flashing back to the clues that were easy to write off in comparison to what I see at work: longer recovery times, a dwindling libido and a paling green tint to his olive complexion.

"What's going to happen if I can't work? What if I can't get this software sold in time? I really meant to tell you . . . I wanted to, but I thought I if I could just clear it up. You worry so much," he says shaking his head and pressing his face into his hands. "Shit, I can't believe I'm doing this again. I'm so sorry, Jen."

"Tell me now, Tom. All of it,"

"I'm so far behind on the property taxes. And the balloon payment is due on the mortgage. I don't know if we can keep the house through this. I wanted to leave something . . . just in case. I didn't mean for it to go this way." He doubles over, quaking with sobs between words. Drips of tears and snot pelt the carpet freely.

The house! Quickly, I shelve practical concerns for later in favor of the rare opportunity to catch Tom.

"Oh, Button," I say. Luckily, my words manifest on the compassionate side of the fence. So easily, it could have been anger.

He lifts his head from his hands and looks at me, showing me his innards. "I'm trying so hard to stay alive. It's just sometimes . . . I'm too tired. Sometimes I just want out. It's too damn hard to keep up." I hold his hand between mine.

"I've been smoking again. Cigars. Thinking I'm doing myself some favor because its not pot, but *I've* always known the correlation between bladder cancer and smoking," he says shaking his head in shameful disapproval. "Why am I doing it when I *know*? I can hardly stand to go the support group anymore. Jesus, I'm such a hypocrite. They count on me."

"It's a *support* group. Tell them, they'll understand," I urge, wanting to fix anything at all that's fixable. There isn't much.

"No, I can't. Not after all I've said. I've made an image and I can't hold it up. Hope is everything and I'd be taking some away from them. I just can't."

He sounds too much like Scott and I can't help myself, I resort to guilt tactics: "Okay, so what, you kill yourself because

Jennifer Allen

you're ashamed and because it's hard? Now *that* would leave behind a trail of garbage for the rest of us to clean up."

"I'm saying it crosses my mind, not that I'd ever do it. I hate that I even think of it. I hate that I can't stop smoking." His admission undermines the momentum of my attack. We're on the same side with this. He leans into my chest and I gather him in, stroking his back, like I do with River when he's skinned a knee.

"I got you, Button. We'll ride this out together," I finally say. Just like back in our climbing days, I try to be good on the belay, sturdy enough for him to fall—even in my own fear. We fall asleep together in a new holding pattern of me spooning him.

Catholics are onto something with confession. When Tom wakes the next morning, he's light and chipper, nothing hiding just behind his eyes. They are a clear, deep black. The side-benefit to unloading such a heavy confession, is that he doesn't have work so hard to cover it anymore with his best-attitude-ever. Nothing wrong with a positive attitude, that is until it holds one hostage from the truth. Then it has become a good thing gone awry. We are both beginning to recognize the steep cost of glossing over what is really going on inside for fear that anything short of a bright-shiny outlook may give the nay-saying illness an upper hand.

Tom wrestles his demons and I wrestle mine. They aren't so different. He had railed against certain aspects of his Catholic upbringing years before at the bedsides of his Auntie Beatrice, then his Uncle Steve, later his Tio Antonio and, finally, his own father. His mission was to convince them all, in their final hour, that there was no hell, never has been. He had whispered it over and over into their ears, trying to undo lifetimes of conditioning that would snag them up with doubt as they left this world. In Tom's mind, the only hell is living in fear of it. His God is benevolent and shows itself through people and serendipity. Now, he must remember this for himself.

Jennifer Allen

9

Tables Turn

Summer–Fall 1996

Angels make the cut amidst the crisis of faith. Not the kind with wings, but the kind that leave me with a knowing—as if they blow messages into the marrow of my bones while I sleep. Having not one, but two children with Tom, is my latest bone knowing.

"Baby, baby, baby." River chants daily, offering up a stash of pacifiers he's never used. My nipples are unusually sore after nursing him and music permeates my pores. All are sure signs, except for the home pregnancy test. A faint pink line makes its way tentatively across the stick, instilling reservation. At night, I dream I'm pregnant and then miscarry. My own crying wakes me. An appointment at the local clinic for a back-up test will be my reassurance.

I'm sitting in one of two vinyl padded metal chairs when the doctor returns with the results. She sits down in the other, leans in and says, "You are most definitely pregnant Ms. Allen-Sanchez." She manages a completely neutral expression, waiting to see if this is good or bad news to me. For an instant, and only because she makes any response fair game, I'm not sure.

I close my eyes and smile: "That's just what I wanted to hear." There are already too many uncertainties in my life I don't need another. I let the knowing prevail. On the long walk back to the house, I busy my mind with logistics like health insurance, prenatal care, and a stable income. The dream slips away.

When I tell Tom, he vacillates so quickly between excitement and looking strained that I can't pin him down. On Fridays the world looks hopeful and we walk down to Migueleno's for the simple pleasures of a Mariachi band and bean burritos. Tom carries River on his shoulders and we talk baby names, fantasizing with River about a new baby in the family. By Monday mornings, the reality of how we'll get by comes crashing down and I've never been so grateful to be employed.

Must keep job. I repeat the silent mantra every time the urge to share my exciting news or to throw up overcomes me. As a nauseated passenger, riding with a co-worker in her smoke-filled car, going from home to home, smelling each patient's unique odor of sickness, I prevail puke-free. It requires swallowing often and a full-screen image in my mind's eye of our family living in the cardboard village behind the hospice house. The worlds of employment and destitution are dangerously close to each other.

Three months pregnant and the first week without nausea and debilitating, decaffeinated fatigue, I'm on the road making home-visits solo. The next hump will come when I can't hide my midsection bulge any longer. That gives me six weeks, at the most, to make myself indispensable. The boss gives me a great start: a noncompliant patient assignment. It's the same label my husband has earned, so I know the type.

Mrs. Tucker lives in a dilapidated trailer, twenty minutes off the highway. A cloud of fine dirt bellows around the car as I pull to a stop. Beads of sweat roll down the back of my dress and I check my backside for embarrassing wet marks. Dogs bark in the distance and flies swarm around the garbage can at the entrance.

Jennifer Allen

This could be us. I want to turn back.

"What the *hell* do you want?" She hollers from behind the screen door. She doesn't care that I'm a good person, or that I'm pregnant, or that my husband has cancer.

"Hi, Mrs. Tucker. I'm Jennifer from the hospice. Just stopping by to introduce myself and see how you're doing." I approach the door with an outstretched hand.

"I'm dying and I don't need your help doing it! G'damn you people, trying to be saints. I didn't ask you to come." She keeps the screen between us and ignores my hand. Odors of urine and coffee waft toward me and I swallow hard.

No, it's quite the other way around. You'd be helping me— keep my job, keep my family out of cardboard boxes, keep me from obsessing on my haunting dream world. Instead, I ask her how she's pulling it off out here on her own and it seems to be the best invite she's had in awhile to tally-off her list of rage items. She starts with the small stuff: the garbage service refusing to come up the driveway to get her cans now that she can't bring them to the road, the raccoons that tip over the trash no matter how many bungee cords the ties down the lids with, and the g'damn child-proof lids on her medicine bottles. When she sees I'm still listening after the first round, she delves into the heftier items: her estranged son who's too busy to call back, her husband for dying first, the g'damn church for promising miracles, and the cancer for stealing her dignity. At the end of the hour, I'm convinced we've made headway and she reluctantly agrees to a follow-up visit in a couple weeks.

I'm not looking forward to it, like I do with patients at the hospital. Her story is sticky with an ugly familiarity—like a possible fast-forward to me in 30 years. I can't get out of there fast enough. Six miles down the road I find respite in the restroom of the only gas station in town. The tears and pee I've held back in the face of an angry woman come flooding forth. Just as I stand to flush and face the world, I see blood.

Mine, this time.

The dream world has been preparing me, only I haven't wanted to hear it. A week ago, I dreamed of a man seducing me in a secluded cabin. I wanted him, but knew he'd kill me, so I told him to leave. Once he was out, I locked all the doors and windows.

He turned into a baby with River's clothes on, lying on the picnic table, completely helpless. Instincts were at war and I decided he was using my maternal drive to trick me into having him. I closed the blinds, covered my ears to the baby's cry, and waited. He turned back into the man and left, cursing.

I was sure the man was Scott, trying to re-enter life via the fetus inside me. On the night I conceived, three months before, Scott had come to me in a dream as himself. He looked up from a monotonous prison task and asked me telepathically (dead people don't talk aloud in my dreams) if he could come back. The old longing had me giving him a thumb's up. In the early morning, I remembered the dream and tried to re-enter it to tell him, "No, no. I'm so sorry. I don't want you back in. I can't save you." It was too late.

Sounds crazy, I know, but the workings of the other realms: dreams, angels, dead people and the like, haven't ever fit snuggly into any box of logic I've ever tried. The best strategy I've come up with has been to ignore them when they tug too heavily on me. So I focus on *real* things like: bank statements, the to-do list, and our busy toddler. There have been spots of blood since the cabin dream. The midwife assured me they were nothing to worry about.

Last night, though, I dreamed of wolves surrounding the doghouse of my childhood dog, Bootsie. She was huddled up in the far corner in fear. An innocent victim to ruthless wild beasts that didn't give a shit that she was a family pet. I jumped out the window into the freezing night with rage fueling me. I swooped down, grazing the wolves' fur, roaring fire at them. They were too hungry and noticed me only as another menu option. They'd kill me as soon as my rage flickered to fear and I lost my ability to fly. So I watched, helplessly, perched in a maple tree as they tore Bootsie out, piece by piece.

The dream comes back to me in the darkness. This time, I hear a voice in the distance: "Jennifer, can you hear me? You'll be all right; you've just lost a lot of blood. We're going to move you to the bed now." A child's scream gets louder. I blink my eyes to the harsh light being flashed in them. Light blue surrounds me. Flesh tones between the swatches of blue showed faces. *Hospital— right.*

Jennifer Allen

I remember calling work from a pay phone at the rest stop and telling them I was going home, sick. Blood saturated my dress, making a slippery puddle on the vinyl as I drove. Once home, I squeezed a towel between my legs, while I called the midwife and Tom. Then I ran to the toilet, surrendering the stream of clumpy blood. When it let up, I bent into the bowl and pawed fruitlessly in search of what was to be our second child, until dizziness overcame me. Vaguely, I remember Tom loading me into the car. River was asking questions from the backseat but I was too foggy to answer. Then, I was being pushed in a wheelchair through the corridors of my workplace. I remember thinking how strange it was to have been in the same elevator the day before as and intact employee, not a bleeding patient. *How quick the tables can turn in just twenty-four little hours.*

The screeching comes again. "Where's my baby?" I mumble.

One of the blue people says: "The product has been disposed of."

I know our baby, "the product," is dead, flushed brutally down into the hospital's sewer system or brought to pathology for dissection.

"I want my son," I plead, empty of new life and still full of mothering instincts. Tom pushes his way between the nurses and hands me River, who is wailing, having just seen Mamma go down in a heap, blood pooling out beside her. He grabs for my breast and I pull the bloodstained johnny aside, cradling him into our familiar position.

The staff scatters, leaving the wrong nurse to witness our emotional wreckage. She crosses her arms and stands over me, nodding self-righteously. "You know you shouldn't breastfeed when you're pregnant."

"Well I'm not anymore, am I?" I bark through streaming tears.

"Right." She raises her eyebrows and turns to leave the room of the crazed mother.

Tom looks on, sad, with no energy to defend me. River snorts and sucks, clutching his Na Na lamb with his free hand. I continue wailing where he left off.

It's for so many things: for losing the fetus who was to be our second child and the faith in the whispers of angels who told me so; for the loss of physical resilience—both mine and Tom's; for seeing ahead to the imminent loss of my husband and our child's father. The places I've invested love and faith have so boldly turn on me, threatening to shred my heart into ribbons.

Tom waits until I exhaust myself into slumber and then carefully peels a limp River off me and kisses me on the forehead.

"We've got to go Jen. I'll call in the morning." It's all he can do to tend to himself and River and I know we can't afford him going down at the same time, so I fabricate a sleepy smile and release them, terrified that I won't see them again.

A few hours later, I'm watching the '96 Olympics and reminiscing about being there in-person four years earlier and suddenly, I feel a massive clot slip out from between my legs like a hot cow liver against my cool, bloodless thighs. The nurses are slow to answer the bell. All I can figure is that they hadn't signed up for maternity nursing to deal with dead "products of conception" and the mothers who feel gypped.

"Yes, Ms. Allen-Sanchez, what is it?" A nasal voice finally responds.

"Please come, I'm passing huge clots. I think my placenta is still attached." I try to use a clinical voice, letting her know I'm a reasonable woman, in fact, a co-worker and not some grief struck woman about to bleed to death.

"Someone will be right there." She answers mechanically.

A young Korean nurse comes in eventually, after my body has contorted itself into a cerebral palsy-like posture. Every muscle, jaw included, cramps in searing pain. I slur out words to her: "Sunkings ong."

Without looking up, she gives a placating "Hmmm?"

I'm familiar with the tone, having a toddler who demands more attention than I have. The blood pressure monitor reads 60 over 30 and I start to panic. *This is it; this is how I die. Alone in a frickin' hospital!*

Urgent animal groans thrusts out of my throat: "Huuuuuuugh, Ahhhhrr!" The sound catches her attention and she looks at me, cocking her head and then moving swiftly to the intercom.

An eternity of pain passes before the blue people rush in, poking me with needles, shoving an oxygen mask on my face, pressing fingers far up into my empty womb and transferring me to a gurney to be wheeled to surgery.

A paternal voice speaks firmly into my ear, "C'mon Pumpkin, breathe! You can do it girl. That's it, slow and easy." I cling to voice and watch the fluorescent lights going by overhead. I want Tom, my parents and my sisters. They're all far away, unaware of what's happening.

Black peace comes and consumes me. I can't fight it even if I wanted to. It's complete respite. Here I have no pain, no memories, no dreams, and no place to be. *If this is death, well, it's not so bad. Think I'll visit for a while.* I drift just above time. Moments and lifetimes are no different here. When I am satiated with all that is nothing, I can feel myself eventually emerge, one layer at a time, until dream images begin pulling me toward consciousness.

I awaken to find that my uterus has been scraped free of the placenta remains that were clinging inside, pumping my body's blood constantly, to the baby who had already left. Somehow it didn't get the message: "Party's over, lets wrap up the bleeding." It just couldn't comprehend life's quick turn of events. Nor can I.

Tom calls the next morning as he promised and I answer the phone, groggy from anesthesia. My throat tightens just hearing his voice and I pinch out, "I want to come home."

"Oh, Sweetie," he consoles. "I'll call Joyce and see if she can come pick you up. I'll come if she can't." He's having a bad day or he'd be here.

I hang up. *But I want you.*

I've sang the Rolling Stones song enough to River in his short life I should know by now I can't always get what I want. Usually, though, I get what I need.

Joyce comes, questioning nurses and insisting on reviewing my medical chart. Her nurse status gets her the respect I was denied. She hovers over me in a protective big-sister-surrogate-mother kind of way. If we stay any longer, she's sure to tell the staff what a cute and feisty little girl I was. She drives me home and brews an enormous pot of blood-building soup, chuck full of bone marrow, to compensate for the transfusions I'd refused. I can barely make it up and down the stairs and Tom is out flat, the stress having kicked his symptoms into a fury. He's got blood in his urine again. As usual, he assures me it will pass when things lighten up. Joyce stays on for a few days until we can get along on our own. She is what I needed.

On the first day that we are both strong enough to make it to the burial site, we pack up some seashells, bird feathers, a redwood tree start and the remains I jarred up from the toilet before leaving for the hospital and head to the State Park. I bring my journal and enter: *July, 27, 1996 ceremony for our lost child.* I realize it's the anniversary of Scott's death. *Sorry, man. If that was you, I hope you find your place to enter.* The car rolls over bumpy gravel and comes to a halt. I close the journal.

"It's over there." Tom points to the incline. Joyce unbuckles River and he runs ahead chasing butterflies, while she helps me up the trail. Tom slowly brings up the rear, a shovel in one hand, a guitar in the other; pausing every few strides to catch his breath. When we find the perfect place, Tom digs a grave and I empty the jar of blood into the hole. We plant a tree that will be fed from the remains and press shells and feathers into the soil, marking this place as special. We sit around the tiny tree sprout in silence: There are no memories to share, only mistaken projections into the future. Tom begins to play his guitar softly: "It's raining, it's pouring . . ." He does the only thing he can and lulls our baby back to the heavens, where he knows he'll be following in time.

In late September, when I should have been five months pregnant, we make a trip back East. My sister, Julie, asked me to be at her third child's birth. My brother-in-law, Andy, has a history of getting woozy at the sight of blood and Julie wants back-up. When she calls me at four a.m. and tells me "it's time" between contractions, my own womb begins to ache and contort sympathetically, with only emptiness to squeeze against.

There's little time to get caught up in my grief. Julie tends to pop babies out with record speed. Her last child was born at the doctor's office, before the ambulance arrived. Besides, the opportunity to witness a life coming in is like nothing else, except possibly witnessing one leave.

As the baby crowns, I try and convince my five-year-old niece that the pain she sees her mamma in, must happen for the baby to come out and she won't even believe how happy her mamma will look in just a few minutes. It's too hard for Haley to trust that scenario. She runs out of the room. By the time I retrieve her, the baby is out and Andy is cutting the cord. Julie is beaming and Haley moves in cautiously, taking in the miracle of birth.

Tom and I return to California inspired and try month after month to get pregnant, to no avail. "Maybe the Universe is telling us something," Tom says.

"Yeah, I guess," I say resigning myself to not knowing anymore. No word from my bones.

Jennifer Allen

10

Un-prayed for Miracles

Winter 1996/1997

"You didn't listen to me, did you? Your father listened and he got fixed, but no you had to do it your own way." Dr. Stinson clucks his tongue and wags his finger at Tom—the bad, bad patient, who's been wandering for years in the wild no-man's land of alternative treatments.

"My father is *dead*," Tom says sarcastically.

"Not from bladder cancer I'll bet," Dr. Stinson snaps back.

Tom stares vacantly like a trapped animal dependent on its captor, and nods. The fluorescent lights buzz and the walls press in on us.

Rage lodges in my throat making it hard to breath. If only we didn't need this man, I'd have let it explode on "Dr. Jerk" for shaming my husband. Better yet, I'd have catheterized him with the same insensitivity he had used with Tom in the early days of local chemo treatments. Instead, I look away. Crucial moments pass. Tom is left to make arrangements for a surgery to have a peek at the beast living in his bladder and ease some of the pain he's had urinating.

We escape into the wet parking lot, but we are not free. Like Tom, I hate the imprisonment of the medical system. Once in, we both feared he'd be at its mercy, with all of his "Tomness" stripped into a medical diagnosis identity: "The Stage Three Bladder Cancer in room 225." And, yet, I know from working in the very system I despise, that it doesn't need to be this way. At hospice, we talk names and family situations and expect healing to happen outside the body's parameters as people neared death. Of course, by that point, all the docs bound by literal healing had peeled off, not wanting to witness the evidence of their perceived failures.

Tom won't hear of hospice. Not yet.

Heavy mist camouflages my tears. "As if you're not vulnerable enough already. He's just got to kick you while your down. Jesus, what arrogance!" I say. Tom nods, puckering his lips off center and biting at the inside flesh of his cheek. He's deep in thought or he's angry; I can't tell which. Guilt abounds. Not only do I realize that he's been enduring medical appointments alone for years, I've missed a prime opportunity be his advocate in this gnarly system—to hold him tight on the belay while he makes a scary move. If I had known what he was up against, I would have understood why he had put off making this appointment until he was pissing blood clots. *Perhaps I would have been a more supportive wife. Perhaps.*

Once we're home, he goes straight up to the bedroom and closes the door, while I see Zoe out and tiptoe upstairs to check on River. From the hall, I hear Tom talking. His voice is low, a few degrees more intimate than the usual phone call, and there are stretches of silence. A half-hour later, he joins me in the kitchen and takes up cleaning beets for the next round of juicing, while I brew and jar up two day's worth of coffee for his enemas.

Jennifer Allen

"Louise is going to stand in for the surgery. She's been a charge nurse there for years and she thinks Stinson will agree to let her be on the case," he says, not looking up from the sink.

"Oh." I weigh the meaning of his move to call on her after years of careful conversations limited to parental logistics. "You actually talked to her, huh?"

"Yeah, she's got clout in surgery. And she's not afraid to use it."

Jealously sears my face. Tom looks up and sees it. "She's willing to help. You just can't be everything all the time, Butterfly—it's all just too much," he says and I feel like his child instead of his wife.

For just a moment, I consider giving him back, making a return. *Here Louise, you've known him since before I was born. Seeing that we're getting into the medical part now, why don't you take it from here?* The possibility of freedom flickers about in my mind.

"Mmmhmm." I rinse and wring out the coffee-stained cheesecloth, hang it over the dish rack and leave the room. I've got to run this one out before I think or say something I'll regret. Thoughts whirl as I lace up my sneakers and head out into the salty air. I run hard. Away at first and eventually, a few miles of grueling hills later, back to my self and my life. Thank goodness for endorphins or my sanity would plummet to unknown depths.

One simple jogging expedition and Louise's entering the picture goes from threatening ex-wife, to potential escape route, to proof that love reigns supreme. If Tom and Louise can remember a love for each other under the thick crust of hurt and resentments that have stacked up between them, then I've got a substantial new faith rising up from the ashes of my Daddy-God. Love is greater than anything: lies, resentment, cancer, death—you name it. All I had read in *A Course in Miracles* years earlier, drops from my head and lands in the center of my chest. *Love really is bigger than life, when fear isn't keeping it small. And God really is love.*

There is one glitch in my new faith. What happens when love isn't part of the equation? Louise coming into our world may mean that she and I actually meet. As far as I know, I've always been "the other woman" to her. I've actually had repetitive dreams of our first encounter, only we are wolves. I'm on my back— neck exposed in submission. She stands over me with teeth bared and fur bristled. Just as I brace for the death-bite, she's overcome with mercy and laps the side of my muzzle.

Still, though, the weeks of anticipation leading up to this meeting, stress me out about as much as Tom's surgery. The big day falls exactly one week before Christmas and it's been a challenge putting on the holiday cheer. In the early morning hours, I drop Tom off at the hospital and know he is under Louise's watch while I'm at work all day. When I return in the afternoon to be with him as he comes-to, I find Tom's mother in the waiting room.

"Why isn't he out yet? Something's wrong, he should have been out by now," she says, looking up at me like I have answers. Her eyes are wild with worry. *Finally,* I think, *I've come across a bigger worst-case scenario thinker than myself.* I try to comfort her but my consolations are dry because I *know* something's wrong.

Footsteps clap down the hall and in walks Dr. Stinson. I feel the residual anger rise up from weeks earlier. This time, I stand tall and face him with a steel façade. I'm ready for him. He's shorter than I remember and I can see the start of a balding patch beyond the brown fuzz that frames his face. He glances at my hospice nametag and for a moment, the power differential is indiscernible.

"Well, it is as I suspected. Tom's cancer has progressed to stage four, meaning it has left the boundaries of his bladder and has spread to other places. We'll have to do more tests to find out where exactly," he says in one running exhale.

Stella covers her mouth and leans onto her cane. I'm still all steel. Dr. Stinson inhales deeply and tilts his chin up. I lose track of the bald spot. He continues, "He'll need the surgery that should have been done years ago. At this point in the game, it won't buy as much time as it could have." Cure isn't mentioned.

"Oh Tommy, not my Tommy," Stella begins blubbering.

"Okay then," I say numbly, offering a handshake to complete the transaction.

He's not finished. "Oh, yes . . . one more thing." He pulls back his hand and cocks his chin on it. Casually, he expands on a detail as if he's reporting on extras he threw into the deal. He tells us he has "roto-rooter"ed out Tom's prostate a little beyond what was discussed and, while it should make urination easier, it will

Jennifer Allen

also cause the sperm to go into his bladder when Tom ejaculates. He goes on, "Of course, that shouldn't be a problem for you two. I mean, he *is* 51 and with cancer. You don't need to be making babies at this point." He extends his hand.

"Wha . . .?" *No babies? But we're supposed to have two!* My hand goes limp inside his firm grip. "Thanks for being direct." I hear myself say, not wanting to give him the satisfaction of a reaction. Dr. Stinson turns on a heel and leaves. I unravel into the closest chair.

"The baby!" I hiccup between gaps of bawling.

Simultaneously, Stella mutters repeatedly "How am I going to get through this? First Michael, now Tommy. How?"

We manage to pull ourselves into the corridor, each wrapped up in our own worlds of grief, red-eyed and wet-faced. A nurse approaches us. Her glasses are cloudy. *It's her.*

Stella moves in close, letting her small frame be embraced by her *other* daughter-in-law. Louise rocks ever so slightly and muffles: "I know, I know," into the crown of Stella's brown hair. I look on, my neck involuntarily exposed. Their bodies finally part and Louise moves toward me. I'm too overcome by the latest loss to care if she hates me. *Go ahead, bite.* At least I know from her acceptance of Tom's request to be at the surgery, she isn't the beast I imagined. When I offer my hand, she takes it into both of hers and looks to me with a sisterly empathy.

Mercy.

"I'm Louise," she says. All at once, past hurts, hatred, jealousy, and guilt are overrode, for the sake of present-time being valued for its fleeting nature and the recognition that life is just too short for anything less. *Now this is spontaneous healing.*

In the following week, leading up to Christmas, Louise comes by the house to teach me how to inject Tom's medicine. We sit together at the bedside with Tom's pants pulled down, exposing his dwindling buttocks. I practice on an orange until I can stab the needle in clean, then she demonstrates on Tom. He's oblivious to the pain, smiling at the scenario of the three of us on the same team. Better late than never.

When I consider that it will probably be his last Christmas, all trivial matters evaporate, leaving behind the true magic of the holiday. We stretch it out and savor every nuance, like a fine wine.

Bone Knowing   139

River snuggles in bed with Tom to watch holiday specials while I bake loaves of flax bread and sugar cookies. On Christmas morning Tom changes out of his pajamas and comes downstairs with a catheter running out his pant leg and his pee bag clipped to his belt.

"What a beautiful tree!" he says sitting down into the couch to take it in. The tinsel and mirrored ornaments glitter with the morning sun reflecting tiny rainbows around the room. River is caught up in the same awe until I tell him that Santa left him the presents under the tree. Every show of delight on his face as he intrigues himself with ripping paper off boxes makes sweet, deep impressions into both of us. Tom squeezes my hand and I am overflowing with bittersweet joy.

A few friends and family visit throughout the day, braving the possible discomfort of sharing what supposed to be a merry holiday, with a slow-dying man and his family. I'm relieved that none of them put out any airs of pity. It's possible that they're all chanting mantras inside their hearts: "He'll be okay . . . he'll be okay." to get them through, but the point is, they show up—and not just in body. We sit around the dining table eating simple fare and laughing, while River dances to the quacking songs of his new stuffed duck.

Tom and I are just beginning to taste the possibilities of allowing all that we hold back to surface. It started when he allowed me to walk his dark valley with him and continues in small increments; each of us taking turns at facing our inner demons head-on. This Christmas we're in the company of those who are doing the same, just by being with us, fully. The hair shirt I've worn around my heart is tattered and has begun to fall away. A nakedness shown though, filling the day with a delicious honesty.

In the spirit of Christmas and finding hope in the darkest of days, we are both granted extensions of holiday highs that last long after our guests leave. The week is a string of Fridays, aided by a break from working. At the end of them, I notice a subtle feeling of ovulation.

Tom has planned his second surgery up at UCSF for the beginning of January, though he's not convinced that the time it *might* buy is worth the quality of living he'd sacrifice. Though we already know his sperm travels only to suicidal destinations, the next surgery would kill the remainder of his offspring potential. We talk "baby" again, from the heart place where anything is possible. Tom understands the hope I've invested in a second child and agrees to try. We agree to give the Universe a final opportunity to voice itself. That way there is no one to blame. Both of us agree to trust that the outcome will be best in the grander scheme of things, no matter which way it goes.

Tom sets about removing his catheter and setting up a turkey baster and bedpan on the end stand in case his sperm sneaks out on a piss. I put River down for a nap. We are on a baby-making mission. Sex has been in the process of redefinition since his symptoms kicked up their ante prior to the surgery. We've both been anticipating and grieving the end of our sex life as we knew it. For Tom, it's not as simple as an erection, but all that it means for him lose that capacity with the next surgery. His potency has been wrapped up snugly with his lust for life. We both desperately need something to shift our hopes to.

With full consciousness of what we are asking for, we crawl into bed together and touch each other tenderly. We know this could be our last love-baby-making. Our eyes lock in communion. Ever so slowly, we merge: body and soul. Tom winces in pain until a flash of ecstasy takes him over. His orgasm serves only to deliver the goods we need to bring about a miracle.

Afterwards, we lie side-by-side and Tom says, "Did you know that plants give out their most potent seed just before they die?"

"No, Button, I didn't."

That's the last we say about it. The turkey baster goes unused. During the waiting month, I'm too caught up in Tom's healthcare regimen and managing incoming medical bills to wonder if I'm pregnant. Perhaps this is what it feels like to have unquestioned faith. At least until I realize that my period is three days late. Then I just have to know.

"I'll be right back," I say, getting up from the table abruptly. Tom nods, keeping his eyes fixed on River and a hand over the corn chip he's performing a magic trick with.

I run out of Pablo's, up to Safeway, and buy a pregnancy test. The checker smiles, "Find everything you were looking for?"

"We'll see," I say and throw the box into my purse. River and Tom are eating when I whiz by to the bathroom. No need for directions, I rip open the box and plunge the stick midstream my urine. A bold pink line crosses it with such confidence I don't even consider miscarriage. *Thank You*, I say to whatever source pushes tender sprouts of grass up through concrete. Today, I'm calling it the Universe.

As I wash up, I catch my reflection in the mirror and notice the glow of pregnancy—or is it the expression of faith renewed? Either way, I return to the table beaming and flash the stick, explaining to River what it means.

"So, the 'force' *is* with us!" Tom laughs. He doesn't have the mixed look I had seen before at the news of a baby. I can see in his elation the hope that if we can defy science with this child, why not his life. It's a tempting jump and I join him in the moment. At the very least, he surrenders this new life to the Universe. That alone seems to take the heavy weight of earthly responsibility off of him. From the high mountain peak of the heart and spirit place, I can see the big picture, with this child's coming being an important part of it, no matter how difficult the day-to-day might become.

My faith is resurrected in a way I haven't known it before. No longer do I pray for earthly outcome. Instead, I pray for courage to trust the whispers of angels and the knowing in my bones.

Jennifer Allen

Months

Jennifer Allen

11

Going Down

February 1997

Once that tenacious seed took hold in my womb, it seemed Tom's final mission had been accomplished. He has begun to slide. A month after the roto-rooter surgery, the tests had come back showing metastasis to the liver and lung. Tom decided against the pending surgery that would exchange his bladder for an outside pee-bag. He rode the fence for a couple extra weeks until it became clear that surgery was a moot point, serving only to make him and his doctor feel like they were doing *something*. The reconstruction of his body was too much to undergo for too little pay off. It wasn't about preserving erectile function. It was about preserving dignity. Instead, he agreed to a round of potent systemic chemotherapy for a shot at some extra time now that we have a baby en route.

"You just never know!" he said, indicating that he, too, held a tiny ray of hope.

Though it's a sickening kind of déjà vu to be back at the place where the pivotal news was broken just a couple months back, I'm trying to cop a better attitude seeing that we are here for his treatment and not prognosis. The room is hospital green and there's a sheer curtain between Tom and the other cancer veteran.

Tom chants in a commanding whisper: "Kill it, kill it," as the potent brew enters his veins from a tube that winds up a pole, to the pouch of toxic chemotherapy drugs hanging overhead.

"Watch it, man. You're the one who's always telling me to be careful what I wish for," I say, from the bedside. "What if the chemo doesn't know you mean the cancer?"

He closes his eyes, exasperated with me. "That's *not* helpful."

"I just want it to work, that's all," I defend.

"Look, I've got a battle going on inside me and the chemo is a cut-throat warrior. This is no time for Mr. Nice Guy to surround the cancer in white light.

"I know, I know . . . just make sure you're clear which side you are on, huh? Remember, you've been calling this stuff poison for a long time."

"Good point," he says, but I know he just wants to end this outer riff so he can get on with what's happening inside him. I'm sorry my fear adds to his minefield of guilt trips, though I've never told him so.

Over the next few weeks, Tom struggles to view chemo as friend versus foe. It's too late, though. His insides have been scoured clean with the Gerson Treatment, only to have the chemo absorb into every cell and deliver a triple whammy. Everything that can go wrong does. He suffers allergic reactions, constipation, hemorrhoids, nausea, vomiting, dry mouth, cracked lips, infections, disorientation; you name it. It looks like the medicine might just kill him before it gets to the cancer. Tom goes from rehabilitation after the first surgery, gathering enough energy to work from home—even officiating a couple wrestling matches, to bed-bound. It's shocking how quickly things have deteriorated. I'm whirling in a frenzy trying to catch up to the implications. For now, Tom can't handle River without help and he probably shouldn't be driving. Often, he's confused and needs me to track his treatment protocol and cancel any work he had scheduled. Every morning, even before opening my eyes, I cross my fingers. *Please, let this be a good day.*

Late Saturday afternoon, Tom calls me to the bathroom in an urgent voice, just as I'm about to change River's diaper. *Not another puke,* I think. *My life is about body waste. All I deal with these days is shit, vomit, piss and blood!* Obligation weights my breath and thudding footsteps as I make my way from one bathroom to the other.

"What?" I say in exasperation. Tom sits naked on the closed toilet with a huge clump of wet brown hair in his hand. Instantly I comprehend and it's as if we both realize, yet again; he really *does* have cancer—as in the dying kind. This isn't a passing flu bug. From this point forward, cancer won't be the secret he can contradict with his appearance until he drops the bomb, blowing people away at social gatherings.

Frowning, I press his head into my belly and run my fingers through what's left of his hair. I feel for his braid. It's secure, though I dare not tug it.

"Your pony," I say, fingering each notch of braid that marks his eight-year cancer journey. He had started growing it as a reminder to himself to live fully—not to wait. Even when it was a wee three-weaves long, he used the rubber bands from Eliza's braces to secure it and showed it off at every opportunity. Coaches at the baseball games would request the Blue with the ponytail. It had become his survivor trademark.

"I know." His chest begins to heave.

River hears us and waddles down the hallway to join us, his diaper swollen. "What's wrong, Daddy?" He pushes his way into the tiny bathroom and picks up a wad of hair from the floor.

Tom pulls away and wipes his eyes. He conjures up his clear, gentle voice: "River, the medicine I'm taking to help me get better makes my hair fall out. I'm sad to lose my hair—especially my ponytail."

"Can me see?" Tom lowers his head for River to examine.

"Jen, can you get the scissors? I want to salvage the braid." He says. Already it isn't *his* braid.

In the cramped bathroom, we conduct a homemade ceremony to cut it off. Nothing fancy, no recipe of ritual to follow. Simply a profound shift in the way we go about the task. Makes me wonder why I don't live my entire life in this state. Time moves much slower than the pace I am accustomed to. Every sense is heightened. The smell of Dr. Bronner's eucalyptus soap on Tom's skin, the silky feel of the brown hair I brush out and braid one last time, the sound of each strand surrendering to the blade as I cut through hundreds of them, the image of Tom's braid lying in his hands and River stroking it as if it were a dead animal and the strange feeling to see something so "Tom" separate from him.

So many little deaths along the way.

River looks up when he hears me sniffle and pulls a hand-towel from the rack and then grabs a washcloth from the shower. Offering one to Tom and one to me, he says: "Here. Crying rags for you."

I kneel down and pull him into me. "Oh, thank you my little pea-in-the-pod. Mamma and Daddy will be okay, don't you worry!" His sweetness overwhelms me and at the same time I'm sad that he is already becoming the "little man."

River helps me clean the bedside table and tie a purple ribbon on Tom's braid. We place it on his jewelry box just below a drawing Tom made at one of his support groups of himself with his braid flying behind him in the breeze. We have an altar in the making.

One of our New Year's resolutions has been to find a church and attend regularly. It's part of an effort to build ourselves a community that might sustain us through hard times ahead and give River the sense of a larger family outside his home life where death threatens to pull the rug out. The side-benefit is having a Sunday family ritual—a constant amongst the frequent tides of change.

Before church, we have established routine of walking to Mal's Market for cinnamon rolls and a newspaper. Today, I stay behind to stock up on juices because Tom feels up to going without the assistance of a wheelchair.

When they get back, Tom huffs, "Hey, little man, come sit. Let's read the funnies." River joins him, hands sticky with cinnamon roll gunk and spit. Tom's dime-a-dozen reading glasses slide down the bridge of his ever-narrowing Romanesque nose. He pushes them up frequently as he reads. River listens and giggles, snuggling into the crook of Tom's arm, completely engaged for the full page of comics. I watch them from the kitchen counter. I'm awed, like I was back when we first met, by Tom's ability to live in each moment. It's a truth about him I'm coming to doubt less lately.

On the drive to church, we talk about the baby that will enter our world in just a few short months.

"What baby's name?" River asks.

"Hmmm. If it is a boy, maybe Zephyr. That means warm breeze," I say, putting one hand out the window to surf the air. "Whenever we call him, we'll be reminded of a angel passing by and we'll think of Daddy." It's out before I can retrieve it.

"Daddy isn't a angel!" River insists, like he's too old to be fooled by the tricks grown-ups play.

"No, you're right River, he's not." I glance at Tom. "You're not, I mean." I figure my cards are already on the table so I may as well explain them. "Daddy's trying his best to stay alive but he *might* die by the time baby comes. When he dies, he'll be a spirit in Heaven—an angel."

"When does Daddy die?" River doesn't go for soft answers.

"Only God knows," I say, digging myself deeper with each word.

"Can we ask God at church?"

Tom turns, resting his arm over the seat so he can see River when he speaks. "Those kind of things are mysteries, little man. The Universe, also called God—by the way—keeps them that way, kind of like a surprise. Don't worry, I'll tell you as soon as I know for sure. We'll just have to wait and see."

"What die, Daddy?"

"Die means my body won't work at all. It won't eat, talk, move—nothing. If that happens to my body, I will have to go be an angel. You will feel me in your heart, but you won't see me or play with me." Tom's voice trails off as his eyes well up. Mine have already spilled over, blurring the road as I drive.

"Why you cry, Mamma?" River asks when he catches my eye in the rear-view mirror.

"It makes me very sad to think about Daddy dying and not being here with our family someday." My voice breaks on the last syllable. Tom puts his hand on mine and we sniffle without words all the way to church. River goes back to his toy, having had his fill of conversation with adults.

We park ten minutes late—our standard. I check my mascara, preparing to face the world. As I open the back door and unclip River from his car seat he declares: "But Mamma, baby is a girl!"

"I bet you're right!" I say, taking his hand, leading him to Sunday school. I put great faith in young children, so close to the source from whence they came.

Upstairs, Tom and I sit through the service uncomfortably. Partly, his back is bothering him again (and that triggers a silent worry of bone metastasis) and partly because the minister is preaching healing by way of positive thoughts again. It was one of our attractions to this church, while we were still riding the bandwagon. Over time, and especially after walking through some dark valleys, it's become an increasingly evident trap.

Ironic, but it's turning us into rebels against good attitudes. Anything glossing over what is real, even the ugly, escalates our cause and turns my ears beet-red. I'm just a hair away from standing up and screaming at Ms. Goodie-Thinking-Minister that she's missing the point. Every word out of her mouth implies Tom's failure. It only takes one good success story; the kind when the person pops off their death bed and into full recovery, to set up a dying person for a million if-only-you-do-this-or-try-that's from well-meaning people who just can't stand to let death happen, as it will, to us all. Even those who are supposed to know better don't

Jennifer Allen

escape the human error. I hope, deep inside where he answers to only himself, Tom knows better.

When the service is over, I'm frustrated and pursue help anyway. If we can't get a supportive message, perhaps some helping hands. Negativity blows it for me: The coffee hour greeter tells me they don't have an organized program of help. I start to regress; thinking they are right. Maybe I caused Tom's cancer with all of my worry and worst-case scenario preparations. It's probably the same reason they don't help me. I'm not exactly putting out a shiny-penny persona these days.

But churches are supposed to help, no matter how one thinks or believes. I know this because I got it loud and clear growing up in a Methodist congregation where my parents gave: taking in a refugee family, mowing the parsonage lawn, and fixing things as needed. I hadn't realized how empowering it was to be on the helper end, until now, when I find myself asking for help.

I'm still recovering from the humiliation of having my request denied, when, out of the corner of my eye, I see a woman cringe as she listens in. As we leave, she approaches me and offers to baby-sit. I keep her number in the "help" file and plan to leave the church after Easter. We'll make our own church at home and our own community with people like her.

Jennifer Allen

12

Getting Help

March 1997

Janice asks the question I most avoid: "So, how are *you*?" Her tone is a blend of therapist/supervisor/mother and I dart for a response that affirms her confidence in my skills as her only intern therapist.

"I'm fine," I chirp, giving her instead the standard red-flag answer. I'm shooting for the survival route, despite the painful incongruence. Truth is, I'm in way over my head with a client I can't help and who I can't give up on either. The theme parallels the roller coaster pattern of my personal life at every turn. If I can't save Tom from getting sicker, the least I can do is help someone who has choices. It isn't working.

A quiver tugs on the corners of my perky smile. Silence. She lingers in that therapist kind of way as if she has nothing better to do than wait out the truth. No doubt, I need to unload the contents of this tightly packed anticipatory grief I've been holding inside me. I long to spread them out across the floor, where they can be sorted and hung in their rightful places. This is, after all, what most therapy boils down to. Only, she isn't my therapist. She's my supervisor. Besides, I still believe help is for everyone else. I rattle on, filling the gaping silence with a monotone update of events: Tom's cancer is stage four, he's not able to work right now, and I'm pregnant again.

Janice's face contorts in sadness, reflecting back to me what I cover up so carefully. "You need help," she declares my obvious blind spot.

A familiar sharp pronging sensation catches in my throat mid-swallow.

"It's okay. I'm okay, really," I squeak out, trying to regain any lost composure. Blinking hard, I glance at my watch. "Can't afford it anyway," I counter, considering the recent medical bills that sit waiting on the counter at home. Our resources go to Tom's illness first and then the basics: roof, food, and diapers. It's unrealistic to consider tapping into those for myself.

"You can't afford not to, for yourself or for your clients," Janice says, holding her eye contact steady. I nod, in search of a subject change. If she wasn't my supervisor and I didn't need to keep the job, I'd blow out of here. She sits back, waiting me out.

"Okay then . . . for my clients," I finally say, making right with my responsibilities.

"It's got to be for you first." Janice alludes to a cliché I heard repeatedly in graduate school: Self-care is the cornerstone to helping others. *Yeah, yeah*, I think. *I can deal with me later, after Tom is better . . . or gone.*

Janice draws the analogy from the hundreds—perhaps thousands— of times she stood at the end of the aisle, demonstrating the yellow cup over the mouth, strap securely over the head, with the reminder telling passengers to place it on themselves first, before assisting others in need. She'd been a flight attendant before her career change to psychotherapist. The concept is pretty much in her blood.

"Here," she says handing me a slip of paper with a name and number on it. "She's a good match and you can count on privacy," she adds. Janice knows the concerns of a mental health

Jennifer Allen

professional getting therapy in a small community. Confidentiality is the rule, but indirect slippage that could tint perceptions of a new therapist could prove deadly to a future practice.

Folding the paper and pushing it deep into my pocket, I smile a tight thank-you and leave quickly, dizzy from restraining tears. At home, I call the number and make an appointment with Marybeth. This round, I know, will be different than the therapy work I did back in Sacramento, trying to shake the monkey from my back, talking incessantly about past and future from a distance. Now, the future I had worried about has come to be.

A few days later I'm climbing the concrete stairs of the medical offices to her suite, hoping she's a large, robust woman— strong enough to hold all I've waited too long to unload.

Turns out, Marybeth is petite in stature. Her presence feels immensely deep, reminding me that depth, not breadth, is what will give me strength to move through the hardest of times. No need to therapist shop. I'm just where I need to be, at last.

As I sit down on the couch and sink into my very own time, I can't deny the needs that have mounted while I've busied myself tending to others. I give her the nutshell version of what's happening and she tells it back, filling in gaps with the losses I've overlooked: not having the slack to be at home baking bread during this pregnancy, not being the at-home mom for my two-year-old, not having a sex life with my husband anymore, and not having a circle of support to help my family. Tsunamis of grief wash over, almost drowning me with rancid tears that spring forth from ancient places. *God, this is so sad!* I think, listening to Marybeth talk as if she's describing someone else's life. Between sobs, I jump in with my own words and things just start spewing from out of nowhere, like a magician pulling scarf after scarf from her mouth. Just when I think there can't possibly be more, up comes another color, another loss.

Self-pity isn't desirable. In fact, I've always thought it pathetic and swore never to do it. Marybeth helps me experience the difference between wallowing in pity and allowing myself to feel fully without the chronic chatter of self-judgment. Wallowing happens in my head, usually instigated by a rut of thoughts. I can feel allowing in my body and it has movement. It's all so subtle. Easy for me to blow off, only I can't afford to. I cling to the feeling of swimming in self-compassion as I go through losing Tom. At the end of the hour, I'm hopeful and about a pint of tears lighter. Marybeth jots down a name and hands the paper to me. I'm beginning to think I was absent the day they covered this handing-off-slips of-paper method in therapist school.

"Call him," she says. "He's been there. He knows how to get a support network up and running. He had to go through it with a young child too."

I tuck the paper away in my journal, knowing full well that I'm not likely to ask a stranger for help even if it's only a matter of telling me how he got through it.

She opens the door and sees me out. "You don't have to do this all by yourself."

Frequently, I look at the paper. In desperate moments, I even pick up the phone. *For God sakes, his wife just died at Christmas,* I think and put it back down. Instead, I call Zoe and ask her for more babysitting—as much as she can pull off after school and weekends and still have a twelve-year-old life.

"Yeah, love to. Let me clear it with the 'rents, though," she says lightly.

Being around someone who's seriously sick doesn't wig her out, like it might other kids her age. MS has been taking her dad down slowly for years. Illness is woven into her reality. She and River have a common thread: dads who need walkers or wheelchairs to get around the neighborhood. Tom liked her from the first moment he met her back when she was just six and shouting a welcome to us as we moved in to our new home. They're kindred spirits—both outgoing and insatiably intrigued by life. The extra spending money is minimal and Zoe acts as if she should pay us for getting to play with our little cherub. Maybe this asking for help thing won't be so bad.

Meanwhile, Marybeth gently nudges me to keep asking, to continue building a support network for my family. Unloading my pent-up grief with her twice a month might keep me from a having a nervous breakdown though we both know I need other help she can't provide.

"How did *he* do it?" I ask.

"Who?" She genuinely doesn't know that I ponder this mystery widower constantly. Maybe she assumes I've called him like a good client and I've been following through on his pointers.

"Your friend. The guy who's number you gave me awhile back. Nick, I think his name is." I say it like I haven't already committed both his name and number to memory. He's been the lifeline I keep for desperate times. "Did he say yes to anyone who casually offered help? Didn't people burn out after awhile? Wasn't everyone afraid she'd die?"

Marybeth smiles. "Would you just call him! He'll tell you firsthand." She tells me about her experience on the outer periphery of this family's support network. In place of the dread I expect to pick up in her tone, her words are flavored heartily with gratitude. "But," she says, "talk to Nick, Jennifer. He's a good man."

She goes on for a bit though I don't hear a word after *good man.* It's not the first time my mind strays to potential future husband candidates. *Damn.* Now I've got a new feeling to shove down for the time being. It would be a bit more convenient if it comes up after Tom dies, and never, if he doesn't.

On the drive home, I think of Larissa, a hospice patient I've been spending a lot of time with at work. She is teaching me, by example, how the giver and receiver roles blur into one; seemingly helped along by the shedding of skins inherent to the dying process. It occurs to me that sharing this potential with others, who sit and watch us helplessly from the sidelines, would be a gift to them.

When I get home, I hurry upstairs to share the revelation with Tom. His eyes sparkle knowingly. "Yes, Butterfly, it's good stuff, isn't it." His voice is loving and patient. Again, I feel like a child he takes pleasure in watching grow, never wanting to impede the process.

"You're going to have to trust that it goes both ways," he insists, reading my thoughts. "We really don't have a choice at this point."

"But . . ." *I do have a choice.*

If only for the control of choosing *when* we get help, I hold out a little longer. Knowing there's a lifeboat in the wings is like the old days of rock climbing when Tom had me on belay. It buys me time to learn new limits. Besides, I'm not sure I could receive help gracefully yet.

Jennifer Allen

13

Still in Chaos

April 1997

Easter has come round again. For Tom it's probably the last revolution. We make our final debut at church with my visiting family. My parents are pleased to see that I've returned to religion after my rebellious adolescence had led me astray. Tom, with his coarse new hair growth sprouting out the sides of his African beanie, sits through the service. His eyes are closed, conserving the energy he's saving for a picnic down the coast. That's what Easter is about for him anyhow: being with friends in the beauty of Big Sur and questing for the golden egg. His spiritual life is becoming interwoven with his everyday living. Any moment or activity is potentially holy, depending on what he brings to it.

As we leave the church, he says a few goodbyes and closes another door. The sermon didn't impress him nearly as much as the view of the Big Sur coastline does as we drive, cresting hundreds of feet above it.

"Now, *that's* God at it's best, huh?"

"Yeah," I answer, distracted. I'm busy contemplating where to hide the golden egg as I'm the honored hider from last year's find. It seems ironic that I should hide what he's been searching for over the past sixteen Easters on the last occasion he'll have to try and find it. For him, it's much more than the egg and a prize.

Slowly, we make our way through the old grove of giant redwoods. A swollen creek pushes itself through the dense ground cover of clover, creating a magical scene straight out of some fairy tale. At the opening of the forest is a hillside meadow where Brian and Lisa have set up the food table from two saw horses and a piece of plywood.

Tom plops himself down on a blanket to rest. Friends make their rounds to him throughout the afternoon, while Brian and I go about cleverly hiding hundreds of eggs. I'm obliged to hide the golden egg at least as well as it was hidden for me. It has to be buried; completely out of sight. The idea is to thicken the tension as time draws out with no golden egg. Most years, the hider has to revert to hot and cold clues to ease the frustration of the frantic finders. The prize is always worthy of the effort. This year, Brian has resorted to a chunk of cash as he didn't have time to pick up a prize. As much as we need that fifty bucks, I've lost my chances as hider and it doesn't look like Tom has the energy to participate. Carefully, I place the egg in a small cavern and replace the stone without turning over new soil. Skillful, like Tom would have been if he were hiding it.

Once hundreds of eggs are hidden, Brian announces the hunt. A feisty crowd makes its way to the edge of the forest where pink vinyl tape borders the perimeter. There's nothing like an adult egg hunt to bring out the child and the monster in everyone. Tom hangs at the back when the tape is cut. He looks pale.

"Tom, come sit down," I say, taking his arm.

"No, I want to do this. I'll go slow."

"You sure?" I ask. He nods unhurriedly. "Good luck, Button." I peck him on the cheek and watch as he cautiously shuffles down the bank to the creek. The backdrop to his slow motion decent is a frenzied swarm moving among easy finds, snapping up spots of color as they go. Tom squats in a patch of sunlight at the edge of the water bubbling by, seeming more mesmerized by the flow than interested in finding anything. He plunges his hands into the creek, cupping them together and raising them to his face. Pearls of sunlit water roll down his cheeks and throat, as he looks skyward. His eyes are closed, as if in prayer. From where I stand, it looks like a scene from the Bible minus John the Baptist. As long as I've known him, Tom has always made his own rituals. I imagine this is his Easter ritual: some kind of rebirth to life in the course of a slow death.

After awhile, and I know it's been a good ten minutes because the finding troops are getting restless having not come upon the golden egg yet, Tom edges downstream and does the same baptism routine. My heart races as he hovers directly over the spot where I hid the golden egg. Running his hands along the moss below him he stops to wiggle and remove a "loose tooth" among the stones. From where I stand, a glint of gold is visible in the gap. He sits above and can't see it. After thoroughly inspecting the rock, he begins to re-set it, but something keeps it from fitting snuggly. Reaching into the hole, he pulls out the golden egg.

I'm smiling so hard my dimple aches. It's true that I've been telling him exactly where to go to find it, though never out loud. Nor has he looked back up the hill at me since he began his quest. I've got to wonder if this is the Universe telling him his path is cleared for take-off or if we have become so close, we are simply telepathic. No matter, he got his coveted golden egg.

Tom doesn't yell out. Instead, he holds the egg to his chest and slowly ascends the bank to declare his winnings. He's quietly elated. This might look suspicious in such a highly competitive hunt if it wasn't evident to everyone he may not be here next year. When all the eggs are found and prizes distributed, the group poses for a picture. Tom stands proud with the gold egg perched just in front of his heart.

Click. Another last frozen onto film.

Brian won't take the egg back when it's time to go. "It's yours, Tom. Please take it." Tom doesn't argue that it's the original egg of the long tradition. He seems to understand this is his long-time adventure buddy's way of saying goodbye.

"Thank you," Tom says and they hug tightly. When they finally part, neither says the standard: *See you next year.*

On the drive up the coast, the horizon grows pink, orange and lavender over the Pacific. I ask him: "So what's your secret? Did you see me come up the bank after I hid it?"

"No Jen, you know I wouldn't cheat, " he says. Instantly, I feel shame for doubting both him and our faith in synchronicity.

"Sorry, just thought with the clock ticking and all."

He shakes his head in sincere wonder. Clearly there's no offense taken.

"How do *you* think you found it?" I ask.

He laughs to himself. "I stopped looking."

Ah, so that's how it works.

My husband is one frickin' good prophet lately. Who needs Khalil Gibran to answer questions when I've got Tom? If nothing else, it's a side-benefit to being end-stage. Needless to say, the golden egg takes its place beside his braid on the altar at home. It's a reminder of what he found once he ceased searching and settled into exactly what was in front of him.

It takes a full week for Tom to recover the energy he spent on Easter. His decline is happening too fast for those outside our daily household to comprehend. When I show up at the wedding of our good friends without Tom, they assume he couldn't come because of an umpiring conflict.

"No," I tell them with a smile, trying to keep the event celebratory. "His mom came down to be with him over the weekend, so River and I could come. The chemo's knocked him flat."

Still, it doesn't sink in. Perhaps it's my smile that throws them off. Maybe they are remembering the last time they were with Tom. Back when he moved in close to listen and spoke with animated gestures. Nobody wants to consider Tom can wilt; that he can be anything other than the livewire, magnetically attracting attention. I move from conversation to conversation at the reception, wishing the allotment for wine while pregnant was three or four glasses. People ask about Tom and I stumble in response, despite practicing in advance.

Rehearsal lines began with the truth: *"I think he's going to die soon. I'm just a hair from falling apart. I hope I don't lose the baby."* And ended with a less-harsh, silver lining version that I voted more palatable: *"The chemo is nailing him, but I guess that means it's doing its job. I'm hanging in there. River is a joy and we're so excited about our new addition. What a miracle, huh?"* I'd pat my stomach, smile, hug, and move on to the next conversation.

It wouldn't be lying, it would be keeping the invisible elephant well fed and smack in middle of the wedding, the grocery store, my workplace, our living room, and in any other place I have to deal with talking about Tom's condition. It's ironic that it makes me crazy when other people feed this denial elephant. Yet I'm playing the same game. And I'm not sure whom it's for.

When others say things like: "He's a fighter, he'll be okay!" or "If anyone deserves a miracle, its him." I know it's really for them. When religious folk offer promises from their position with God like: "I'll pray for him to be cancer-free" I know their intentions are good also. Nonetheless, I want to take each person by the shoulders, shake them and scream: "Yes, he *is* a fighter, and guess what? He's *not* okay!" and "So, if he dies from this, was he undeserving of that miracle? Or did God just not give a rat's ass?"

I've concluded there isn't really a right thing to say to me about Tom right now and I've sold out to the elephant conspiracy. I'm tired of maintaining everyone else's comfort level around illness, death, and grief. What I need most right now is good listening sans guilt trips or judgment, beyond the one hour I get with Marybeth every two weeks.

My parents are just the people. Mum was brought up in a loving but constricted religious household. No smoking, no drinking, no dancing, no rock-and-roll, and no food before the blessing. The constriction stuck in that Mum had all five of us children trained to go on emergency ashtray patrol when our grandparents unexpectedly pulled up the driveway. It had more to do with her parents' beliefs than her own. Mum is religious and holds her beliefs firmly, but converting people in the checkout line or even her closest friends isn't her thing. Her beliefs haven't kept her from listening. And though I won't be sharing my latest disillusionment with the Daddy-God with her, I know she can hear my worst fears about Tom without offering up some quick fix that's designed to shut me up.

Dad, on the other hand, wouldn't bat an eyelash over my firing God. Even with his being a faithful churchman since he and Mum got together in their teens, his grip on beliefs seems looser— open to questioning. Though I've never heard him query aloud, let alone prompt conversations of depth on the topic, I've never felt an ounce of judgment from him, either. Lord knows I've given him plenty of material over the years. He's got a keen sense for listening when it's really important. And now is that time.

We have the four-hour drive back to Seaside from the wedding in Santa Barbara and a few days to follow for such business. My parents are still on their annual visit out West to see their three stray daughters and fading son-in-law. On the return, I ride with them, unloading while River naps in his car seat. Dad drives, eyes on the road, nodding every so often. Mum turns to the backseat frequently with such an intense look of empathy on her face, I want to cry for me. I'm afraid if I do, I'll come undone and tangle in a heap just when it's time for them to leave.

When we get back to the house and relieve Stella, Tom is picking invisible nits off his skin. Stella is shaken by Tom's frailty and medication-induced disorientation. After years of imperceptible decline, things are sliding fast. None of us know whether this is a temporary result of the chemo or if he is really going down for the count. It definitely doesn't look like he'll be getting out to the ball field anytime soon.

In quiet acknowledgment, Mum and Dad bring River out to the playground and come back with a full sized color television to replace the portable black and white one with the aluminum foil antenna. Dad sets it up in our bedroom and when Tom wakes, it's like Christmas. The ballgames come to him now.

Over the next couple days before they leave Dad scoops River up and carries him every chance he gets. He bathes him and changes his diaper; something he never did with my sisters and I. And he growls, chasing River on all fours, just like he did with me at that age and just like Tom and I did with River before I got too pregnant and Tom, too sick. Mum reads to River and makes him tuna sandwiches. When Tom's oncologist reports he needs blood transfusions, Mum and Dad bring him up to the hospital and donate their blood to him. My eyes water in response to each gesture of love they offer.

Their departure day comes too soon. I don't feel old enough to handle what's coming. The house is quiet and I'm back to a slue of internal conversations that I'd like to be having with another adult. It's time. I retrieve the neatly creased paper from my journal, lock myself in the bathroom, and dial.

I'm blowing my nose when a man's voice answers. "Hello, is this Nick McQuay?" I ask, sounding like a telemarketer. He doesn't hang up. Awkwardness and guilt, for asking a stranger for advice on such a painful subject, overtake me as I bumble through orienting him as to why I'm calling.

" . . . and he's pretty sick, I mean it's not looking good." I tiptoe around the big "D" word. "Tom is forever the optimist, so we don't talk about the potentials much. Lately, he can't even focus to have a conversation." I feel like a traitor, confiding in a stranger about Tom—a male stranger.

"Mmm. It's really hard isn't it?" Nick invites me into a place he knows well. Intimacy hangs over the phone line, between two people who have never met. I cough, shooing it away.

"Tell me about how you managed." I shift us to the practical, afraid of falling into his lap with all of my problems. Nick speaks slowly, leaving gaping spaces, which I feel obliged to fill with specific questions.

"What did you do for childcare while you worked?"

He tells me his son went to preschool and the half-dozen-or-so people who helped with Conrad while Wendy was sick are still helping. He hired a cook and a housekeeper as well. That gave him time to be with his family when he got home.

"Oh, I see," I say, realizing the difference money can make. *Maybe he can't understand.*

Genuinely unaware of any wedge between us, he goes on, until I forget as well. He talks about how the leader of his men's group prompted him to rally a support network for both the emotional and practical needs of his family. Fortunately, both he his wife were involved in large overlapping social circles, resulting in an abundant list of eager helpers. Two friends, Russ and Emily, alternated orchestrating the wide range of help.

How bold to ask for so much, I think. "Didn't you worry you were overwhelming people?"

"They're adults," he answers matter-of-factly as if having boundaries correlated with the cessation of bone growth. "It was up to each person to decide how much they wanted to help and how. Our job was to receive the offers," he says. "Let me give you Russ's number. Ask him how it was on that end of things."

I call Russ immediately after I hang up with Nick, while my courage is building momentum. Russ has a smooth, earthy voice, the kind that have women trusting him completely on a first date.

He doesn't lie: "It *was* tough. And it was long," he says. "You know what? I wouldn't have traded that experience for anything."

"What do you mean?" I ask, wanting something more to go on—something to boost my campaign for help.

"Being able to do something—anything— in such a tragic situation felt important. Like it really mattered. And it wasn't just me. There were a bunch of us doing all sorts of things," he says. He is silent for a few moments and then continues: "We hoped she'd live, but it didn't go that way. Being on board, through to her death was . . . intimate. I'm not sure how else to explain it."

As soon as I get off the phone with Russ, I start making a list of anyone who has ever even casually offered help. That's as far as I get before a stubborn streak of independence sets in and has me wait until I'm sure we're sinking before I drop the lifeboat.

Simultaneous to the seemingly endless downhill swoop of Tom's health roller coaster, I've been slinking into the bowels of the hospital before making my art therapy rounds, checking for the rumored posting of a full-time position as Child Life Specialist. It

Jennifer Allen

would be a ticket out of the Medi-Cal welfare system before the baby comes and Tom crashes completely. Every day that passes counts as my belly grows. I don't want the pregnancy to kill my chances, nor my chances to kill the pregnancy. The seventh time I check, it's posted and I apply immediately.

For the interview, I wear a long vest to cover the gap of flesh bulging out between the linking safety pins securing my pants. I talk about the long-term vision I have for the position. Carefully, without bringing personal experience in, I demonstrate a grasp of the issues families have while coping with illness and the medical system.

"Would this position work for your situation?" asks Linda, my potential boss. Despite her kind eyes, my guard stays up. She knows Tom is sick. Word travels at light speed in the tight circuit of hospital and hospice.

"You mean because my husband is sick?"

She nods, "Well, sure —and you have a young child."

What should have been frosting qualifications for the position suddenly sour my candidacy simply by way of being too close in proximity to my daily life. *If only I could fast forward and this was all past tense, she'd be sure I'd have the wisdom from the experience without the emotional slippage.*

"It's perfect," I say. "My husband works from home, so he helps with the childcare (translation: He's too sick to work now). Our son has just started an early preschool (a.k.a., daycare that I swore I'd never send him to). He just loves it—perfect age for socializing. Speaking of which, I had an idea for the playroom. We could have open play for kids daily, so they're not isolated in their rooms." I segue from a wishful reality to the job at hand. Truly, I believe all the advice I'd give families would be sound. Only it would be for them, not for me—the helper.

Linda smiles sincerely as I shake her hand upon leaving. I'm pretty sure I have the job, unless she noticed the safety pins when I got up.

Within a week she welcomes me aboard.

Two days after that, the morning I've painstakingly come to the decision to give my notice to hospice and maintain contact with Larissa as a volunteer, she calls with regrets reporting that the funding for the position fell through. Back to square one. At three safety pins across the belly, a co-worker at hospice pulls me aside.

"Honey, it seems you've got something cooking. Look, I've got some great maternity dresses I've hung onto, just in case we have another. You'd look beautiful in them and they're roomy—discreet." Lola winks, her punk-model face softening with concern.

"Thanks, that'd be great." The burden of one less secret is lifted and I glide into the day.

Nurse Gerry enters as I'm packing up my briefcase. "Hey, Jennifer. How's the hubby tolerating the chemo?"

"Put it this way, he could write the textbook on side-effects. The bald thing, though, that really does it for me," I say, winking.

"Kojack, oh yeah. I can get that. Just got to tweeze the stragglers and wax the bulb," she says.

"Now you're talking!" I call back as I head out the door, laughing past the lump in my throat.

I'm getting pretty dang skilled at separating business from personal, until they bleed into each other and personal becomes a numb business plan for survival. Though it keeps me functioning, the price of losing closeness with Tom is high. When I update people on his condition, I'm starting to sound like his social worker instead of his wife. Life is pushing me flat up against the wall to come up with other options. Larissa is showing me how, but I'm a slow learner and time is of the essence.

Jennifer Allen

14

Along for Her Ride

May 1997

Larissa and I met back when she had a mane of dark curls bubbling over her shoulders. Before she knew.

She didn't get to ask the discharge planner about me and then walk in on my life, like I had hers. Really, it wasn't fair for me to know the pain she was admitted for was end-stage cervical cancer before she did. The doctor hadn't been able to break the devastating news to this single mom of three. Not yet, anyway.

Before entering her hospital room I took a deep breath, unclipped the hospice nametag from my blouse, slipped it into my pocket and entered as an art therapist.

"Habla Inglese?" I asked.

"Si—sure, what do you need?"

"Oh, I work here doing art with patients. Just thought I'd stop in and tell you about our menu of art activities," Even as I spoke, I felt like a double agent doing the undercover work of establishing rapport for the long run—assuming she'd be on hospice services soon enough.

We talked easily until the third visit when she *knew*. She sat straight up in bed, staring into nothingness. It was hard to tell if she was angry or in shock. I stayed for a grueling ten minutes before I couldn't take the silent tension and I left.

Our visits continued weekly at her home in a neighborhood I usually avoided because of its gang violence. Larissa endured me at first, and then, through the season of her hair dropping off and then returning as wiry stubble, things changed. Comfort grew from the predictability of our time together—one sure thing amongst too many uninvited changes.

Each week, the atmosphere was different. Some weeks I'd find a cheerful Larissa, carefully making her way around the small, dark room straightening up stacks of magazines and hanging clothes on the water spigots sticking out of the wall. She'd make chitchat about her kids and the what plans they had for the summer as she shuffled around.

Other weeks, she lie flat and silent, eyes sunk in deeply, as if surveying her inner landscape and looking for herself within it. Sitting with her in silence was often the extent of my visit. Though it felt increasingly sacred to spend out time this way, it was a challenge to come up with progress notes to satisfy her Medi-Cal coverage. No clinical language fit what was happening in those visits. She was moving slowly from body to spirit and I was riding along as an open witness.

Interspersed with the quiet, sinking visits were angry ones. Larissa went from being irritated with me, her kids and her mother; to downright enraged at the doctors who couldn't fix things and at God, whom she thought sent her this punishment for violating Catholic codes. Guilt and heaps of confession spewed forth, especially after she dared to question the justice of God's motives. With her, I was open-eared; receptive to all of her humanity and unthreatened by any of it. It's a different ballgame when one is not married to the confessor.

Jennifer Allen

When I've tried offering Tom the same kind of listening, I can't help interrupting him with wifely concerns. Almost all of his confessions have potential impact on our family. It's like walking a tightrope trying to find the balance between absolute compassion without judgment and giving him a reality check on the implications of his choices. If I were one-hundred-percent sure he'd die from this cancer, things like warrants for his arrest and overdue property taxes would be moot. Sure, we'd lose the house, but at least I wouldn't have wasted precious moments being angry with him for things he doesn't have time or resources to right, anyway. Larissa gives me a chance to practice and learn. The way I am with her is exactly how I want to be with Tom. Death seems so much closer to her doorstep, though I sometimes wonder if I have a massive blind spot with Tom.

Since our visits began a few months ago, Larissa has taught me more than she'll ever know about how to simply be with someone who is leaving this world.

I'll tell her this today, I think, just as Alicia, Larissa's ten-year-old daughter, answers the door.

"Hi," she says, quickly turning to usher me through the hallways past the kitchen where Larissa's mother stirs a pot.

"Buenas dias!" I have to practically yell to be heard over the game show blaring from the living room.

She nods with a smile. This has been the extent of our exchanges from the get-go. Either it's because she can tell by my accent that this is about the scope of my Spanish or because she doesn't want to talk about why I'm here.

Alicia opens the door to the back room, where her mom lies on a cot with thick layers of Mexican blankets pulled up to her chin, despite the warm weather. As small as her bed is, each week it seems to swallow her up.

Larissa asks her daughter something in Spanish and Alicia answers in English "Okay, okay! I will after I finish this show. I promise," she says. Larissa tries a firmer tone, only her voice has little tooth to it and Alicia closes the door mid-sentence. It doesn't stop Larissa from finishing. She mutters something in Spanish that sounds like a string of satisfying cuss words.

Their mother-daughter habit doesn't stop just because Larissa is sick. Neither does the husband-wife thing I have with Tom. I wonder how close death must come to break down the useless bickering. *What will it take for me to love him without resentment for breaking the twenty-year promise?*

Larissa clears her throat, pulling my attention back to her— the easy one to love free and clear. She frowns, looking resigned.

"What?" I ask.

"I can't do this anymore," she says.

I don't know if she means mothering or living. Instantly, I superimpose Larissa onto Tom and conclude how tired I must make him with all of my petty earthly concerns. He probably can't do a relationship on top of trying to stay alive either.

"What is it you can't do anymore?" I ask, hoping for more on the inside scoop, something to help me know what is going on with my man.

"This," she says, fingering the rubber tube that runs from a bag of milky fluid hooked on an I.V. pole, entering her body through a vein in her neck.

"Oh?" I ask, comprehending as I go and reminding myself she is not Tom. It's not fair for me to glean clues from her and apply them to Tom.

"I can't do the feeding tube anymore," she says. Her voice is sad and clear. Initially, she had gone along with the strong preferences of her family. Everyone has avoided talk of an endpoint to the artificial eating. Tom would never do the feeding tube to begin with, no matter what I had to say about it.

Stop already! I force myself back to Larissa.

"They think this is going to save me," she says. "What if I die when they take it out? It will be my fault." She shifts her focus from my eyes to the space between us. "How can I leave my children?" Larissa's mouth is dry, making little snapping noises as she speaks, and her eyes look tired. She doesn't wait for an answer because it's not me she's asking.

"My mom won't let me talk about dying to her or the kids. They can see what's happening. I don't want to hurt them." Now she looks to me.

Jennifer Allen

"Oh, Larissa," I say, frowning. "They're already hurting and it's nobody's fault. They've been losing you a little bit at a time over the past few months. Not talking about it leaves everyone alone in their hurt, including you," I say, giving her something I know from experience, not textbooks.

"Then what if I don't die?" she asks.

"Great. What's the harm in that?"

"Well, then I've gone and upset everyone; robbed their hope. They'll think I gave up."

"Larissa, if you live through this—I don't think anyone is going to be thinking about how you gave up." Her face softens momentarily.

"On the other hand, if you end up dying from this cancer, are you going to be okay with having not talked to your kids?" I ask, trying hard to maintain objectivity.

"No, I need to tell them some things. And I need to talk to my brother about helping take care of them. He's worse than my mom," she says shaking her head hopelessly.

"Every time I try and talk to him about this food-tube, he says, 'Leave the praying to us, your job is to do what you can to get better and that means you must eat. If you can't do it with your mouth, then get what you need from the tube.' It was okay at first, but now my stomach hurts so bad all the time and I'm losing weight anyway." She catches her breath. "What am I going to do?"

"It is your call, Larissa—the feeding tube, talking to your kids. Those are your choices. Whatever you decide, though, I'll back you. If you want help in either case, I can be here or we can get a nurse.

"He only listens to doctors," she says.

"We'll get Dr. Miller to come," I offer.

"Yeah. Let's do that. Let me get through for one more week. Okay?"

"Sure. Whatever you want Larissa."

She looks at her watch, "Ah, it's General Hospital time. Turn it on, would you?"

I switch the channels and tweak the antenna until her show is at least audible. We watch together for a while and then I rise to leave. As I'm going out the door she asks, "Jennifer, do you think there are cows in heaven? I'm just dying for a glass of milk."

Bone Knowing   173

"I'd like to think everyone gets just what they need most in heaven."

On the drive back to the office, I stop at Dairy Queen and order a strawberry milkshake. Each sip I think of Larissa and send a quasi-prayer out to the Universe that there are, in fact, cows in her heaven.

All along, I've been reporting back to Tom about "this woman" I visit. Larissa is nameless to him and yet, he feels for her more vividly than he seems to feel for himself. When I tell him about the feeding tube dilemma, he says: "How can her family not see that the artificial feeding is for them not for her?"

"It's complicated," I say, not wanting to argue. But then I can't stop there. "It's one of those things you just can't understand until you're in it."

"Please tell me that doesn't mean you'd be rigging me up to a feeding tube," he says, half serious, half joking.

"Who knows, maybe you're the one who would want it. You did do chemo when you swore you wouldn't, right?"

"Hmph," he answers, nodding. "You tell her I'm rooting for her to have it *her* way."

"Sure," I say, smiling.

Larissa has been a catalyst for Tom and I to talk about hard things. It goes both ways. She asks me about him often, especially how he reconciles Catholic beliefs with what is happening to his body. Since I don't lie, when she asked point blank about hell, I had to tell her Tom is adamantly opposed to the belief—in a God-inflicted kind of way, anyhow. Earthly suffering—yes. A fiery inferno—no way. It is as if she and Tom have been linked through me, coaching each other along this final journey, without ever having met.

Back when she first learned my husband had advanced cancer also—after about a month of visits, she was pissed. We were talking about kids being tuned-in to adults. I told her how my son, at two-and-a-half, could call it when his Daddy was getting sicker.

"His Daddy? You mean your husband?" she had asked.

"Yes. My husband—Tom, has cancer." I had said, suddenly realizing I hadn't actually mentioned this before.

Jennifer Allen

"Why didn't you tell me?" She looked betrayed, like she had in hospital when I showed up with my hospice pin.

"These visits are for you, not me," I had said.

"Oh, that's how it is?" The anger in her tone had caught me off guard. She had no idea how much I wanted it to be otherwise. *But* there were boundaries to be kept. It was my job.

"If you think it would help, I'll tell you anything you want to know," I had said.

"Okay, now we're getting somewhere," she had said, her scowl giving way to a slight smile.

That was the day my job became more than a job and Tom and Larissa began their invisible relationship.

Now though, Larissa is too far into her dying process to relate outside of herself. Dealing with her family is more than enough. She manages two weeks of wild-eyed anxiety and discomfort before she can take no more. We have a meeting in her back bedroom to discuss her wish to remove the feeding tube. Her brother, mother, and children stand around her bed. A painting of the Virgin Mary hangs on the wall above her head. Larissa forces her focus on each family member, gasping after every word or two. When she finishes, there are no more secrets, only tears—her brother, Juan, included.

As her death nears, my boss grants me free reign on visits to Larissa, without having to consider her insurance coverage. I'm visiting daily now, though she is often asleep or inside a pre-death reality where she can see people and things I cannot. A few days ago it was a crocodile in the room, then an Uncle who had passed years ago. Today, she is awake and looks full of purpose.

"Come," she says in a rough whisper. There is a necklace on the bedside stand and she's pointing to it. "For you." It's a string of black hematite beads with three red stones spaced at center. I hold it up and then latch it at the nape of my neck. She smiles and her full gum line is visible, as if she has false teeth about to drop out. Her body is thinning around its bones, the flesh giving way each day.

Twirling the bead between my fingers, I look to her. "It's beautiful Larissa, thank you." I lean in close and kiss her forehead lightly. "Thank you for letting me in. Our time together has meant so much to me," I say, pulling back to look into her eyes.

Bone Knowing

She nods and mouths "Me too." Then she pulls me close and whispers into my ear: "Goodbye for real this time." For over a week we've had a running joke as to what number goodbye will be the final one.

It's awkward to hug her fragile body propped up so precariously on pillows, so I press my cheek to hers and say, "Goodbye dear Larissa." From the door I ask her to send Tom a sign on whether he can count on milk in heaven. She smiles to one side and closes her eyes.

For the next three visits, Larissa is unconscious. On Friday, when I show up at work and see her name on the list of deceased patients, I return to my car to cry.

We had let each other in at the risk of feeling. Sadness and gratitude mix together inside me as sweet grief. Larissa has gifted me with the experience of growing closer to her as she approached death. Our relationship has helped me recover my heart, bring it with me to work and back home again—where I'll desperately need it in times to come.

Jennifer Allen

15

Using Lifeboats

June 1997

It's a good thing the secret is out at work with this pregnancy because I've had a major growth spurt in my waistline that no amount of safety pins can accommodate. I'm not positive it's all baby with the slue of Dairy Queen Blizzards I've been putting down in honor of Larissa. Either way, I'm growing uncomfortable right alongside Tom, only the bigger I get, the smaller he gets. There is a time frame and a motivation for my discomfort. Tom has no idea how long his will go and he's at war with the source of it. At least we are both done with nausea—mine from pregnancy and his from the chemotherapy. Since he finished treatment a few weeks ago, he's been milling around the house, driving River to daycare and taking care of his own juicing.

When good days come, we seize them. Last weekend it was the Boardwalk. Donning a Moroccan beanie to keep his bald head warm, Tom lifted River onto the rides. All day, Tom's eyes never left his son and a smile never left his face. In the name of normalcy, he even ate french fries with River. It cost him three days of bed rest and digestive rut.

Today, I picked up River after work and have come home to Tom standing at the door with a picnic dinner packed and a rolled up inflatable boat in tow.

"Let's go out on the lagoon, Rio!" he rallies, shooting me a quick check-in, after the fact. My aching back has been screaming for recline all day. It will have to wait. Tom has a number on his good days and I don't. Besides, there is nothing sweeter than being present to every last drop of quality time with our family before it changes.

River shrieks in glee. I have to wonder how confusing these days of extreme fun peppered sparsely among those of fatigued and overwhelmed parents who say "Sorry, not today," must be for him. *Better confused than depressed*, I think, as I grab sandals and sweaters for the three of us.

As evening turns the light a lovely Tuscan orange, we drift about the lagoon that joins the Carmel River to the Pacific Ocean. A swarm of pelicans pass over us, blessing us with the soft pulse of their wings. My eyes well up from the joy that is palpable between us. Moments like this make everything worth it.

Later, sleep comes hard and fast to Tom. Sometime in the wee hours, though, I hear him get up and I know something's wrong because he usually pees in his bedside bottle.

"Tom, what's happening?" I mumble, fighting my way out of sleep.

Slam!

In the half-moon's light, I see the outline of his body flop backwards into the closet doors. He's down by the time I jump out of bed. Slumped in a stupor, Tom utters nonsense between dry heaves. When he comes to, he's confused and doesn't remember falling. What he is clear on is that a trip to the E.R. isn't an option.

178   Jennifer Allen

"It's okay, Jen. I've got an appointment in a couple days. It can wait," he says as I wedge myself under his armpit and help him back into bed.

Something is very wrong.

It's June 12th and I have no idea what is happening in the world other than President Clinton is in office and the California medical marijuana law has been upheld, though it makes no difference now that Tom is adamantly opposed to using it. The only thing significant to me is that it's Tom's 52nd birthday and likely his last. As promised, he calls me at work after his doctor's appointment.

"Got myself one hell of a birthday present," he says playfully.

I'm hopeful "What?"

"Got a brain tumor the size of a pea, right in the brainstem. Can you believe it?" His tone contradicts his words.

"What? Are you kidding?" I'm confused.

"You've got to come with me when I get my radiation mask. It's a fascinating procedure. They press this net against my face and it makes a replica. And I'll need to come daily for six weeks. Oh yeah, I can't drive anymore. They have a ride service. We'll have to get the schedule." He speaks fast and sounds like a kid reporting birthday scores.

No! Don't you give in to being a patient! I heave a sigh of exhaustion, already anticipating the implications of a brain tumor. "Shit Tom! Why are you all happy?"

"Simple, Jen. It's my birthday, maybe my last, and nothing is going to blow it. Besides, a brain tumor isn't all bad. It could be my best friend if this gets real drawn-out and painful. I could just drop dead."

"Let's talk at dinner," I say, feeling a lump already congregating in my throat. I'm not ready for him to die suddenly. At least with an illness there is time to adjust, to plan. In the time between work and what is supposed to be his celebration dinner, I make frenzied efforts to accommodate the news. Since this morning, logistics have become impossible: He can't drive at all and there's no chance he'll be going back to work. He can't be left alone with River and shouldn't be left by himself.

For dinner, we pretend we're tourists with money and go out to a restaurant on Cannery Row that overlooks the bay. Zoe isn't available, so River comes along. Our conversation is limited. I just stare at Tom as he converts the napkin into a puppet for our son's entertainment. Nobody would ever guess this man was diagnosed with a brain tumor today.

The reality check comes within a week's worth of compensating for all he can't do anymore. River enters into the full-throes of his two-year-old rebellion and Tom has taken to the bed between daily radiation treatments. The household stress level has blown out the roof, my temper is hair-trigger and I fear breaking. Breaking down. Breaking my child's arm. Breaking Tom's heart. Keeping up with a spirited two-year old, while my belly grows between us; picking up and administering medications; juicing, juicing, and juicing more for Tom's regimen; going to work; coordinating childcare and Tom's care; making food, cleaning up puke; nursing; paying bills; and (sometimes) walking the dog has brought me to my knees.

It's time to make some calls. Tom's therapist, Patty, is first on the list. She's been coming to our home occasionally for his sessions and agrees to facilitate the meeting. With her on board, I'm committed to making it happen. Methodically, I move down the substantial row of names, dial, and spit out my spiel before I second-guess my invitation for help.

What I need most is a Russ kind of person: someone else to run the show with organizing the actual help. The very idea of trying to do that myself, while I'm bouncing unpredictably around the full gamut of emotions, is part of what has kept me from pursuing help for so long. Talking on the phone, answering the endless questions about Tom's health status, and asking for help directly, rank down there with dog-poop patrol and taxes.

Back in April, when I first called Nick, he had referred me to a book: *Share the Care*. I've been plugging along through it in time for the meeting. It has forms to copy in the back for organizing the intricate web of help I'm weaving to catch my family's fall. During the meeting, the papers will give me a focus—something in writing that will keep me from forgetting what we are meeting for. It'll be all too tempting to say we're just fine once Patty discloses the pitfalls of helping.

On the afternoon of the initial support network meeting, I order pizza and sit on the couch with multicolored stacks of forms spread across the table and a basket of pens. I close my eyes and imagine Russ telling me again what an opportunity it was to help. *Rewind again and louder this time.* His face is huge on my mind's screen. I've pictured him handsome, with dimples and orange hair, like an old college buddy who's nickname, Rusty, came from his brilliant rust-colored hair.

Drrring! The doorbell interrupts. *Here goes.* Big smile. *Do we have an offer of a lifetime for you!* I open the door to the pizza guy. Good practice, anyway. The difficulty isn't only asking for help and admitting I can't do it all anymore, it's also letting people decide if and how they will take this offer. *What if nobody shows?*

Impulsively, I call Nick last minute and leave a message; certain he couldn't get a sitter in time to make it. Over the next half an hour, our tiny living room fills to maximum capacity. Tom drags himself downstairs to be with his guests, as if to prove he's worth investing help in. I overhear him tell a friend, "Oh, I'm feeling better. I'm going to get through this. It'll just take time."

So much for our game plan to be honest and talk openly about the possibility of him dying, I think. Making himself likeable is in Tom's blood, like independence is in mine. He can't tolerate the perception that he has given up. If people need to see a battle, well then goddamn it, he'll show them one! The crowd brings him to life, making it easy to overlook his sagging clothes and protruding clavicles.

Patty starts the meeting before Tom has everyone convinced this is a cocktail party and not a desperate cry for help. She's mid-stream introducing the concept of a support network when the doorbell rings. Eliza lets in the late guest. A man enters, his red hair glowing from the afternoon sun streaming through the door behind him. An orange glow continues a rough edge around his shadowed face indicating a beard. *Hmph,* I think, *must be Russ. Funny I don't remember inviting him.*

"Welcome," I say approaching the stranger with an outstretched hand. Time is stubbed upon our contact, breaking itself up into frames: hand, warm, man, light, orange, deep sound.

"Jennifer? It's Nick. Nick McQuay."

"Oh . . .Oh, hi. Come on in."

Morse code vibrations tap tenaciously from bones to heart before I can intercept and think right over the flush of knowing. It's the kind of knowing that has led me to now. *Please no. Not yet.* Though I've promised to listen when it comes, this isn't good timing. I push it away, but the realization that Nick is going to be a significant figure in my life is undeniable. It has me bumbling through introductions. My ears are hot and I can only imagine the contrast of these crimson crescents against blonde hair. *Why did I wear my hair up anyway?* Quickly, I point Nick to the food and take my place on the floor between Tom's bony legs, making it clear to myself and to anyone who witnessed the time warp: It wasn't anything. I'm with my man: 'til-death-do-us-part.

Patty has a few words with Nick and, the next thing you know, he's in the center of the circle, clearing his throat to speak. It seems as if the room has been waiting for him and he for it. As he steps into the spotlight of the afternoon sun and begins his story, everyone hushes, captivated by the heart in his telling. There were the endless ups and downs in his wife's journey, just as there have been with Tom's. Listeners seem to easily translate his story to our situation. Only, unlike us, Nick had asked for help early on and really knew how to use it. From picking up their three-year-old son from preschool to helping his wife adhere a huge butterfly tattoo onto her bald head; there were so many places for those watching from the sidelines to step in and be one less degree helpless to a possible tragedy unfolding right in front of them. That is where we are. The tension in the room thickens in anticipation of what happens next.

They don't know.

Nick smiles, accounting the celebration they had with their support network when Wendy had gone into remission. Everyone had been thanked heartily and let off-duty. An audible sigh passes through the room. Relaxed brows quickly contort with concern when Nick inhales deeply and resumes. His eyes water and his voice grows determined as he moves into telling the *whole* story.

Jennifer Allen

Tom's legs stiffen in anticipation of his cover being blown. Nick talks about how the network had reconvened when Wendy's cancer had returned a few months later in a more aggressive form.

"The grace was in the way people showed up for us and for each other," he says.

"One of the hardest things for all of us to get, was that even when she was looking so sick and completely out of it, she was still Wendy—alive until dead." He looks at Tom and Tom blinks in recognition of a truth that is out before he can make it more palatable to others.

Nick continues, "It's challenging to be around someone who is getting better one minute and dying the next." Nick scans the group suddenly aware that some people may not know this helping stint may not be about Tom getting better.

"Just try and be with Tom where he's at, no expectations," he says, looking at me. He's clearly been on this path with greater consciousness than I feel capable of. A pause for emphasis is broken by one of those snorts-coughs people with post-nasal drip do every other minute. When he picks up again, death is undeniably in the room.

The story doesn't end with her last breath. Nick talks of how the support network had gathered at Wendy's deathbed. After a long silence, tears, and consoling; a few close friends had helped to bathe her, paint her nails, and dress her in the outfit she had ordered for Christmas, just a month before she died. He tells us how everyone had participated in putting together a celebration of her life just weeks after, so he could be free to feel his grief.

"It was an incredible gift to feel such support through my wife's illness, her death and even now, as I rebuild my life as a single parent. Still, it astounds me that it was mutual," he says. Heads tilt and eyebrow raise.

Tell them how, I urge him on like he's got telepathy or something.

"I keep hearing from friends how profoundly the experience has impacted them and how grateful they are for having been allowed into Wendy's dying process. It was her last and greatest gift," he says, looking around the room at each person. Some nod in return and others look away.

Bone Knowing   183

I'm right there with him, until he stops speaking. Then, I fall flat into this reality where such things don't seem possible. The pace I've taken, just to keep up with my life goes much too fast for such a heart connection. Slowing down as things get more difficult doesn't seem like an option. It saddens me that this grace feels just out of reach.

Tom knows exactly what Nick is talking about only he opts to take care of those who don't. "No worries, things are looking good here. I'm getting radiation treatment now. Who knows what the miracles of modern medicine are capable of these days!" he says. Only a couple people, who were prepared to help with a quest toward cure and not a potential death, fly with his statement. At the break, they check their watches and declare they are late for appointments.

Better they peel off now, I think. Those who stay to fill out the endless forms seem to have resonated with Nick's words. They're on for the long haul. Paper noises hum in the background as everyone fills out their information sheets, preferences for ways of helping, and availability. Meanwhile, Patty goes over the pitfalls. She encourages helpers to avoid being martyrs, use good boundaries, take care of themselves first, support each other emotionally, and respect our family's privacy. Eliza and Ed raise their hands to tag-team the coordinator's job. They'll be the bridge and the buffer between our family and all those helping. My job will be to fill out a calendar of needs each week and they'll do their best to fill them. They (and not me, thank God) will initiate the phone tree for updates of Tom's condition. It's a lot to ask of anyone, but I know dang well if it's left to me, the calls won't get made. We'd remain struggling in isolation.

I let go. Hope enters like a tendril of jasmine luring me into graciously receiving the sweetness it offers so freely. It has me considering the possibility that I could stop this crazed pace of keeping up with life and simply *be* with Tom for whatever time he has left.

The pizza is gone, the forms are filled out and I have thanked everyone for coming, and people are slow to leave. They are friends and acquaintances from different pockets of our lives. It's as if they need to orient themselves with this new circle—one that might take them to unknown places. When they do finally depart, what lingers is a sense that we aren't alone. *Hallelujiah!*

Within a couple weeks, our support network is up and running full-bore. Roxanne comes over daily to walk Kizma, who has been pacing the confines of our tiny backyard for weeks. Bob isn't comfortable watching Tom's body fade. He helps by writing an article in the local paper highlighting Tom's contribution as an umpire and announcing a fund being set up to help our family with medical expenses. Ingrid shops at the farmer's market, gathering a hearty list of juicing vegetables and delivers them every Tuesday. Nick brings River on play-dates with his son, Conrad, so Tom and I can have some time together. Stella begins a regular schedule of visits from Hollister, to stay with Tom, while I do errands. Eliza picks up her little brother and brings him to her mom's house for a couple of hours so I can take respite in a good swim at the local pool. A woman from Tom's cancer support group heard about the network and signed on for a pot of her famous chicken soup every Thursday. Tom sips the broth, while River and I put down seconds and thirds. I'm left feeling nurtured, built up enough for another day.

When Tom's hives aren't flaring up, Sean comes over and gently massages his weary body to sleep. Even *I* get some pre-natal bodywork occasionally from a massage therapist who heard about us from a mutual friend. The phone has stopped ringing and this is a *good* thing. It's phenomenal to be on the receiving end of so much generosity. Once we start getting it, though, I realize how much we actually need. I'm careful not to ask too much and chance burning people out too early on. After all, none of us know how long this could go on.

Just when things begin to seem manageable, a nasty green vine creeps up my leg and winds itself tightly around my chest. It has me in its clutch, like it or not. Jealousy sucks. Everyone who gets to go home to (what I fantasize as) a normal life is a target. Worse, it sickens me to be anything other than immensely grateful, so I've got a heap of guilt on top of it.

Vicky drops off a casserole on the doorstep and then returns home to her healthy husband and secure future. Her dancer body moves gracefully across the driveway. It's hard to believe we have the same due date.

Bone Knowing

We met back in February at a meeting for those considering home births. I recognized her husband, Evan, who was an old friend of Tom's. Evan asked why Tom hadn't come along and I brought him up to speed. He winced and said, "So sorry."

By the end of the meeting, it was clear to me that we couldn't afford a home birth. I told them I wouldn't be back. They walked me to my car and Vicky said, "We'd like to help, really. Here's our number. Call us."

When I did eventually call, they eagerly joined our support network. Vicky and I have talked more. I really like her. *She is so sharp and together—like I was at one time and maybe still would be if only Tom had stayed in remission.* These thoughts have me caught in a downward spiral. Before long I'm jealous of everyone who doesn't have a sick husband. It's getting ugly. I dread coming home to other people in our house when I can't hold together a social façade for a moment longer. I resent having to trade our privacy for help at a time when I want to hide in a closet and scream. Instead of biting someone else's head off mid-way through a second explanation of Tom's medicine regimen, I bite off my own. A brutal internal dialog ensues, gnawing away at any shreds of self-compassion I've cultivated with Marybeth's help.

How can I be so damn ungrateful?

Before I sour our help, I release them from duty.

Jennifer Allen

16

Hope Redefined

July 1997

Marybeth thinks I'm crazy and she's probably right.

"Really," I tell her defending my sanity, "it's not just because of my bad attitude. It's summer. Come September, we'll have a newborn added to the mix. *That's* when we'll really need help."

Marybeth nods, "Hmmm." She's not completely sold.

"Okay, this is the deal: If I cut the support network, I'll have no choice but to head back East," I say, surprising both of us.

"Go on," she encourages.

I tell her it isn't that I don't want to go. Quite the contrary; I've longed to take respite in the comfort of my large family so far away, but I've been dreading what it means.

"What *does* it mean?" she asks.

I'm bawling before she finishes the question. "G-goodbye," I stutter out between sobs.

The remainder of the session is spent imagining having to leave once there, having to witness the last time my family—now his family—and Tom would see each other. It breaks my heart. Feeling for everyone else is the entry to my own grief. At least it's a start.

There's no hiding my puffy eyes once home. Tom asks if I'm okay and I tell him I talked about going back East at therapy.

"We are going, right?" he says, concerned.

"We just can't afford it," I say, screwing up all the good therapy work I just paid for from our overdrawn medical bills budget.

"Who cares? It's too important," Tom argues.

"What if you have a health crisis there, or what if I go into labor early?" I ask, making a second round of valid points that miss the mark.

"Maine's not that remote. There are doctors and hospitals. Jen, it's probably the last time I'll see the family."

Bingo. The tears re-start. "I know. It's just that . . . well, I don't think they do," I say. There. It's out. This will be his last trip—a goodbye trip. And they won't really know it until they see him. He motions for me to join him on the bed. As I lay alongside him, he strokes my bulging belly.

"Every second is a last, Jen," he says and I cry harder.

"You're their family," I say.

"And they're mine. That is exactly why we have to go." He's resolved. "Put it on the credit card and I'll skip the Zophran for awhile. It'll even out, " he says.

"You'll be puking the whole trip without it," I remind him.

"I'll be okay." He pats my stomach and kisses my nose.

The next day I charge the tickets to overlap with the family's time at the beach cottage and make a plea for last minute vacation time at work. Both bosses are gracious and we fly out a week later.

Jennifer Allen

Tom requests an aisle seat close to the bathroom as we board. The culminating side effects of radiation paired with his decision to ditch the only medication that kept his puking under control, makes bathroom access a must.

Squeezing into the window seat beside him, I realize there isn't space for River. No laps. Mine is huge with baby and Tom's needs to be unencumbered for dashes to toilet. River runs down the aisle. He is not to be bothered by space limitations. Most everyone else is seated, waiting patiently for us to get settled. Tom puts his arm out and intercepts River on his next fly-by, but he's got no energy to entertain him into staying put for takeoff. He looks to me questioning, his skin contrasting with the many healthy pink and brown faces around him.

"Sorry, it's the last time he can fly free," I say, pulling our screaming child across my knees, wedging his body between my belly and the seat in front of me. He pulls away. I'm desperate.

"Time for nursees," I say, unbuttoning my dress. River pulls my breast to his mouth and suckles voraciously, like a newborn upon waking. He occupies his free hand with the long strands of hair that have fallen loose of my bun. All the efforts to wean him from day nursing are blown in one takeoff.

We make it through the first leg with River asleep and Tom only puking twice. I begin to see our situation from other's eyes as we deplane, on show for all to see: the big pregnant lady with the toddler on her hip, struggling to steer her sickly husband's wheelchair with one hand as she hurries to the next terminal with diapers dropping from her bag. It makes me want to disappear.

Matters deteriorate when the wheelchair never shows up on the last leg and our plane is boarding at another terminal.

"I'll try and walk," Tom says, wobbling on each step.

"No, Tom. You can't afford the fall. Just wait here, I'll find someone to help." I snatch up River and hoist him onto my back, pretending with all my might to be a prancing pony and not an overwhelmed caregiver. I gallop, sweaty and out of breath, from one counter to another; only to be forwarded to yet, another. Finally, amongst an incoming crowd, I see a young airline rep pushing an empty chair and I signal him over to where Tom is sitting.

"Hurry, please! We're going to miss our flight!" I urge when he gets closer.

He swings the chair around behind me. "Have a seat Ma'am."

"No, no—it's for *him*." I point to Tom, who tries to smile over his humiliation.

"Oh, I see. Sorry." His pimpled face turns crimson.

"It's okay. It's just the way it is," Tom says. This youth is getting a basic life lesson: Things don't always work the way they're supposed to. He pushes Tom's chair briskly to the gate where we are last to board.

I negotiate an aisle seat with a passenger at the bulkhead, hating to resort to pity. "Please?" I whisper. "He needs to be close to the bathroom. He's got cancer and . . . you know." I have to look away.

What is normal to us suddenly seems so heartbreaking, maybe even pathetic, as I look in on it from the perspective of strangers. All three passengers in the row surrender their seats and take our two seats and a vacant one at the rear of the plane. Tom nods appreciatively at them and I thank them profusely. We're utterly dependent on the goodwill of others. *All that's missing is the cardboard house.*

Only one puke the second leg. River is entertained standing in his chair and making faces at the passenger behind us. We land and my parents whisk us up into their care. It's only been a few months since they've seen us. Still, I can see their shock mixed among the hugs. Chemotherapy and radiation treatments have caught up with Tom, shrinking fast-growing tumors and the rest of his body along with them. And I've gained the forty pounds he's lost. They turn their attention to me.

"You sure you're only seven months?" Dad jokes.

On the drive from Massachusetts to Maine, Dad tells us we'll have the RV to ourselves. He's parked it in front of the cottage so we'll have an ocean view.

"I bet the neighbors aren't happy with you. Isn't that illegal?" I ask.

"Let's see 'em move it if they don't like it," he says.

They know it's a last. My father isn't a rule-breaker.

Jennifer Allen

As we drive down Mile Road across the marshlands to the sandbar, where a long row of cottages line the ocean, I can smell the familiar sweet musk of beach roses mingling with the low tide. It brings forth a lifetime of nostalgic memories of family vacations spent here. This time, though, the building anticipation doesn't hold the flavor of excitement it has in the past. Dread is the flavor of the day. I can't bear seeing everyone's hope die the instant he gets out of the car. On the other hand, I can't endure pretending things aren't as bad as they are.

Here it is about to unfold, as it will. As we park I squeeze Tom's hand. He gives a quick pump in return and pulls away, as if he's gathering energy to buffer the blow.

"Look, Rio, the cottage!" He rouses River from a nap.

Sisters, brother-in-laws, nieces, and nephews who have come from near and far for the reunion, pour out to greet us. We look like Jack Sprat and his wife standing at the car. Dad unloads our luggage and Mum picks up a sleepy River and carries him up the stairs.

They look and they see it. Tom is grey and gaunt. The only color on him is his beanie. It covers the tiny bit of grey-black fuzz that has grown back after the chemo, only to be fried off in patches by radiation. It's clear he's no longer the suave blackjack dealer or the athlete, going down only ever to one knee. Now, he goes down completely and often, with seizures from the brain tumor. I ask my brother-in-law, Ryan, to spot Tom as he climbs the stairs.

"We borrowed Gram's old wheelchair if you want to take a stroll on the beach while the tide's low," Mum says.

"Oh, I'm good. I just need to lie down for a while," Tom assures her. He's got to be feeling awful if he bails when the attention is on him. They can see that Senior Sanchez, the magician from previous years' talent shows, is long gone, as is the storyteller who has enchanted them late into the summer nights with tales from adventures past.

The family is graceful, trying to catch up with all the changes. "What about the lobster feed?" My sister, Julie, asks.

"He can't eat right now. I think he might be obstructed. Everything just comes right back up. He absolutely wants us to go ahead. Really," I say. When I tell her about the nausea medicine she insists on filling the prescription. It's a way to help, when there isn't much they can do, even with Tom right in their own backyard.

Over the week, a tension of frustration and guilt hangs in the air when we are inside the cottage having a good time—playing cards, eating, or preparing the scavenger hunt, while Tom lay alone in the trailer, miserable. He can't tolerate even one visitor, unless it's me. When he does emerge from the trailer, it's only when he can manage interaction with a smile. Still, he wants them to retain memories of him as the vital man he was. And he knows I need a break.

"Jen, go be with your family . . . just go. I'll be fine. Please, Butterfly, take it while you can. You need it," he says as bravely and sweetly as he can muster. It's the blessing I need to take care of myself and remind River that life goes on, sick Daddy and all. When I leave the trailer, I leave the world of illness. It has become a matter of sanity for me. I'll do my duty of reporting his condition to the family and reassure them he wants the show to go on. And then, I'll do my best to be on vacation.

Late into the trip, after many an enema to free an obstructed bowel, Tom wakes with a mission. "I'm going to make it to the Jetty today," he announces. He's been out a few times to try and lasted only a few hundred yards before needing the wheelchair. Walking the two-mile round-trip is a bed-bound person's miracle marathon.

Word spreads and the family gathers after breakfast, eager to be along for his quest. The sun glitters diamonds off the morning waves as the group of us cascade down to the firm sand of a waning tide. We break into small constellations as we migrate north toward the rock piling in the distance, talking and laughing as always, with occasional cheers for Tom: "Lookin' good!" or "Already halfway, you can do this!"

Tom wears navy sweats with the hood draped over his head, while the rest of us are scarcely clothed. His steps are slow and deliberate. The kids run circles around him with the wheelchair. Amy walks backwards, videotaping and interviewing on the fly. When he makes it the full mile and come upon the huge rocks, Tom presses his hands on them.

"Wait Tom. Hold right there. I want to capture this," Amy says, recording what we all recognize as a "last."

I'm thinking: *How strange to know each last of a lifetime—lucky and unlucky.* Tom raises his fists over his head and we all begin clapping and hooting. Today it's lucky.

Tom makes it back to the trailer and sleeps 24 hours, waking only to pee. Time is closing in and the goodbye moment is just a couple days away. The children make cards that say "get well" only the images of suns crying and trees dropping leaves, clearly express "goodbye" and it doesn't take being an art therapist to see this. Tom's eyes had welled up when he found them pinched in the screen door. The cards have prompted him to come into the cottage and be with everyone. He lies on the couch watching the world buzz on around him. Dakota crawls over and pulls herself up to get a close look at her uncle.

"Such a big girl," Tom says caressing, her downy head. "Do you know the last time we were here, was when you came into the world?"

"Baa!" Dakota exclaims in response. Her arms wave wildly, grabbing for Tom's beanie. He bends forward so she can succeed. It's hard to believe how many changes happen in ten months time—for her and for him.

"Dakota, you've got a little cousin coming to join you soon. Next summer, you'll have a playmate when you come to the cottage," he says moving into future territories that don't include him. Julie squats down with them, tears streaming down her cheeks.

"Oh, Tom," she muffles out, trying to smile.

"Mhmm," He sighs, reaching his hand out to squeeze hers.

Others come couch-side throughout the evening, daring to edge closer to that painful place. I strain to hear the exchanges at first as if I could throw in a towel if it got to be too much, but it isn't my place. These are his goodbyes. *Unlucky or lucky?* I wonder.

Amy organizes a healing ceremony for Tom in lieu of the annual talent show on our final night.

"We have to do *something*. It's a last for him and us," she says, calling the elephant by name. I'm relieved, though I feel a twinge of failure for being too exhausted to make his every last special. I've resigned myself to letting things be what they are.

Tom is touched by the idea and pulls himself out of bed for the shindig. On the picnic table stage, shreds of his former identity surface for one last hurrah. Spontaneously, Tom makes up a song about our family and sings it in a raspy whisper as he hunches over his guitar. The melody is the same one he sang at his father's service with the words changed. There isn't a dry eye in the room when he finishes. We applaud and then dim the lights for the ceremony.

Tom lies down on the bed of pillows and we take our places around him. The children squeeze in front and everyone lays a hand on Tom. Amy gives protocol to the foreign experience our East Coast family has willingly stepped into. She guides us to send him our love and prayers—whatever form they take, as we touch him. Tom's job is to receive. Eyes close and, after awhile, a palpable buzz grows out of the silence. I can't tell if it is sound or a sensation. The power of it is undeniable. All sixteen of us are generating a lightning bolt of love and Tom lay in full reception of the infusion. It's difficult to say what time has passed. My guess is that it can't be more than ten minutes because I've never witnessed River simultaneously awake and still for this long. The kids start to get antsy and Amy wraps up the ceremony. The clock reads 7:35. Twenty-five minutes have elapsed. Again, I realize how much of an illusion time can be. We look around at each other in soft gazes, sniffling and nodding lightly and I feel as if I have come to know my family in a new way.

Tom sits up and rips a honkin' trumpet fart and we all laugh, cheeks tight from dried tears. Simple things become sacred and sacred things become simple. In his illness, Tom has offered this gift to the family. They—we, are letting it in. Over the course of two weeks time, hope is reeled in from a distant miracle to the immediacy of each opportunity to love him.

Tom sleeps peacefully and, in the morning, I pack us up for our return West. An assembly line takes scattered form between the living room and the porch. Tom moves to each person, taking his time, giving long hugs. Eyes meet and hold as he faces each person and each goodbye. He goes through the entire family, including the youngest children. Moments are so direct and final I can barely tolerate them, yet, I'm so proud of his courage.

Grief, some vicarious and some undeniably my own, has been catalyzed inside me. It's all I can do not to begin wailing on the return flight. If it wasn't for the distraction of a rambunctious two-year old, I probably would. Tom is quiet. Peaceful, in a content kind of way, as if there could be no better way to end his story with these people, who had surely become part of his family and he theirs.

Jennifer Allen

17

Parting Paths

August 1997

If Tom were not my husband, I surely would have opted for the slip-out-the-back-Jack kind of goodbye. I would have compensated more comfortably by paying respects at the memorial. With our family, he has shown me how to *do* goodbye. Now, as he leaves for Mexico with no guarantee of returning, it's my turn.

When we got back from Maine, Tom, full of confidence that he could still travel, began a mission to check into the Gerson Clinic. The doc there told him the same thing his doctors here have been saying for a while now: His cancer is too advanced for cure. Tom told them he had a baby coming; that he had to at least try for time. I didn't think he was serious until I heard him ask his mother for an advance on his inheritance, which would get him to Mexico for a month of treatment.

Asking for money in the last chapter of his life, when he needs to review it and come out feeling like he's okay, humbles him. As much as he wants to be, he isn't free from the cultural conditioning of men being measured by their wealth and accomplishments. Stella agrees in hope of a miracle. Tom knows she'll do anything for chance of him outliving her. Arrangements have been made. He leaves tomorrow—possibly for good.

Suddenly I find myself scrambling to make sure I've covered all bases. *Have I left anything unsaid? Is he ready for a "Do Not Resuscitate" order? Has he hidden anything that needs disclosure? Do I know exactly what he wants for final arrangements? Does he want to leave a message for his unborn child?*

Hospice work has given me the benefit of witnessing the course of terminal illnesses in other people so I know things can turn quickly. I may not have a chance to squeeze in some important tidbit that may ease Tom's journey. Still, it has come down to waiting until death is walking in his direction to start the important conversations.

They can't wait. Eliza will be here in the morning to bring him to the airport. I stretch out beside him on our new king-size bed. It's a bargain I found in the classifieds. A few people from the support network helped launch it up over the bedroom deck. Tom has been spending far too much time in bed not to be comfortable and it's hell to sleep in close proximity to him when he isn't. He opens his eyes as I cuddle in close.

"Button, can we talk?"

He blinks to attention. "Yeah, sure. Go ahead," he says hoarsely.

The pressure of time has me talking straight. "So, you're sure about cremation?" I ask.

"Yes . . . yeah." He gazes off as if he can see through the closed blinds.

"Should I wait before? I mean in case it takes some time to fully leave your body. I couldn't stand to think . . . well, you know. I've been reading the Tibetan Book of the Dead and maybe there's something to waiting a few days."

He cuts in: "You do what you need to—whatever makes you comfortable. I don't care at that point. No service though."

Jennifer Allen

If I were to be honest, the first thought that comes to mind is: *Whew, one less thing to plan, especially if he dies in Mexico.* I don't even want to *think* of how I'd coordinate a long distance cremation and actually get *his* ashes back to California. Regret follows in quick succession. *No, I need a service so we can all begin talking about him.* I've lived with an elephant in the room for far too long.

"Don't you want something? Button, I don't want to guilt-trip you, but the rest of us *need* a service," I plead.

I sit up so I can see how he is taking things and it dawns on me: "It's the Catholic thing isn't it? Tom, you tell me just how you want it. It's *your* life and *your* death, *you* decide," I say, getting downright pushy. "And you're not going to hell if you don't have a Catholic service."

"You're sure about that?" He looks to me and smirks.

"Look man, I'll remind you of what you adamantly insisted on with your Catholic relatives when they neared judgment day: no hell, no devil. It's an inside job. Hell is worrying your whole life about that God who you thought was so benevolent, deciding in the end that you should go to hell." I step off my soapbox. "You're a good man, Tom," I say, running my hand over the newest ribs that have surfaced. "Give us a chance to talk about you that way. Besides," I grin, "it will ward off any doubt St. Peter might have at the pearly gates."

"Humph." his eyes shift all directions and he bites at the inside of his cheek. Finally, he says: "I've always pictured a memorial—a celebration of life. I'm not sure if my relatives would attend anything outside the church and that's half of Hollister."

"Well, if they're too damn Catholic to celebrate your life then . . . "

"Jen, Jen," he soothes. "It's just the way they do it."

Inadvertently, I've upped the ante to the ongoing conflict he has hoped to die his way out of.

"I know," I sigh. "I just want your service to reflect you, guilt-free. My vote is that we follow *your* wishes. Your family will get over it. I might not, though, if they no-show." Playing on his need to impact others, I add, "You'd be expanding their horizons—leaving your legacy."

Suddenly he has no energy for argument or contemplating the pro's and cons. He belts out clear-cut decisions. "Okay, I want a celebration of life. Hold it at the Elk's Lodge in Hollister, so it is easy for my family to come. Don't expect anything. You decide the details. I want half my ashes in the ocean at the same site we got married in Carmel. Spread the other half at Lakes Rose and Marie in the Sierras. That's it." He closes his eyes, seeming exhausted.

"Wait, let me get a pen," I say, scrambling to the bedstand. Between pregnancy hormones and caregiver stress, I can't rely on memory anymore. It's the kind of thing one doesn't want to mess up. *Was that Lake Mary-Jane or was it Violet something?* Not that he'd ever know if his remains got spread in the wrong location, but I would and that would be worse.

"Ask my brother. Mike will help you find it." Tom says with his eyes closed. He's had enough, just as I get started.

Questions start to pop into my head like popcorn kernels that had met ideal temperature—all at the same time, competing for space. Time ticks seconds off loudly in my head. I review a mental list of questions, prioritizing so his energy isn't wasted with things like who to donate his umpire equipment to or how to access files on the computer.

The baby. "Tom, c'mon just a little more. Please? Let me ask and you can think on it and get back to me before you head out tomorrow. "

"Shoot," he says, eyes still closed.

"What about the baby? We haven't got a girl's name yet. I've been poking through this book on spiritual midwifery and the name Oceanna was in it. I like keeping the water theme and now that we live by the ocean . . . what do you think?"

"Perfect. Oceanna. We married at the ocean. Good knick-name options: Shana, Oshi, Anna," he continues with simple clarity, sounding rather Dali-Llama-ish.

I push for more. "And a middle name?

"Hope," he answers matter-of-factly.

"Man, Tom, that is beautiful! Oceanna Hope. I love it! Thank you, Button!" I kiss his forehead and release him from twenty questions, content with having something from him to offer our baby. This child has already been through our many redefinitions of hope, in-utero. For me, my children secure hope in a future. My investment has already begun shifting from Tom's future to my own.

In the morning, I send him off alone to a faraway place, knowing I might have the baby while he's away and that he may not make it back. Barely able to stand vertical for more than a few minutes, he leans against Eliza's cranberry colored SUV and pulls me to him. With the baby pressed between us, we kiss like old people in the movies. No more tongues.

"Wish me luck. I'm going to need it." He smiles, pulling a handkerchief from the waist pocket of his gray button down sweater. He presses it to his eyes and turns to climb into the car.

"Good luck, Button." I'm so caught up in the visual contrast I miss the feeling cues. He looks like Mr. Rogers, minus all but a few patches of hair, dwarfed and muted by the bright, muscular vehicle and aged by the beautiful youth in the driver's seat. I stand outside the moment to frame the slice of life and it keeps me from being in it. This is exactly why I gave up photography. The habit sticks, especially when moments are too difficult to be in.

As Tom drives off into the peach-lavender sunset, I can already feel our paths clearly diverge. He's got a death approaching and I've got a birth. As much as each of us wants to give the other our full support for the upcoming life passages, we are magnetically pulled by our instincts and physiology to our individual paths.

Later that night, Tom calls from the clinic. I can hear the distance in his voice, caught up in his quest, as he should be. In the morning I send him a letter telling him about the change I feel and that we both must forgive each other and ourselves for not being able to be there in-person.

"This is our practice at long distance love," I write. Though I've thought about him constantly since he left a couple weeks ago, I don't have the usual worry as when he's here. Instead, I feel unconditional love building momentum, as if he were already gone.

River and I are on a trial run of life without him. It surprises me how easily River accepts it when I answer his frequent question: "No Daddy today?"

"Nope, he's still in Mexico, trying to get his body stronger."

"Okay Mamma. Can we get french fries at McDonalds?" he asks. Life marches on for him.

"Sure, little pea. Let's bring Kizma for a walk on the beach after," I answer, colluding with all the fun and freedom we can have without a sick person or a new baby to tend. Our brief window of opportunity makes it evident how my precious little boy has taken a backseat to the daily crisis of getting by with a sick spouse. He'll soon take it again, when this baby inside me will divide my attention even further. I'm not the mother I intended to be. There just isn't enough of me to go around. More than guilt, I feel helpless. All of my efforts won't change my son's losses. A large chunk of hope is reserved in my heart for River being okay down the line, once Tom is gone and the baby is old enough to play.

Fifteen days into our freedom, Tom calls. His voice is faint. "Jen, I think this is it. I'm so scared. I want to be home with you. I'm so weak."

"It's okay Button," I say soothingly, feeling only immense love for him. No panic.

"I'm sorry I'm not there with you, Sweetie. I'll call Joyce. She offered to go if needed and Mike can drive from San Diego in just a few hours. You've covered all the bases. It's okay to go . . . really, I mean it." If it's permission to die he needs, I want him to have it.

The following morning he calls back with more grist in his voice. "Whew, Jen. That was a rough night. Scared the hell out of me. The strangest thing happened. Around midnight, this man came into the room playing his guitar." Inhaling deliberately, he continues, "He sang the same lyrics over and over so softly, like an angel: 'Listen, listen, listen to your heart song, I will never forget thee, I will never forsake thee." He sings the melody in a jagged whisper. "It was beautiful. They send him to help those who are transitioning." He draws another strained breath, "Jen, please remember those lyrics. They're important. I can't explain."

I repeat the lyrics as I write them down. "Got it, Tom. God, I'm so glad you're through that rough part. Joyce is in flight and

Mike left San Diego about an hour ago. Please remember they are there for *you*. No need to entertain."

"I'm past that, Jen. No choice. Listen, I need rest. I'll try and call in a few days. A couple more weeks left. I'm going to make it back. Keep our baby in until I get there!"

"All right then, you come back alive, and I'll hold it in," I say, mocking our attempts at control.

On Friday, co-workers are crowded around my cubicle when I come in. They present me with cake and a giant baby bottle filled with cash. I'm moved to tears and find myself repeating "Thank you, thank you so much," throughout the day. In my growing vulnerability, I am able to receive more fully. *Tom would be proud,* I think.

The very next day, the support network surprises me with a baby shower. From the way I'm waddling around, I guess everyone thinks this baby is coming sooner than later. Ingrid tells me it's the only day they could reserve the church, otherwise they'd have waited until Tom returned.

So many of our family and friends crowd into the sunroom of the Unitarian church. Everyone is there, except Tom. The void feels like a vacuum throughout the day: A sneak-preview of what's to come.

It looks that way for River too. He and Conrad have been playing easily together in the sanctuary. The boys are like opposing puzzle pieces that synergize when they come together. River, with his long curly locks tangled in a pile on his head and his saggy jeanie-pants and mismatch t-shirt, waits to pounce and wrestle anything that moves. Conrad, with (what I'm guessing is) his mamma's fine blonde hair—cut by his Daddy into a practical helmet, exposing his sweet, freckle-spattered face; defies his three-and-a-half years with a deep voice and grown-up questions. Over the many play dates they have had together as part of Nick's help, an understanding of loss has bonded the boys. Conrad knows what River is in for with the dying of a parent, having lost his mother just eight months ago. River is well into his losses and Conrad is like a beacon of survival. When I check in on them, they are playing with figurines from Lion King. I hear River say, "Help, my daddy is died," as he pounces the Simba character on Conrad's monkey.

"It's okay. I'll help you find your mommy," Conrad says. Tiptoeing out, I leave them to their most important business of play.

It's the end of August and I've successfully held this baby in until Tom's return from Mexico. His homecoming is quiet. Eliza drops him off and he walks on his own to the door where I greet him. After a lifetime of defying his age on the side of youth, he looks a decade older than his 52 years. We hug tenderly. I'm afraid of hurting him. Mostly, I feel grateful to have him home where I can love him though his death. Yet, some small piece of me sunk when he arrived. The carefree schedule River and I have been keeping has come to an end. As we part, holding each other's faces, Tom's eyes are determined. Hopefully he can't see the trace of dread in mine.

"It's good to be home with you," he says.

River hears his voice and bolts down the stairs from his afternoon nap.

"Daddy!"

"You made it, Tom. You really did it," I whisper to him.

He smiles, bracing himself against the wall as River tackles a leg.

"Oh little man Rio, how's my boy?" He squats and pulls River to him. They hug until River squirms away to show Tom the latest painting he's made at preschool. Just like that he's back to having a daddy. No questions asked.

Tom moves back into the routine of Gerson therapy from home, only now that he's had clinic experience as comparison, it's even more intense. I'm back to being a nurse, social worker, therapist, food producer, mom, pregnant woman, and wife. Thank goodness the support network is revving itself up again.

Thursday afternoon Joyce and Amy put on an intimate Blessing Way ceremony for me. It's a time to nurture the mother—fill her cup—before she becomes the nurturer. The timing's good as I'm running on empty in the nurturing department. I've been counting on biology to hand some over with the birth of this baby. Even that may not translate over to Tom. So I'll take whatever I can get.

Joyce and her midwife friend, Tina, drum and chant birthing songs, while I lay on the carpet with my feet propped up in Tom's lap. Lovingly, he rubs almond oil into them. His energy has perked up. He needs to take part in preparing for this baby and a chance to take care of me. It's been lopsided for too long, no fault of his. Amy massages my scalp, pressing in all the right places, gently pulling sections of hair. This is absolute heaven.

The doorbell rings between drumbeats and reluctantly, I pull myself back to time. River lets himself, Nick, and Conrad in. I forgot he was due back from his play date. He bustles into the living room, checking out what's going on. Seeing nothing unusual with the candles, drums, and sage smoke (no doubt, he's a California native), River bolts up the stairs with Conrad in-tow. Nick stands awkwardly in the hallway.

"Oh, hey Nick," I greet him from the floor, my eyes barely open. I'm not trading this bliss for social etiquette. "Can you stay—I mean with the boys?"

"Sure, yeah," he says, disappointment flashing over his face for a millisecond.

He wants to be part of this. It's too weird, though, I can't.

Nick stays with the boys upstairs until the drum beat stops, bringing the ceremony to a close. We call them down. River begs for them to stay longer. Nick reassures him they'll play again next week. Tom thanks Nick and holds River for a long while after they leave. As much as we both agree it's important to hook River up with his own support to cover the slack from Tom's declining energy and my caregiving, it is so painful for Tom to watch River start taking his Daddy-needs elsewhere.

It's the second hit in a week. Mike visited a few days ago and challenged River to a wrestling match at Tom's bedside. River was all too eager, having been told for the good part of his second year: "Be quiet and still you want to cuddle with Daddy and watch T.V." Tears streamed down Tom's face and he broke into a sob. Mike startled and stopped, apologetic.

"No, go on. Please go on. I just wish I could . . . " Tom pleaded.

It is clear that even his son has begun a separate path. A selfless hope eases Tom's mind, while it breaks his heart.

Jennifer Allen

18

Surrender

September 1997

Time is closing in. The pressure in my pelvis is unbearable and I'm sure this baby will crack me open at any moment. Just after midnight on September 11th, two weeks after Tom returned from Mexico, five days since my leave from work, one day since Allison arrived from Maine to help, and two weeks early; a hot tsunami rushes out of me and into our warm bed. At first I'm confused. Even though I've had contractions for four days, it doesn't sink in that the baby is coming—now. As I'm changing into dry clothes and stuffing a hand-towel down my pants, my insides contort and I double over.

"Tom wake up! The baby is coming!"

He blinks, orienting himself as he moves about the room faster than he has in almost a year. When the contraction lets up, I grab the bag I had packed a week ago.

"Ally, it's time! Things are happening fast," I shout, rapping on Allison's door.

Tom gathers River out of sleep and Allison carries his droopy little body to the car.

"Did you call Eliza and tell her to call the others?" I ask Tom. He nods. "Did you tell her we couldn't wait for a ride?"

"Yes, Jen. It's taken care of, " he says. Our roles are changing quickly. Allison gets behind the wheel and Tom navigates, from a barely conscious state. The hospital is 20 minutes away—that is if the car doesn't pull one of its stalling fits. From the backseat, I groan low and deep. I focus on River's face, lost in dreamy slumber, trying to remember the precious reward that will come out of this pain. The car sputters.

"Press the gas pedal down hard two times! C'mon! Two times, it'll catch," I shriek urgently amidst the clenching in my pelvis. Tom and Allison murmur words back and forth. *Okay, nothing I can do. They have it under control. Trust the rope.* The old rock climbing mantra resurfaces, allowing me to drop into my body and ride the currents of birth.

It's surely the longest twenty-minute drive of my life to date, but we do make it without breakdown. *And that's something,* I tell myself. At this point, I'll take any shred of evidence that things are going to be okay.

The aid has seen too much gore to appreciate how much I need a bed right now. Nonchalantly, he wheels over two chairs, while I breathe quick bursts of: "Hurry, hurry, hurry."

Déjà vu of the airport a couple months ago, only this time there's no mistaking that Tom needs a chair as well. He ignores his chair and gets behind mine, pushing slowly, painstakingly so. None of us, not even me—mid-contraction and desperate to be horizontal, messes with his mission. By the time I have my clothes off; one midwife, two doulas, and three sisters present; I'm fully dilated and still keeping my focus. I'm figuring this baby will be out and in my arms in 30 minutes tops. *I can do this.*

Thirty long (definitely the longest) minutes of intense pushing and bursting blood vessels pass. Eons later it has been an hour. At least a lifetime later, it has been two. Nothing. At three hours and at least five position changes later, my focus has melted into a swamp of desperation.

Jennifer Allen

"I can't do this anymore!" I begin sobbing; completely losing the breathing rhythm I've been clinging to up to this point.

"Get this baby out of me! Help! Please, somebody help!" Any physical limits I've known up until this point—childbirth, bike accidents, marathons, judo matches—all of them have been busted through, pushing me to unknown territories of pain. Becky tells me I'm too far along to intervene with medication.

"Please! I can't . . ."

Tom lifts himself up from the bed beside mine, places a cool hand on my back and whispers as loud as he can: "Jen, you *can* do this."

Having him here, urging me on when he's barely in-body, renews me temporarily. It can't be passed over, as if there will be other opportunities in our marriage to give me this. Looking at him, I know it's true for him too: The only way out of the pain is through it.

I'm riding a wave of surrender, when Becky insists on checking me.

"We need to find out what's happening. The baby's heartbeat is fine, don't worry," she reassures. But she looks worried. Her fingers prod into the vortex of pain. I gasp.

"Mmmhmm." she nods at one of the doulas and then looks up at me. "You've got one big baby who wants to come out sunny-side up. It's too late to reposition." She talks me off the bed for a try at squatting over the toilet when the last thing I can imagine doing is moving. I make it there, knives stabbing in a belt of pain around my hips. Still nothing.

"I want this to be over. I just can't . . ." I moan, head in my hands.

"Jennifer," Becky says, squatting down, her face in mine. "We need a doctor, things aren't progressing. We can try vacuum extraction first. The baby's head is right there. Or we go straight to a C-section."

C-section sounds good. *Anything to stop this pain,* I think, until I flash on Tom's theory on C-sections. I can't do it.

"Okay, vacuum. Hurry, I can't take this anymore!"

She phones for the doctor on-call and reverses instructions, telling me to ignore the huge currents surging through me. As I try to hold back, I begin to worry that in some other realm, both the baby and I resist the passing of life's baton. It's causing us both great suffering. This birth means moving on. As irrational as it might be, I don't want this child or me to ever feel responsible for Tom's death.

Inside, I begin talking to my baby. *You are your Daddy's parting gift and your timing is perfect. He knows you'll keep me wrapped up in living.*

My body goes with the words, surrendering again, to what is to come. Bear-like growls vibrate through me as I let the constricting pressure turn me inside out. Amy and Allison press deeply into my palms and foot arches, altering the pain pathways. In the periphery, Joyce steps away with an aching expression.

In August, she miscarried at four months. I recognize her pain. In a space between contractions, I flash back to almost exactly a year ago when I witnessed Dakota's birth after losing my own pregnancy. As I watched her purple head crown from Julie's body, I remember yearning for the pain—*this* pain—just to bring forth what should have been.

I'm sorry, Joyce, I think and then shift all attention to the baby who has made it this far—alive. *God, we're so lucky.*

Dr. Diaz arrives, says a few words, rigs up a contraption between my legs and flips the switch.

"JESUUUUUUUS!" I scream, as he extracts the baby's head and leaves it there, waiting for the next contraction to dislodge the remainder of its body from its tenacious grip on my pubic bone. Bright lights warm the inside of my thighs, mixing a hint of pleasure among the overwhelming pain. In the shadows, I can see a crowd of faces in awe watching a life before it breathes air. Jessica, Eliza, and her boyfriend, Devon, bring River in from the lobby to witness the grand finalé.

The wave crests as Dr. Diaz pulls and I surrender to the ripping of my most tender flesh around the shoulders of our second child. With one last scream to my good brother, Jesus, it's out: a plump, juicy, blood-stained baby, with a head of thick black curls, bubbled to an oblong shape from the suction. A girl: Oceanna Hope. River was right. Her eyes pinch tightly as her mouth stretches wide with a rebel screech.

210   Jennifer Allen

"You did it, Jen," Tom says, leaning in to kiss my ear. Dr. Diaz holds her up, for all to see, shooing away the nurse who insists the newborn be taken to the nursery for observation.

"She stays," he says, placing her on my chest and tucking us in with a warm blanket.

Thank you. I nod appreciatively, never taking my eyes away from our daughter. Her skin and my tears are hot and comforting. Tom steadies himself and gives River a boost onto the bed.

"Hi sister!" River says, poking at her to see if she's real.

"See *my* baby?" he asks, pushing his new doll into her face.

"Oh, what a nice baby, River," I whisper, intercepting the plastic arm before it takes out an eye. Snuggling him in under an arm, we gaze at our new family member together. Oceanna strains to look around as if she has already sensed something is missing: *Mamma—check. Big brother—check. Lots of extended family— check. Daddy—Daddy, where are you?* The hand-off is a success and Tom's presence wanes almost the instant our daughter takes her first breath.

Over the next half-hour, the rising sun sends gold lasers across the room, illuminating the exhausted faces of those who have rode out the night with me. It's time for rest. Allison scoops up River and catches a ride back to the house with Joyce and Amy. Tom hugs his girls and Devon, thanking them for their support. He'll stay for some time alone with the baby and me, promising he'll be okay to drive himself home later. I'm too exhausted to argue or make ride arrangements. We sleep—Tom in his hospital bed and me in mine, with Oceanna grunting in satisfaction as she nurses. At noon, he gets up to leave, taking the brief window of energy while it lasts.

"Rest," he says, kissing the top of my head.

I watch him hold the railing as he shuffles down the corridor. He's on his own and so am I. Well, except for aides who bring endless streams of cranberry juice and nurses who help tend Oceanna, while I hobble to the restroom to check the damage. My motto is changing quickly: *if insurance pays, I stay!* The hospital buys me time to indulge the instinctual desire of staring into my daughter's eyes as she nurses, before I return to my gig as caregiver. The cable T.V. won't go unused either.

Oceanna sleeps for a few hours, nestled into the crook of my armpit, while I get lost surfing channels with the remote. A post-childbirth high kicks in and I'm on vacation. Everything feels normal and I'm convinced my husband will come to visit later with our son, trailing an "It's a girl!" balloon behind them. They'd be just in time to share in the celebration dinner, reserved for those who bring in new life.

A young guy, maybe twenty-five tops, enters my room late into the afternoon. He's dressed to the nines. His skin is tan against his crisp white collar, like Tom's used to be.

He smiles wide. "What can I bring the parents of this lovely baby for dinner?" It's obvious he loves his job. I click off the T.V. and with it, the fantasy.

"Salmon for one, please," I answer.

"Oh, you've got to get your husband or your mom or someone in here. It's a great spread—champagne and everything!" he says. This guy reminds me of the young flight rep at the airport: well meaning, but not yet comprehending that life doesn't always come in neatly wrapped packages.

"You don't understand." I stop before I start crying or launch into the drama that is my life. "Just one," I insist dully.

If I were better at asking for help and I hadn't already kept every possible candidate up all night, I'd have called somebody. An hour later, the elegant meal arrives set up with real linens, a candle, and fancy dinnerware—set for two. That's it, no escaping reality. I pick up my substantial little bundle, place her in the bassinet and limp over to the table. Sitting down carefully, I look across, through the candlelight, to what should have been Tom. Instead there is an empty chair framed by the muted flesh-tone of the wall color. Champagne-is-a-calling. As I contemplate the bottle, regret for announcing my emotional vulnerability with a thorough birth plan posted on the door, which included our situation, enters my mind. *Would they think I had a problem and deem me an unfit mother? Would they send a social worker up to chat with me?*
Halfway through the second glass, I don't care what the hell anyone thinks. I fill the aching void with most of the remaining champagne, two Caesar salads, two salmon filets, two scalloped potatoes and two slices of lemon cheesecake.

Jennifer Allen

Satiated and buzzed, I return to the bed and sink into a joy-laced sadness. My body quakes as I wail into the pillow. Unfamiliar sounds boil up from deep within. Sweet liberation fills me while my defenses are preoccupied, spinning circles around the room. Somewhere along the way, I fall into a dense, timeless sleep. Dreams fly through me like commercials, one after the other. Far away I hear howling. It grows louder, penetrating the dreamworld, only it doesn't match the images.

Baby!

With my eyes still closed, I push my body toward the sound before it's ready and I fall back onto the bed, my head throbbing and piercing pain darting about my entire pelvis.

"I'm here, sweetie. I'm coming, Oceanna," I repeat to her as I edge over to the bassinet. Cradling her, I meet her rooting with a warm breast, only she doesn't settle long enough to take it in. I turn the light on to orient. Her tongue sits like a communion wafer, suspended purely by sound waves, in the center of her gaping mouth, as she shrieks. Nothing consoles her. This little soul has felt my grief all along. To top it off, I checked out, just as she checked in. Suddenly I understand Tom's attempt to ease his pain after River's birth, though my grief has different origins. I've already jumped ahead to witnessing our daughter's milestones alone and having her know her daddy only through pictures and stories.

The next morning, I feel nauseous and cloudy. Despite the discomfort, I decide food and beverage hangovers are a good thing. The comfort they gave me last night scares me. Things are complicated enough without returning to the addictions I'm already primed for.

Allison comes to pick me up. Reluctantly, I check out of the Ritz, bracing myself for how this will all work now that I can barely walk without busting my stitches.

"Home again, home again, jig-idee-jig," I sing the ditty I always sing River when we arrive home, only now the tone tentative and sarcastic. It isn't anybody's fault, it just is. Allison looks over at me with an empathetic smile-frown. The expression makes her look even more like our Mum. She and Joyce both have Mum's warm brown eyes and it's as if they got the look of compassion with eye color gene.

Allison unlatches Oceanna from the baby carrier and coos to her. Though she is younger than me, she is an experienced mother with two school-aged sons. I'm comforted having her here. She's the buffer I need while I adjust to a new routine and let go of all the things I can't control. A prayer of surrender spreads across my chest as I turn the doorknob.

The house is quiet, except for tiny voices from the television upstairs. Three papers are taped on the fridge: Tom's treatment schedule, a calendar of the week with names already filled in to help, and a Do Not Resuscitate order. *The irony*, I think. We ask for loads of help to keep the clock ticking for him, and yet, if death comes knocking, Tom doesn't want anyone to stop it. He seems obliged to give life his maximum effort so nobody, he included, could mistake his surrender for giving up.

Mostly for Tom, I'm glad I birthed this baby vaginally. He needed to witness this rite of passage, in all of its difficulty and he needed to know this child would have a strong will. Having been a C-section baby himself, he was sure it was the culprit behind his struggle with willpower. He really believed the easy in robbed him of the instincts to rise up in hard times. Finally, as I scan over the contradicting papers, I comprehend. Choosing treatments requiring so much discipline was partly an effort to cultivate what he thought was lacking. It looks like death is giving him the opportunity he believes he missed at birth. No easy out.

Allison runs up and down the stairs for a week straight, tending to all of us like a live-in mamma. When she leaves, her goodbye to Tom is clean, having already made closure back in Maine. It's Oceanna who is having a hard time. Colic, grief—whatever it is, it has possessed our baby girl and has her screeching for hours each night. By day she sleeps with a strawberry pout facing her daddy, the two of them off somewhere together in peaceful slumber. Come the bewitching hour of four o'clock, she transforms into angst baby. Tom doesn't seem to hear her howls. He just looks at her and smiles, while I come out of my skin.

By the tenth night of this routine, I'm well out of my skin from exhaustion. If I thought it was safe to leave Tom and River

Jennifer Allen

alone, I'd go out for a walk with her. She loves the cool air and I need the freedom. It isn't an option anymore, so I open a window and hold her while I bounce on the gymnastics ball until my thighs burn. Nothing helps. The louder she shrieks, the more helpless I'm rendered.

"Shut UUUUP!" I scream to the ceiling. "I can't do this for one more frickin' minute!" I'm counting on my words being obliterated by her chalkboard-scraping screeches, until I see Tom grimacing in the blue light of the television. I lay our flailing daughter in her crib and go to him. His voice is too weak, outweighed by the mega-decibels coming from the crib. Just then, I spot River in the doorway, rubbing his eyes and carrying his Na Na by the ear. All too often he has been last, despite being the easiest to help.

"A nightmare? Oh, my sweet boy! And you want nursees?" At last, redemption for all I'm helpless with.

As I lay with River until sleep overtakes him and I can pry his little suction-cup mouth off my deflated breast, I slip into fantasies of a post-Tom future. I imagine getting a double stroller and bringing the kids for walks to the park everyday, my body slowly retrieving an athletic form. I'd rent out Tom's garage office as a bedroom in trade for childcare so I could keep my job. I'd go out once in awhile, catch up with old friendships I haven't had time to feed in ages . . . maybe even a date. A groan from the other room interrupts my flight.

Woah! I drag myself out of River's big-boy bed and out of a time that doesn't exist yet, and go to my man. Oceanna is sleeping quietly, now that it's after the blessed hour of eleven.

"I'm sorry, Button. I must have dozed off. What do you need?" I ask. *I'll give you anything—another fentanyl patch, water, a little love, huh? It's so hard to love you, when I'm going out-of-my-skin-mad. I'm sorry, Tom. I don't know how to do this.* He's restless, but asleep.

A few days later I'm kneeling down in the kitchen, packing the vegetable press under the sink and thinking how nice it would be to box this stuff up and store it away, when a hand on my back startles me. I turn and meet Tom's knees.

"Jesus, you scared me!"

The last thing I expect is for him to be upright and downstairs. Neither has happened since the baby came over two weeks ago. His emaciated face beams down at me.

"My goodness! Look at you!" I exclaim trying to tweak my expression of shock into one of delighted surprise.

"It is a good day, a *really* good day," he says, sitting down at the kitchen table. There's some heft to his voice.

"You won't believe this, Jen, I think I've turned a corner. Something feels different. If I could just keep up a year or two of impeccable treatment, I bet I could beat this thing. Really, I think the month at the clinic gave me the upper hand." He looks to me for cheerleading.

Too late, though, I retired my pom-poms a while back when it looked like he wasn't going to get better. I traded them in for candles, believing the attitude of a hallowed light would be more helpful as he moved into dying. Even he had agreed it was too difficult to be around people who couldn't accept his impending death.

Busying myself with dishes, I keep a back to him. "Mhmm, wouldn't that be something?" I say, straining for zeal. Meanwhile, thoughts pound away on the inside of my skull: *Look, I thought we had established that you are dying from this cancer. You know I'll never leave you and I can't do this for two more years. I simply can't.*

These are the kind of things I fear will slip out into words any day now. With full force, I push them back, again, and search out the pom-poms, like a good wife and caregiver. Betrayal weighs thickly on my enthusiasm.

Just when I get past your twenty-year promise, you decide it's back on? Even I can't believe I'm actually angry with him for getting better. For so long it had been my prayer to the Daddy-God I let the prayer go along with the disillusionment. Guess I'm jaded.

He stands by his convictions without even a flinch. I step back and try and see this scene from my hospice social-worker perspective. *Oh yes, I've seen this before: Lazarus Syndrome.* Patients just hop off their deathbeds with a burst of energy before

Jennifer Allen

the final crash. It really messes with everyone, including the patient. Even when they're told to expect a second wind before the final decline, they still believe they've won the battle and the bargaining with God has paid off. It just goes to show the power of a good day in a string of suffering.

I check the tiny scribbling on the pink sticky note I keep on the fridge to remind myself what medicine gave him. *Hmmm, a fresh fentanyl patch at 2 a.m.* Usually, he'd be a little disoriented following a new patch, but this doesn't look like the usual. He's oriented, all right—to living.

River pads down the stairs full of sleep, rubbing his eyes as if to be sure it isn't a mirage he's seeing.

"Daddy!" Clearly he hasn't retired his pom-poms. "Read me the funnies!" Though it's been awhile, River doesn't forget their couch position. They cozy together behind the paper and go about bringing back a ritual I thought was long gone.

"Man-oh-man, Rio! Daddy's doing good today." Tom says, folding up the paper. Let's go to Mal's for a cinnamon roll and I'll push *you* in the chair! Sunday, Shmunday, everyday is a cinnamon roll day!" His eyelids rise higher than they have in a month. It's sweet and yet, I want to warn Tom not to bring our little boy on yet another swoop of this roller coaster. They'll both have to lose all over again.

We have shifted our language with River from "sick," to "might die," to "going to die." Back when Tom had his near death experience in Mexico, I started preparing River, telling him that Daddy might not come back. When Tom did return, River looked confused for only a fraction of a second before the leaped onto Tom's legs. At almost three, River treats each day as its own entity; making it obvious the worries I have are my own.

In the evening, when Oceanna begins her colic, Tom rocks her and hums softly, immune to her shrill cries. His second wind lasts into another day and he grinds his own juice and packs a picnic for all of us to go to the park together. Old hope shows up and I start to fall in with him. *Okay then: live, but only if you can take part in this family. And no tricks, huh?* It would be good to have my co-parent and adventure-buddy back again.

Just as I dare to consider believing in outcome miracles again, I remind myself about the Lazarus thing. I can't afford the disappointment when he crashes, so I back off, urging him to use his energy to make audiotapes or write letters to each of his four children.

"They could open them on future birthdays," I suggest.

It becomes clear to him that I'm not on-board. "Why use a dose of life on the business of death?" he retorts.

Hmph, so he does know it's a dose and not a full-meal-deal.

"Because you can't do it when you're feeling like shit," I answer.

"I'll get to it. I actually have an idea of putting my short stories together and binding them—one for each of the kids. I can work on that over the weekend. Right now, I've got a little boy who wants to hear a story," he says, patting the couch for River to come sit with him.

For the hundredth maybe even thousandth time on this eight-plus-year journey, I have to release all expectations and accept that he will do what he thinks best. It's too risky to start an argument with him when he could be gone at anytime, so I try and bring to mind all that he *has* done. I soften to his ways remembering the beautiful letters he has written to his grown daughters on each birthday since his cancer diagnosis; the trips he's taken them on to introduce them to the world, the lullaby he wrote for River and sang to him every night when he was a baby; and all the trinkets he has stashed away for his son "when he's older." Oceanna is his final gift and seeing her in will have to be enough. Using time to be with them is his best offering.

The book of short stories doesn't happen. His body crashes hard on the third day and his hope collides with fate. I'm guilty of being the naysayer, not willing to take a last ride. Flip side is that my steadiness makes it possible to catch him.

"I really thought . . . just maybe," he whispers, lying in bed staring into space.

"I know," I say, kissing his forehead. "You've made the best of what you were given, Tom. That's all you can do on this ride." My heart busts wide open for him while, for me, it maintains an arm's length.

We continue with the treatment protocol, though it seems empty, as if out of obligation to those who still believe he'll recover. Talking becomes difficult again and Tom holds his language to present tense. He coasts along without gravity, in limbo, and ripe for another layer of surrender.

Jennifer Allen

Days

Jennifer Allen

19

No Turning Back

October 1997, Day One

The first day of October Tom calls me to the bedside.

"Jen, I think I'm cachexic," he says, his dark eyes penetrate mine with importance.

"What do you mean?" I ask, even though I've heard this term from both him and nurses at work. Bottom line: Cachexia means he's *actively* dying. I hold my breath as if doing so could stop the process.

He waits for me to exhale. "There's no coming back. My body is feeding off itself. I'm dying, Jen."

"Oh, Sweet Button," I climb into bed and hold him to me absorbing the impact of him saying it versus me thinking it. Despair, then numb, then relieved, then helpless, then hopeful, then numb again. A dizzying roller coaster of emotions ensues inside me as I spoon him in silence and he surrenders to sleep.

"Maaamaa! I hungry!" River calls from downstairs.

Disorientation overcomes me as I rise from the bed. Things are moving too fast. As I move down each step, I transition from a caregiving wife, to a multi-tasking mother and finally, a calm social worker. The phone is wedged between my ear and shoulder as I slap together a peanut butter and jelly sandwich and call work. It's *that* time.

"Thanks, baby's great . . . no sibling rivalry yet," Pushing through personal niceties, I get to the point. "I've got an appropriate referral here who needs a home visit from Dr. Miller A.S.A.P. to avoid a potential autopsy."

"Aren't you off on maternity?" nurse Katie asks.

"Yeah. I'm talking about my husband, Tom," I say, already imagining how obvious my denial sounds. Not about Tom dying, but the feelings I'm keeping in check. I'm textbook. And I can't imagine getting through the day without a hearty dose of it.

"Oh Jennifer, I'm sorry. I didn't realize," she says empathetically.

Her tone alone has my throat cinching up. I can't finish the request. *See this is why denial works. How else could I make this call?*

"I'll get Dr. Miller out tomorrow," Katie assures me.

"Mhhm," is all I can get past the cinch before hanging up.

Hospice has had the heads-up on Tom since July, when he and his doctors decided they had maxed out conventional treatment with little result. Tom, like many patients, resisted hospice service as if to do so might undermine his hope.

"Button, I called hospice. Dr. Miller will come tomorrow to check on you."

"Don't' bother. I'm done with doctors, Jen."

"I know, I know, but listen: If you don't want to risk an autopsy, you need a doctor to sign off. Besides, you still have benefits through Medi-Cal for hospice, it's time to use them," I say, ever the social worker.

"No medical intervention, okay?" He looks concerned, like he's already losing his say.

"Exactly, that's why we get hospice on board now and give them your advance directives. Only problem is I haven't seen them since you left for Mexico." I get up and paw through his dresser, feeling myself spinning faster, not wanting to be caught unprepared.

"No, they're in my desk. Top drawer," he says, wearily.

"Of course," I say, escaping with a task.

Jennifer Allen

20

Days

October 1997, Day Two

*D*AYS? *What do you mean days?*

I try and comprehend what Dr. Miller says. *Wait just a minute! I'm not ready, River's not ready, Oceanna doesn't even know him yet. Yes, I'm near breakdown, but no Tom?* I feel like a top spinning recklessly close to the edge of a table that someone has just put their hand on to stop.

Tom looks relieved. He even smiles. "Yeah, I can feel it," he tells her. Finally, no more struggling to stay alive so no one left behind thinks he's given up. "The doctor said so" is enough for him now because it's enough for his critics.

Seeing the peace in his face pulls me to the periphery of my skin and away from a self-centered internal chasm. It looks to me like we have our reactions mixed up. Off and on for almost a year, I've felt alone in knowing he was dying. Now that we have the official word, I'm not ready to hear it. Meanwhile, Mr. I'll-get-20-years-out-of-this looks to Dr. Miller as if she's his savior.

She's a gentle giant: tall and robust with large hands and a thick waist. Half of her success, I have always thought, was that she wasn't what patients expected. Plain clothes are enough for her—no lab coat needed to establish authority. Her voice is clear and direct, with compassionate undertones, like a wise mother. This is a quality I have appreciated about her during staff meetings. Only this time it isn't our team sitting around a table, it's Tom and I in our bedroom. I can see her mouth moving as she sits on our bed leaning in occasionally to hear Tom's hoarse questions. I was lost after the "days" part.

Maybe she assumes I'm leaving the room because I already know the spiel about what to expect or maybe she recognizes the news hitting me after months of patiently going along with the cool front I have put on at work. I'm awed by how many layers of denial and acceptance there have been. *This better be the last one.* I think, heaving and sputtering as I walk around the kitchen trying to orient myself by naming utensils.

River gets up from his train set, marches over, and pulls a fresh dishcloth from the drawer. "Crying rag for you," he says, handing me the towel.

"Thanks, baby boy." I wipe the snot dripping from under my nose.

"I not a baby!" He demands recognition for having to leave his baby-ness behind.

"No, not a baby." I hiccup a row of inhales. "And not a man. Not even a *little* man. You're a boy. And such a sweet boy." He looks up at me from under his blonde curls and I notice his eyes have changed from army green to dark brown. *Just like your Daddy's,* I think, bursting into another round of sobs.

Dr. Miller comes downstairs and I stop long enough to see her to the door. My head feels like one of the tight, bloated ticks I plucked off Kizma earlier in the morning.

She looks at me with concern and says something, only it all sounds like Charlie Brown's teacher: "Mwap, mwap, mwap." From the couch I hear her drive away and I start up again.

River picks up the snot-cloth from the floor, throws it on my lap and goes about pushing his train around the tracks. I spin and whirl until I wear out and my circles become looser, eventually coming to a stop. A dense sleep overtakes me.

"Chshshshshsh!" River's train noise wakes me. I check my watch. Only 16 minutes have elapsed since *the news* and it feels like a lifetime. The baby coos from upstairs and I go to check on her.

"Riv, c'mon up with me." I stand, feeling light— even high. The last of the elephants is out; free to exit the living room at last. River leaves his play easily, seeming to know something important is happening. Upstairs, Tom opens and closes his hand above Oceanna and she is mesmerized. River lays next to the baby for the show.

"Go get the video camera, Jen. Take some footage of me with my babies," he says.

"I not a baby!" River's tired of not getting credit where it's due.

Please don't call him little man, I plead in silence. Our pet name for River is turning on us. It's bad enough to lose a daddy but not a childhood too.

"No. You're right. You're a big brother now, River," he says in a low articulate whisper, seeming to know instinctively what to say. River closes his eyes and smiles with pride. The sun beams down on the bed enveloping the three of them in light. I let the camera run until the batteries die.

Tom props himself up and speaks with concise clarity, just as he did before the trip to Mexico.

"No more treatments—at all. Just pain relief and keep it minimal. I want a Papa Chano's bean burrito while I can still eat. Call people and have them come say goodbye." He makes his final requests and then tenderly answers River's litany of "why"s.

After years of limbo, "to die or not to die" being juggled about from one day to the next, we have an official direction. I call Ed and he alerts the family and friends in our support network that we are shifting to closure. It comes as a relief to report something we can all adjust to. For so long, we have all strained with prayers and hopes for Tom to recover and it just isn't in the cards. Waiting for the big miracle had begun to get in the way of what was real. The news frees all of us from the possibility of having control over the cancer. It allows us to look aloud at mortality—Tom's and, indirectly, our own.

Jennifer Allen

21

Weaving

October 1997, Day 5

With an end in sight and the rigorous Gerson regimen retired, the practical part of caregiving qualifies as doable. At least it does from the slightly euphoric state I've been in since digesting the prognosis of *days*. Tom has begun transitioning into whatever lies beyond this life. It reminds me of active labor—early on, when there is no doubt something big is happening and one is still able to crack jokes or make requests between contractions. Only I keep forgetting there won't be a new addition to the family afterwards. Instead, there will be an end to Tom and his suffering.

Each day into the dying journey Tom edges further into another realm, testing the waters while keeping one foot in this world. From the in-between place, he seems to be doing some kind of voodoo, weaving lives together in ways he wasn't able to as a mere mortal. Louise has been over with their girls for the past two afternoons. They gather around the bed for hours as the unit they once were, inadvertently mending wounds of the divorce. When Louise and the girls leave, they're eyes are puffy and red, but somehow satisfied. It's as if they have found a missing piece to a puzzle even though the picture is sad.

Tom isn't talking much. What he does say has punch. People who have come to say goodbye tell me how poignant his message is, but never what it is. He gifts each visitor with something very real from just beyond the awareness we all live in day-to-day.

Nick comes by with Conrad one afternoon to pick up River for a playdate. "C'mon in, he's still napping, but he'll be up any minute," I say, opening the door and making room for Nick to pass with a child-appendage stemming off of his hip. He puts Conrad down near the toy bin and Conrad looks it over before carefully picking a big yellow bus from the top of the heap.

"That's one of River's favorite toys," I say. "Here, push this button and it will turn on." I squat down with Conrad, suddenly feeling awkward at the three of us alone in the living room. I've been working up the nerve to ask Nick more about what the dying part was like with his wife, only the time is never right.

"Hello, Nick. Hi, Conrad." Tom rasps from behind me.

"Woah, Tom! Here, let me help you," I say, shocked that he's out of bed, let alone made it down the stairs in one piece.

He grabs the end stand and then the arm of the couch. "I got it," he insists, maneuvering awkwardly onto the couch. Sitting upright as if nailed to a two-by-four, he smiles at Conrad.

"Wow, you can chew gum, huh?"

Conrad looks up and nods proudly.

"Good for you," Tom says. His ability to relate to children is still fully intact. He puts a hand out, inviting Nick to sit. His head sways a bit as he gathers himself to talk.

Jennifer Allen

"They're a joy aren't they?" Tom says to Nick, still watching Conrad.

"Yeah, they sure are." Nick grins and I can see the indentation of dimples beneath his beard.

"Is this your first?"

"Oh, no. I've got two grown sons from my first marriage—before Wendy. Twenty-three and twenty-five."

"Interesting," Tom says. His bony finger curls around his chin in thought, like he used to do over long dinners with friends. Only now his arm quivers to hold it there, making it look like way too much effort. "I have two daughters the same ages as your boys from my first marriage," Tom finally says, smiling and dropping his hand as if Nick is scoring better than expected on some sort of test.

"What line of work are you in?" Tom asks, his usual curiosity only lightly masking an agenda of some kind.

"I'm a forensic pathologist," Nick answers.

"As in autopsies?"

Nick nods.

"Fascinating, I bet." Tom catches his breath. In the old days this kind of subject would launch him into a milieu of questions. Right now he hasn't the energy. "Guess you'll never need to worry about being out of a job, huh?"

"There's no shortage of unnatural deaths these days—so no," Nick says.

"How are the hours?"

"Not bad, thank goodness. It makes single parenting do-able."

Tom glances to me briefly and takes a full inhale as if he's got one question left in him that must come forth.

"That's got to be hard."

It comes out as a statement that hits me in the solar plexus.

"It's an adjustment. I'm lucky I have a lot of help."

"Yes," Tom says, starting to fade.

Nick is no fluff and Tom seems to appreciate this.

Silence ensues as we all watch Conrad play. It seems I'm the only one uncomfortable. Tom conjures up a final burst of energy and kneels down with Conrad.

"Have fun with River today," he says and then excuses himself and hobbles back up the stairs.

"I'll be right back, Nick. I think River's awake," I say, hurrying to follow Tom in case he loses his balance and to find out what the interrogation was all about.

"Jen, he seems like a good guy," Tom says while I'm tucking him into bed. "He's not stupid, you know."

"*What* are you saying?" I exclaim, trying to look as if the thought had never crossed my mind—not even come within a mile of it. Elation that I might be getting even a faint blessing on any potential man in my future wins out, creeping through the corners of my mouth and turning them upward.

"Jen," Tom waits for me to stop tucking. "You're a catch. Let's hope he is too." With that he rolls over and drops instantly sleep.

I'm left hunched over the bed, fighting off the smile that wants to take over, for fear he might see it and misinterpret my loyalty. River is awake, talking to his Na Na lamb in the next room. I scoop him onto my back and skip down the stairs with just a little too much prance in my step. *No matter,* I think. *River needs a happy Mamma.* Nick seems oblivious—an innocent bystander to the drama. He leaves with a little boy on each hand.

Later, once River is back from his playdate, fed, bathed, kissed goodnight, and Oceanna's colic has run its course, I join Tom in bed. Painstakingly, he shifts his body, bringing his bones to rest up against all of my extra flesh. He presses his face into my back and begins a dry, silent shudder. I reach for his hand and press it between my leaking breasts, against my heart.

A parched whisper comes forth: "Jen, I don't think I'll make it until morning. Just know I'll always love you."

My body responds with its own wet, noisy sobs, keeping rhythm with his. It's a new lovemaking with love separated from familiar physical pleasures. The ceiling we have bumped our heads on for years is suddenly gone and all of the old squabbles are moot. Heaven's the limit. We've made it, but with so little time to revel in it. *So it is—the bittersweet.*

Jennifer Allen

22

Lasts

October 1997, Day 11

Not only did Tom find himself alive the morning after the matchmaking weave, his voice was full with enough vitality to form full sentences.

"Guess you're not ready to go yet," I said, relieved not to be waking up to a corpse. I've been trying to warm up to the good possibility of such a scenario. Just the thought of it has kept me awake listening vigilantly to his breathing, night after night.

"Maybe I'm not and maybe other people aren't either. Doesn't matter. I'm here and I'm feeling okay for now. Think you could make me a pancake?" he asked casually, as if he'd actually been eating since the two bites of bean burrito five days ago.

"Anything for you, Button, just name it."

"Anything?" he joked, looking down at his crotch.

"Now that'd kill you for sure."

"But what a way to go!" He grinned exposing a gum line I hadn't noticed before then. "I miss that part of us," he said.

"Me too." I smile-frowned.

"Look what came of our last big shebang," I said, caressing our daughter's head as she lie between us, her face angelic with sleep.

"A little big miracle, huh?" he whispered to her.

"Yeah. What if you're just not finished with miracles yet? Not the getting better kind," I said, heading him off mid-sigh.

"Or perhaps *they're* not done with *me*."

"Something like that," I said. "The first one will be getting a pancake down." I rolled out of bed with a mission of importance.

Real maple syrup and melted butter saturated the pancake I presented to him. Anyone in her right mind would have salivated on the aroma alone. Tom, however, couldn't even look at it, when, only fifteen minutes earlier it was his heart's desire.

Each time he has rejected my efforts to fulfill his last wishes, I've had to remind myself that it was an expected part of the dying process. The body starts to close up shop, while the mind is fondly attached to the pleasures of food. It started with the pancakes on Monday and followed with the baked garlic pate' on Tuesday, the figs on Wednesday, the huevos rancheros on Thursday, and the eggplant parmesan on Friday. All were cast aside after a bite or two.

Five days of non-stop trips up the stairs to answer my dying man's wishes and I'm losing patience at the same rate I've been losing post-pregnancy weight. Between sleep deprivation and the unhealed stitches that sew me from one end to the other, stair climbing wouldn't otherwise happen. In an ideal world, I should be the one in bed, snuggling with our newborn and being waited on by Tom. The world isn't ideal, and lately, it's just plain unfair.

More than making special dishes all for not, it is the helplessness. When he asks for food, it is *something* I can do. Otherwise, I haven't found a niche in his homestretch. The insult strikes deeply when he spits out my offerings, no matter how much I know better.

Jennifer Allen

It's day eleven since the official dying prognosis and I'm actually feeling ready for him to die. If this goes on too much longer things are going to get ugly and I don't want Tom to leave on that note.

Peeling potatoes over the kitchen sink for the request du-jour at least gives me time to breathe and renew myself. The house is quiet, until I hear Tom's raspy whisper calling for me. Oceanna starts bellowing in quick succession, drowning out his words.

Breathe. No use. I'm already jacked up on the cusp of overwhelm, clenching the potato, and fighting the urge to peg it across the room at the merciless box, when the other monitor chimes in.

"Maaaaama!" River is up from a late nap.

What was I thinking buying two sets of baby monitors?

"Shut up!" I aim my frustration safely at the device, the potato cocked, threatening to take it out. Practical thoughts of affording a replacement save the damn device from destruction and me from the raging fire of injustice building inside me.

In the best interest of everyone, it reasons. My arm goes limp. I release the potato responsibly into the sink and, with it, a stream of hot tears. I'm on an edge without belay—no one to catch my fall. Teetering on the brink of breakdown, I try to remember the life lessons I've learned from rock climbing: Look only at what is directly in front of you and trust the next move.

The monitors keep on. I wipe my cheeks with a shirtsleeve and climb the stairs. River has missed the potty and Oceanna is starting her nightly run of colic. Puddles of piss and screaming babies can wait. It's Tom I tend first now.

"You want pasta with garlic? Lots of garlic. Okay. And milk. Got it." I mop up River's accident and shuffle back downstairs, careful not to bust my crotch open with too bold a step. I put Oceanna in her swing and the water on to boil. The calendar of help on the fridge indicates Nick McQuay is signed up to drop off dinner.

When he shows up, I intercept him in the driveway so he doesn't smell the garlic and think his efforts are wasted. The foil pan he hands me is warm. I stumble over a thank you and he nods knowingly. I'm a hair away from inviting him in to pick his brain about how to get through this part without going stark-raving mad, but I can't bring myself to be any more dependent on an almost-stranger than I already have been. Besides, I might just unravel into him and that wouldn't be good.

On the way back into the house the soft scent of jasmine twisting itself heartily up the entry trellis stops me. I feel the moment, just as it is, before I pluck a sprig off and move back into the bittersweet chaos of my life. The flowers embellish Tom's dinner tray, along with a cloth napkin folded like a king's crown. I pour a shot glass of milk, toss the pasta with garlic and butter, and empty a small portion onto a leaf of romaine at the center of a glass plate. It's a five-star presentation if I've ever seen one and worthy of being his *last*, last supper.

In recent form, I bring the tray up and rouse Tom. He pulls himself to a sitting position and says: "What's this?"

"It's exactly what you asked for, Button," I reply, hoping against the odds that he'll remember this time and comment between each savored bite how the meal is heaven on earth. This one, I'm sure, will be the meal left in memory.

Unhinging the legs of the tray, I press them securely into the bedding on either side of his body. He rolls his fork into the pasta, strains to bring it to his mouth and then drops it. Strings of pasta fly onto the bed. Things aren't looking good.

"Can't do it," he says, grimacing.

"But you said . . . " I don't bother to finish. The milk spills as I pick up the tray. I usher myself out before regretful words pour out of my mouth and taint another last.

Downstairs, I poke at the food, too resentful to eat it. This last supper thing has got to stop. It's turning me into a martyr and that isn't in anyone's best interest.

River pads up to me, "Me hungry, Mamma."

"Good," I say, lifting him into the booster seat. With a British accent, I present the rejected last supper: "I have some delicious pasta on the menu for your Royal Highness this evening."

River laughs, pulling fistfuls of pasta to his mouth and I'm satisfied. Growing boys need food; dying men need other things—though I'm not sure what yet.

Jennifer Allen

23

Leaving Behind Names

October 1997, Day 14

In the days following the pasta ordeal, Tom's requests for food wane, synchronizing with his dwindling presence in the reality I live in. Whether it was because he sensed obligation in my sighs or his body is just finished eating, I'll never know. All my hospice training conveniently convinces me it was the later. After all, I'd spent many an afternoon educating and comforting families who's loved one refused food. I've been replaying the spiel in my head about it being nature's way of closing up shop so as to gloss over guilt implications.

The short-order-gourmet-chef apron is retired. River and I settle into cereal, yogurt and PB&J sandwiches plus whatever surprise is brought by for dinner. Nothing tastes better than food someone else has cooked. The woman River calls "the chicken soup lady" drops off a pot every Thursday and I don't think I've ever tasted anything as nourishing. Enchiladas, lasagna, and quiche—the food just shows up on our doorstep multiple times a week. I feel cared for by angels of the flesh.

Two weeks into official dying and Tom is only interested in liquids. Dr. Miller guesses he might last weeks if he keeps up a steady flow of them. It surprises even her that he's plugging on. His name on the board at work will likely outlive all the other cases whose names are one-by-one becoming smudges of dry-erase marker. In the trenches of all it means to have his name is still up there, I find myself disappointed—scared, really. I'm afraid I'll run out of care before he dies.

I've begun to ration the caregiving, keeping it ultra-efficient. Oceanna nurses while I take advantage of the downtime to read every other page of Lyle the Crocodile to River, before Tom needs something. River fills in the blanks. He's heard this story dozens of times in the last week alone. Midway through the story I hear Tom rustling about.

"Water." His voice is gravel-like over the monitor.

"I'll be right there!" I call from the couch, closing the book.

"Wait, Mamma! Why is Lyle crying?" River insists, trying to re-open to the page we left off on, where Lyle storms off from the birthday party in self-pity because he wants a celebration for himself and can't ask for it.

"You remember. He's sulking because it's not his party." As I say it, I feel a resonance with Lyle, like neither of us have enough reserve to let things be about everyone else for even a moment longer.

"Poor Lyle," River says empathetically. I stop and marvel at his ability to empathize with this personified crocodile when his innate two-year-old "me"ness has been swiped inadvertently by his daddy's illness, his sister's arrival, and my preoccupation with both. Pulling him into me, I kiss the crown of his head.

Poor River, I think.

"But you, my little pea-in-a-pod, have a birthday coming soon and we'll have a big celebration, just like Lyle wanted," I say, knowing there is no backtracking on my word no matter what day

Tom's death falls on. Too many promises to River have been severely bent, if not broken.

"Water . . . water, please." It's Tom over the demand-box again, pulling me back to priorities. *Dying first. Clean up the collateral damage later.*

Wedging a finger between mouth and nipple, I de-latched Oceanna from my breast. Her head flops back in a drunken sleep.

"Here." I hand River a stack of books to look at and head up the stairs to put Oceanna down for a nap and bring Tom his third water bottle in an hour. The last one had rolled under the blankets and today at least, he's regressed to the stage of development when a baby thinks something doesn't exist if it isn't in sight. Only *his* sight now includes another world outside of mine. I lift the blanket to show him the hidden bottle as he mumbles something about a train coming. He's looking through me as he pulls the bottle he's been using as a bedpan from beside his pillow and begins swigging down the yellow liquid. Not that it is that far out of range for him. Months back, it had been part of an Ayurvedic treatment he practiced.

"Tom, wait. Try this one," I say, offering clear beverage in exchange. "I think this'll be better."

"Oh, its *you*," he says with a warm smile as he pulls the bottle of pee away from his parched lips and looks up at me. "What's your name again?"

It's so innocent I laugh at first, until I realize he really has no idea.

"Jen—as in Butterfly. Remember? I'm your wife and we have two children—River and Oceanna, remember?" I lay Oceanna down onto my side of the bed, showing him the proof, hoping the children will at least stick if I don't.

His eyes glaze over and he ventures off. "I'm waiting for more children, five hundred pounds, before I can leave with them. Why must so many children leave?"

"Tom, listen to me." I get in his face. His eyes stare through me. "You have four children, two grown and two little, and they are not going anywhere. You're confused." Screw everything I've learned about talking to a dying person within their world of metaphor. This is *my* husband and he's forgetting *me*.

He's oblivious to my efforts to pull him back. I see it clearly: the passing of being his wife, specifically me—to him. And Tom, as I know him, has been leaving in slow motion, readying his own butterfly wings for flight. Things are changing and there is no more stopping this process than there is preventing a child from learning to crawl. Time is messing with me, slowing down when I want it to hurry up and moving ahead in leaps that leave me spinning. Remembering he's doing exactly what he needs to in order to leave his body, ego, and life at exactly the rate he needs to do it, helps me settle into the small spaces between clinging to the last time I heard him say my name and fantasizing about a future beyond caregiving.

Jennifer Allen

24

Future Presence

October 1997, Day 18

About a year ago Tom looked into a Waldorf preschool for River. It was too far and too much money. We let it go and settled for a daycare close by. Tom sunk a little with that. He wanted assurance that River's fertile imagination would be nurtured and his innocence spared from the cultural push of early academics. Neither of us said it then, but we both knew it was another attempt to make up for the collateral damage River would suffer from possibly losing his daddy at such a tender age.

Making this happen now is a tall order, but I am on a roll of gathering successes as offerings to Tom each time he touches down into this world seeming anxious. Sometimes his brow smoothes out and he rests quietly, in response to the news I bring. Occasionally, he'll even be conscious enough to ask details, though names haven't returned. Other times, he doesn't seem to even hear me and goes about his waking nightmares revolving around losing money and being falsely accused. The game plan is to reassure him that our earth-bound future is secure so he can fully focus on his transition and feel the love part. This is for me as much as it is for him. I, too, need to believe we'll be okay without him. I make an appointment for River to visit the school and say nothing to Tom until it is a go.

River is giddy on the drive there. It's another change for him and I'm gambling the improvement will be worth it. A cottage at the edge of a forested park matches the address scribbled on a sticky note attached to my dash. *Sweet.*

A middle-aged woman with a French accent introduces herself and welcomes us in. She is older than I pictured from her voice. It causes me to wonder how she keeps up with so many kids when I live in chaos with only two. About ten children are at play. Some skip around in pastel capes and felt crowns and others are on the floor earnestly building a tower with wooden blocks. Dominique makes room on a couch for me to nurse Oceanna and returns to playing softly on her flute as she moves around the room. It's a small space, with a strong feel of order and a soothing buzz of little people at the work of play vibrating in the air.

River spots his play-buddy and sputters, "There's Conrad!" He bounces over to him like Tigger does Pooh. Conrad merges him into the fold. A group of them ride pretend horses around in a circle acting out some storyline I can't quite follow. River seems to know exactly what is going on. He's completely engaged in being a child. I'm certain we've found a place that can hold our son through hard times.

By the time we leave, I've maneuvered logistics allowing him to attend on a part-time basis. River can't wait to get home and tell Daddy about his new school. I'm just as eager to tell Tom he had been right: It is just what River needs right now. He'll delight in the synchronicity of Conrad being there. All the way home, River is caught up in wonder, humming melodies Dominique had played on her flute. When we get there, he unclips his own car seat and bolts into the house.

"Daddy, Daddy!" I can hear him shout, stomping up the stairs. Unlatching the baby-carrier, I trail in behind. Monica gives me a heads-up as she's leaving.

"He's way out there, right now," she says.

I sigh, marching heavily up to our room where River talks excitedly at Tom, who swats at the air, looking pained.

"C'mon, River," I say. "Daddy can't hear you right now, he's in a dream."

"No, he's not. His eyes are open!" he insists. "Daaaaaddy!" he shouts in Tom's ear. "Daddy wake up, wake up!"

"Stop it!" I yell, scooping River up and running him out into the hallway. I'm not sure whether it's Tom or River I'm protecting.

"We'll tell him tomorrow. Promise," I say, searching for a soft tone of reassurance.

He bites his lower lip and runs downstairs. Oceanna is screaming, overdue for her feeding. This time, I opt for her first. Once she has dozed off, I place her in the crib. Our bed isn't safe when Tom is hallucinating. It's quiet—too quiet. I rush downstairs with a dull gnawing in my gut and find the slider open.

"River!" I holler out into the yard. Nothing. I check the front door and gate. *Locked—good, but no sad little boy.* The gnawing turns to adrenaline.

Forming my hands into a megaphone, I yell: "RIVER! I'm counting to three. No cheese doodles for snack if you don't come out! One . . . two . . . three!" Still nothing, except for the sound of demolition next door.

Frantic searching ensues and becomes increasingly irrational as I go from slapping open cabinets, to yelling into the washer, and throwing off the couch cushions. Outside, I check for holes in the fence. Anything bigger than the size of a baseball warrants a search. I check the gate again. It hasn't unlocked itself over the last five minutes. In the silence between breaths, I hear a muffled voice. Images of my son buried alive or trapped under piles of laundry, struggling for breath, fill my fertile imagination. I hold on inhale, straining to hear his distant voice over my thudding heart. The source comes from the corner of our tiny back yard, where Kizma pokes a nose out of her doghouse.

"C'mon, Kizma!" She won't budge. I pull at her collar and she backs further into the house. Too late, the cover for her ally is blown. I spot River's pant-leg. The relief is short-lived. Rage follows in quick succession.

"God damn it, River! Don't you *ever* . . . "

Just as I start in on him, something plucks me up abruptly and shuttles me into the living room. The invisible force has me pick up a pillow from the floor and unload a primal scream into it. Meanwhile, River's little voice continues on, singsong, likely telling Kizma all of what he can't tell his daddy or his mamma. Whatever it is that keeps me in line, I give great thanks for.

At bedtime, I tell him the truth. "Daddy is getting ready to die . . . to leave his body behind. He's practicing right now, so he's not always there even though we can see him," I say over the book River is pretending to read. "I think his spirit visits other places, kind of like in a dream. If he comes back before his body dies, I'll make sure and tell him about your school, okay?"

"Tell him about Conrad!" he insists, putting his book down and sputtering in my face.

"I will," I promise.

It's eleven by the time Oceanna is through her evening round of colic. My thighs are burning from holding her while I bounce on the gymnastics ball for hours. Despite being utterly fatigued, I can't sleep. In the low light of candles, I pull out my drawing pad and sketch Tom's profile, willing him to wake up so I can carry out my promise to River. He turns to me suddenly, opening his eyes.

"I want you to write this down," he whispers.

"Okay, okay. Go ahead," I flip over the drawing quickly, feeling lucky to be here when he has touched into this world.

"I want it to be known I will return in a form that you, or our descendants, can recognize," he whispers monotone like he's reading scripture. "If they are still existing, which I think they will be, I'll communicate."

"How?" I realize he's bridging worlds.

Jennifer Allen

"By mail," he answers, from his world where logic is a lower function.

"Won't work. What if we move?" I ask from earthly logic.

"Newspaper," he says, finishing the thought I interrupted.

"None of those are permanent," I argue. "What if I don't get the paper the day you communicate? How about dreams?" I ask, hopeful I've found a possible eternal link to him.

"Okay, I'll try. If I make it through the night, I'll try for another . . ." His eyes float out of focus.

"Wait, Tom-Button, I need to tell you about River's new school," I plead, wanting to secure a future plan for him to release us into.

"There are people on my chest traveling very fast. They're joking, telling me to answer the phone," he trails off, his eyes shift rapidly behind partially closed lids.

Too late, he's off between worlds somewhere. I sigh, looking down at the drawing pad and read over the strategy he has just given me. I realize he's been making plans too, only his are for a future in spirit form. We're both rushing to get it all in before he touches down for the last time. So much so, we sometimes miss the few moments we have left. I'm torn between being completely with him in this bubble of slow-motion time holding his passage and preparing for what's ahead.

Nick knows this place.

Jennifer Allen

25

Loving Him Well

October 1997, Day 22

I've dialed Nick's number a dozen or so times over the past four days; hanging up before it rings. I'm not sure what it means to be going to him for answers.

In usual form, I wait until I'm nearly drowning before I let the call go through. When he answers I say, "Uh, oh it's me, Jennifer—Allen." I feel close to him by way of common experience and keep forgetting I barely know him. "I just . . . um, I wanted to ask you something." My voice quivers. "How did you do this part with Wendy?"

He knows that *I* know that *he* knows Tom is dying. And I need more than dinners delivered.

There is a long silence on the other end of the line, a sigh and then: "All I can tell you is to be with him where he's at and love him well."

I wait for more. The one thing I do know about Nick is that he is set on a slower speed than I am. He doesn't feel the need to fill space with an abundance of words.

When my tolerance for dead air space meets capacity, I ask, "That's it?"

Doesn't he remember needing detailed directions for this part? Something more on par with: Ten easy steps to get through your loved one's final weeks. It is becoming increasingly difficult as Tom takes extended leaves of absence from reality and I keep slipping ahead into the future.

"That's it," he replies. No road map from Nick, or at least, none I can read right now.

"Thanks." I try and sound sincere as if his one sentence of advice had opened up a new world for me. Really, though, the words hadn't made it past my latest preoccupation with affording the cremation. I hang up thinking he must just be a better person than me.

I need to get out—escape the confines of the house and breathe un-sick air. Maybe then I'll understand Nick's counsel.

Monica agrees to cover me. She has re-entered her big brother's life for the homestretch, after years of chance-only contact in the same community. It wasn't due to any stale conflict left over from childhood. In fact, Tom and Monica have always been the free spirits of the family. Before Tom's cancer, Monica fell on the freer side. This left Mike Jr. shining in parental approval and weighted with the role of being responsible. Monica rents a place across the peninsula. She's an easy ask and Tom doesn't feel the pull to maintain his wit with her. Since I never had brothers, I can't speak to that. But a sister—that's who I'd want changing my piss towel.

When she arrives, Tom is sleeping. River is eating snack and I've got the baby packed up to go. I hurry out, walking as fast as I can. Before I know it, I've crossed Broadway and I'm

Jennifer Allen

climbing the stairs to the mortuary. A man in a charcoal-black suit opens the door just as I raise my hand to knock.

"And what may I help you with, young lady?" he asks, as if I must need directions and certainly not funeral arrangements for my husband.

"I'd like to purchase insurance." I sound cavalier, like I'm ordering a pound of beef at the butchers. I've tricked myself into believing that I'm advocating for someone else—some caregiver on my caseload at work. This is the only way I can complete such transactions.

He tilts his head, perplexed, and then catches himself. "Of course, come right in." He escorts me further into the dark corridor, flicking lights on as we go. "Will this be for yourself or a loved one?"

"My husband." I keep it simple—another hospice tidbit I can use for myself. If I don't offer, he can't ask. Besides, we all have pre-existing prognosis of death. It is just that no one can really say *when* it will happen.

"Oh?" he asks, pushing for more.

"Mhmm." I nod, no cracks visible. "What do you estimate I'll need for a basic box and cremation?" I ask.

"And a service?" he adds, checking off boxes as he runs a pen down the dense list of small print.

"No, thanks,"

When he glances up at me suspiciously, I realize I'm too cool. He has it all wrong. I'm not a vengeful wife cashing in on my sugar daddy. Angry—sometimes; ready for Tom to die— sometimes; but not vengeful and there isn't sugar, anyhow. Not even a life-insurance policy, since Tom missed payments a few months back.

Like I said, angry, sometimes. Resentments I covet about the business he hasn't taken care of have their place. They serve to intercept the incoming guilt I might otherwise feel for burying my husband alive. I remind myself this is the same protocol I advise other caregivers to follow in order to avoid the overwhelming stress of planning and affording arrangements once the patient dies. I cut a check for a fraction of what we couldn't afford, gambling that next months' payment will be moot, and march down the stairs cooing to my baby girl: One investment in a future down, many to go.

Back on our block, the pervasive pounding and high-pitched creaks of nails being pulled out after years of holding a home together, dominate the warm air. Carl's old place is being torn down. We heard through the grapevine he had missed too many monthly payments and now lives in a tent at Veteran's park. I've seen him on occasion pushing a shopping cart around Sand City. The one time I did speak to him, he was his usual easy-going self. I was painfully uncomfortable, unable not to take him on as a charity case. For a few days after, I contemplated inviting him to take the garage office as a room in exchange for help. In the end, the idea felt too dicey and I let it slip away.

The new owners have plans to tear down his funky place and build a massive box that will take up every square inch of the lot. We'll be able to pass a loaf of bread between bedroom windows. Back in August, when Tom was in Mexico, I attended a city council meeting to fight their permit, if only to hold off the noise of construction just outside our bedroom window until Tom died. When it came time to stand at the podium and present my case, I got all choked up at the sheer pity I felt coming my way— massive with pregnancy and pleading with them to let my husband die at home in peace. Not only was I mortified to be crying in public, but the letter I got in response a week later indicated I might have been playing to the councils' hearts. *That* is not how policies are changed.

I stand in the driveway watching Carl's house disappear, cursing change, at least this particular change. And Carl, he was like us. Now he's like *them*—the other unfortunates pushing overloaded shopping carts down the bike path. We could cross that line all too easily with the missed property taxes. The penalties and the balloon payment due on the mortgage tally up to a couple year's worth of my current salary. Postponing foreclosure until he dies is the most I can hope for. At least Tom has kept things in his name so my credit won't be tainted when he's gone. He knew himself too well.

Each time I come home to a foreclosure notice on the door, I rip it down and throw it away. Money stress has been the substance of Tom's waking nightmares—the snag that keeps him from dying in peace. These days, it's ranking high on my resentment list.

I look up at our cute little house, remembering back to when we moved in after our Europe trip: the many nights talking in the hot tub and sleeping on a futon under the stars on the back deck. As I enter, I'm suddenly nostalgic about even things that have chronically annoyed me. The snake grass growing up through the concrete is *home*. The dingy stain of dirt along the hallway where River runs his hand and Kizma brushes past is evidence of a boy and his dog. Instead of the fence, just outside the kitchen window, I notice morning glories struggling to make beauty from what is. All of it is home. All of it will soon be gone.

I want time to stop. *And* I want it to fast-forward me past this torturous anticipation of losses.

Conflicting wants stretch me in different directions like the saltwater taffy machine I remember watching through the glass as a child. Monica and I tag-team care. I try to freeze the machine on "wanting time to stop," so I can be with my family right now—as is.

As the sound of her car diminishes, I line up diapers, towels, and wipes on the bed and begin the changing routine. Catching River's eyes, I hold a smile to them and tell him what a sweet boy he is, while I swipe the soiled diaper from beneath him. For a moment he just stares at me, as if he can't believe I finally got it. Then he laughs and takes Oceanna's hand into his mouth, pretending to eat it, in the same way Tom used to do with him. Shifting now to Oceanna, I run my hands down each of her soft fleshy legs and kiss each toe. She rotates he head around looking at each of us. Our whole family is on the bed together.

My God, I am lucky.

Tom is between worlds. He tries to focus on the children, smiling for moments before he returns to the drama behind his lids.

"I'm just going to change your towel now, Button—no diapers, I promise." I tell him before I begin. Diapers haven't worked for him as he tore to shreds the only one I managed to get on him. Pulling a chucks pad from a stack beside the bed, I carefully roll Tom to the side and slip it under him and then drape a fresh towel over his groin. His torso is covered with scabs from the hives he's been itching. They feel like wounds of battle beneath my hand as I caress him.

Oh my sweet, sweet Button. Tears pelt the back of my hand. The sharp pain in my chest begins to melt. Tom is somewhere else. He grumbles insistently, eyes shifting about behind half-mast lids.

"The money. They want the money." He frowns. "They don't understand. I don't have it. Tell them I lost it. *Please*, they're coming to get me and they're taking everything!" his eyes widen with fright as if mafia men surround his bed, guns cocked.

River has moved on to play with his Tonka truck downstairs and Oceanna is dozing off on my side of the bed.

I squeeze in beside Tom and soothe him: "It's okay, Tom, it's okay. You're safe here." A déjà vu of Morocco passes through only it's not me he is afraid of. Now it is his angst over losing money or not making enough of it.

An enemy has arisen and I can see the importance of making it common. Money matters just aren't worth suffering about on the way out of a life full of loving people well. More than anything, I want him to know he is so much bigger than money. I wish for him to leave this life feeling at peace. His grip loosens on my arm and turns into a familiar stroke. He's back in this reality.

I tell him tight snippets of news, hoping to lay his angst to rest. "Tom, I got insurance to cover your funeral arrangements. It is all taken care of," I say, slowing my pace for his full absorption. "The kids will get the maximum monthly social security benefits until they are 18. Louise has a life insurance policy for you that will go to Jessica and Eliza. We're all going to be fine." His body relaxes with the last few words. More than the facts, I bet it is the message he needs most.

In slow repetition, I whisper: "Your love is all that has ever mattered. Your love is all that has ever mattered . . ." He nods ever so slightly and drifts into a steady snore.

I am loving him well. Now I understand what Nick meant. In the greatest way, it is *that* simple.

26

Sweet Acceptance

October 1997, Day 24

A few days ago, Tom's mother brought River over to her car and handed off a bunch of candy, looking up to see if I noticed. Of course I saw her. Still, she pretended they were pulling off some kind of heist, though it looked more like a drug deal. My initial requests to stop the sugar flow had been met with Stella's insistence that it's a Grandmother's job to spoil her grandchild, followed by a game of secret candy deliveries. If I didn't have other things demanding my energy, I'd have taken a firmer stance. Anyway, I know all too well the desire to make up to River for his losses. For Stella, it seems to be the next best thing to giving to her own son something he won't let in—her way of loving.

She whispered to River and then hugged him snuggly to her breast. All at once I got it: She's losing a child. Worse, Tom's father, Michael, is gone and she has no one to share her grief with. At any other time, my heart would have welled up with a continuous supply of empathy for her. These days my supply is bone dry, taken up fully with Tom and the children.

I walked over to her, ignoring the chocolate smears on River's face. "He's not going to make it, you know," I said, trying to get through before it was too late.

Her jaw tightened. She looked away and changed the subject. "I'll see you next Wednesday. Tommy's Aunties are all praying for him."

I shook my head as she drove away: *She doesn't know what she's missing.*

It's Saturday and Stella has popped over ahead of schedule, offering to be with River and Tom so I can get out with the baby and pick up some groceries. I'm sure she knows. I return and find her standing in the bedroom door staring at Tom who lay on his back, eyes closed. She startles when I nudge her with an elbow.

"My Tommy, oh, my Tommy." She sobs.

"Go," I whisper. A gush of empathy comes up out of nowhere. "Sit with him."

"I can't," she says, wiping her cheeks with a lace handkerchief.

Steam from the bowl I'm patiently balancing, ascends between us, softening both of our worn features. Tom hears us and looks over.

"A bath?" he mouths.

"Yeah, finally, huh?" I say. "I'll do your legs now and the rest later, okay?"

He nods and closes his eyes. Stella remains frozen in grief.

As I kneel at the foot of the bed, I'm glad we chose a Captain's bed. This way I don't break my back giving an unknown number of sponge baths and he doesn't have far to fall the next

Jennifer Allen

time he thinks he can make it to the bathroom. I roll up the blankets to his mid-thigh, lift his knees under one arm and tuck a towel beneath him. Tenderly, I run the warm sponge down each of his withered legs, remembering how strong they had been in our days of rock-climbing. Now they are grandpa legs—pale and almost hairless, unable to hold him upright. I pat each leg dry, tuck the comforter around them and begin massaging lotion onto each foot poking out at the blanket's edge. Stella stands motionless in the doorway.

"Come on over to this side and take a foot," I encourage. Hesitantly, she finds her way to the end of the bed beside me.

"What do I do? Won't it hurt?" She whispers, fumbling his foot self-consciously between her arthritic hands.

"Just touch gently, like you would a baby," I say.

She stays with it, her caresses gradually lengthen and smooth out with maternal instinct.

From the head of the bed comes a delirious groan laced with panic: "Ohhhhh . . . I can't feel my feet. I won't be able to walk. I won't . . . "

His feet are modeled purple and white and don't warm no matter how much we massage them: a sure sign that death is knocking.

"Oh, Tom-Button," I answer feeling a love so wide beyond my bodily parameters, it can hold his dying separate from my grief about it.

"No worries, you won't need those. You'll be flying free soon enough," I say. "Sweetie, let your body and spirit separate. It knows how to do this."

Tom exhales slowly, seeming to remember that he's in the labor of dying. There's no fighting it anymore. The task comes in repeated surrender.

Stella sniffles. She is in the trenches, like it or not. It's raw here in the most beautiful, real way. An aching expression covers her face and she doesn't get up and leave. Denial must have grown so painful to her that it was worth trying something else. Especially when she sees the relief on her son's face. Stella's pleading has stopped long enough for her to really see Tom beyond all of her ideas about him and beyond her own loss. Simultaneously, I see *her*—another human being witnessing the slow death of a son. A thread is being woven between us. I hope it will be strong enough to connect us long after Tom is gone.

Though his face has sunk dramatically over the past weeks, Tom has the satiated look of a baby who is drunk on Mamma's milk. Stella has offered him a love he can accept, if not purely because she has accepted that he is dying.

Jennifer Allen

27

Light Homefront

October 1997, Day 28

The way I've been feeling in our home lately reminds me of going to church as a child. Back then, upstairs was the place of prayer, candles, and carefully chosen words. Downstairs held casual conversation over coffee hours, feasts of five-table-long potluck dinners, and Monday bible school, complete with Ritz crackers, Skippy peanut butter, and the latest knock-knock jokes. The feeling of sacredness I had held in my ten-year-old budding spirituality was present in both places—linked by the very same staircase that divided the activities.

It is the same now.

People come and go throughout the day, visiting Tom and continuing support for us in various ways. The house is like Grand Central as we wait out the big moment. Those who said goodbye almost a month ago, when we first had the concrete news of what direction Tom was heading, are back for second and third rounds of goodbyes. My parents had made plane reservations, hoping to arrive before he departed. I had told them they'd likely miss it. But they have made it and Tom labors on. Mum keeps snacks out and offers guests beverages. Noise of conversation, laughter, utensils clattering, and the baby swing tick-tocking fills the downstairs.

Climbing the stairs to our bedroom transitions one into stillness, the only sound being the continuous play of David Whyte's poetry CD or Hilary Stagg's harp-music. The smell changes from food to antiseptic, urine, and sage. There's only Tom to be with, his body barely detectable under the flannel sheets of our gargantuan bed. Pictures of those he loves, drawings he has made in art therapy experiences, trinkets from his collection of miniatures, and his braid all mix amongst medical paraphernalia to create an altar at his bedside. The room is light, with the blinds open and the sun pouring in.

Come evening, the religious votives I found at Longs take over. Then, the feel is more like a Catholic church, with the stained glass sticker of a guardian angel lit up from behind, casting a compassionate orange hue over Tom. I've taken to gesturing the symbol of the father, son, and Holy Spirit each time I see her in respect of the miracle that she, and numerous others just like her, has provided by way of a continuous flame at Tom's bedside for twenty-eight days straight now.

I'm not the only one graced with such miracles. Visitors come downstairs after some time with Tom looking themselves in ways they hadn't before. Tom's persona—his social-self —has shed itself along the way. We are left with Tom in his truest essence. Even his clothes had to go due to the discomfort they caused him. Simply witnessing the nakedness of *being* so evident in him is enough for others to ditch their facades. It's a potential gift in dying Tom has realized and extends to anyone who is receptive. He's our local Jesus, these days.

Jennifer Allen

Like Jesus, I imagine, he's all forgiving. Just last week he gave me a sermon on patience, through the metaphor of fixing his razor. I suppose it was in response to my neglect of not shaving him for a week and being caught up in a frantic buzz, one step removed. He showed me how to be with him through this: one human to another in the sweetest way.

Ironically, the result is that this dying business has started to feel uncharacteristically light. Infrequently, when he touches down into consciousness, we joke about when the big "D" is going to happen. After weeks of having Carlos Nakkai flute music cued up for his last breath and worrying he'd die alone each time I left the bedroom, I decided—again, to let his dying be what it is, when it is. We're both good to go: Me, to pick up some groceries and him, to die.

Although Tom is like a son to my parents, he isn't comfortable with them tending his personal needs while I step out. Monica is the only other person he'll allow to change his pee towel. If I weren't so desperate for a hit of other realities every so often, I'd ask other people to shop for me. A simple venture down the aisles of a grocery store keep me from floating up and away.

Miracles are everywhere. Monica's busy vet-assisting schedule has freed itself up over the last weeks, enough so she can cover me at the drop of a hat. Within half-an-hour of my call, she's here. The bedroom door is open and she peeks in.

"*Still* hanging in there, huh Tom? What are you, trying to outdo Ghandi?" she says, teasing.

"MmmHm." Tom acknowledges her with just a slight lift of the chin.

"Yeah, he's on day twenty-eight with no more than a few bites of food," I respond for him. Then, careful to keep him in the loop, I say, "Button, you know, Halloween's in a couple of days. You'd make a great living skeleton! You could really freak out the trick-or-treaters!"

He's with us, parting his dry lips in an effort to smile.

This is different than my childhood church. Humor wasn't considered holy. In fact, just because of the taboo, I found myself magnetically pulled toward hysterical laughter over just about anything the minister had to say. Inevitably, my snicker would begin a chain reaction among the children's choir. For some reason, the more sacred the event—communion for instance, the more hilarious things were and the more trouble I'd get into. I'd argue that God wouldn't make things funny if we weren't supposed to laugh. Though I'd argue the same point now, it didn't get me off the hook then. Thinking of this now, I'm grateful my husband feels like one of the other kids in the church choir, relieved to be finding humor in such serious matters.

Tenderly, I rub vitamin E over his lips and run a wet sponge-brush over his gums, reminding him that if he wants to die without me here, this could be his window of opportunity.

"You do what you need to do, Button. I'll be back in about an hour. See you later, sweetness. Dead or alive." I wink.

He looks genuinely relieved, like he's really starting to believe I'll be okay.

Jennifer Allen

28

Hallowed Time

October 1997, Day 31

Halloween is here and so is Tom.

Joyce came from Santa Cruz to bring River around the neighborhood trick-or-treating, freeing me up for a bedside vigil. I have it figured that Tom is taking the next train out tonight, when the veil is thinnest between worlds, as the story goes. At most, he might be waiting for the height of Dia de los Muertos—Day of the Dead, which runs over the next two days. It's a Mexican tradition of honoring loved ones who have passed over by luring them close to the realm of the living with altars of brightly decorated sugar skulls and favorite foods.

We've definitely got plenty of tasty morsels downstairs. After tonight, River should have a few sugary treats to donate to the cause. Of course, I don't really know how this works—the dying/dead thing, but I'm willing to try anything that could aid

Tom's passage. Lord knows, he has helped many a relative from this side as they've headed into the great mystery. I'm hoping their spirits come by for a whiff of paella and reveal themselves to Tom in the most benevolent ways. Soft whisperings of reassurance as he leaves the confines of his body to join them would be ideal.

Jessica and Eliza have maneuvered their work schedules because they, too, think their dad's time is close. Jessica has come down from the city to stay with Eliza and their mom, a dozen blocks away, making it possible for the three of them to squeeze in as many last-moments as possible. Tom's brother, Mike, and sister-in-law, Suzanne, are up from Southern California and are waiting in the wings at Stella's. They came up early in the month, when the prognosis was days. The vigil felt premature and had ended up in "see-you-later"s instead of goodbyes. My parents are here for another ten days. They'll hold down the fort while bedside circles form, break, and re-form.

Our home is aglow as All-Hallows Eve sets into darkness. It's the spookiest place on the block. Candlelight flickers upstairs, casting a shadow of Tom's frail profile against the slider drapes, while a menagerie of costumed visitors cackle and shriek with laughter from downstairs. Eliza and Jessica are dressed past recognition. Once River discovers who they are, he's ecstatic with the idea of being incognito. A colorful clown midget spins circles around me, begging permission for he and his big sisters to go upstairs and see if Daddy knows who they are. Before long, there is a potential parade of costumed loved ones who want to bring the Halloween party up to Tom.

I can't let them go. Not because he won't recognize them, though. As far as I know, Tom hasn't placed any names with faces, even when they're not disguised, for a few days now. If he talks at all, its been mumbling about the other world he visits. Today that world has been a waking nightmare. The last thing anyone needs is for him to be freaked out by a slue of almost-familiar characters roaming about his bedroom. No one wants to end on that note.

Besides, things have changed from even yesterday. Offerings of reassurance don't calm him anymore. He seems to have successfully let go of the worries holding him back in the tangible realm of our daily lives and has dropped into dredging up his eldest of unresolved fears. Perhaps even things that have haunted him from other lifetimes. One minute he's being cornered by gangsters, accused of a betrayal he swears he didn't commit; the next he's witnessing the deaths of hundreds of children with no way of preventing them. Deep in my bones it doesn't feel right to intervene with his visions. I've promised myself I'd listen to such cues. I don't want to impede him while he's hanging in his body by threads, trying to empty as much baggage as possible before he loses the human vehicle for tending such business.

It helps to remember a story I heard once about a man who saw a butterfly struggling to break out of its cocoon and tried to help it by peeling back the silky covering and freeing it. He was a good person with good intention. In the end, though, the butterfly couldn't take off because its wings weren't fully developed and it died. The man had unknowingly robbed the butterfly of its natural process whereby its wings would have had time to mature in the challenging course of working its way out of the cocoon's tight confines.

So it is with Tom, struggling with panic at times as he births himself into spirit. I've become his labor coach, like he has been mine through the births of our two children. He's getting to the nitty-gritty of transition, where things can get pretty dang scary. Most of the afternoon, now, I've sat with a hand on his shoulder, whisper occasionally, "You can do this, Tom."

So, no, I'm not about to let Halloween descend upon him in the form of clowns, witches, and geishas, as much as it is another loss to his children. He's in a hallowed state and our entire household—the party downstairs and his nightmares upstairs—are all happen simultaneously in this hallowed time.

Jennifer Allen

29

Birth/Death Day

November 1997, Day 33

I'm torn. The birthday party I've promised River and Tom's last breath look like they'll fall on the same day—today.

Between Tom's sinking features, a consciousness that is now about ninety percent devoted to the other world he's been visiting, and his fish-out-of-water gasps every thirty seconds, I can't imagine what is keeping him alive. Not until I start blowing up balloons and Mum is decorating River's clown cake, do I realize Tom has been holding out for his son's third birthday. I've been planning a party for River at a nearby park with a big Simba jumpy house for a few weeks—never mentioning it to Tom. If he didn't have names anymore, I was sure dates wouldn't have stuck.

Besides, I didn't want to keep him obliged to his body for a drop longer than nature intended. It looks to me like dying gets tangled up with one's will and emotions the same way birthing does. It can't be stopped, but slowing down or speeding up seem to be options.

Amy and her boyfriend, Brett, don full clown regalia and sneak out before River sees them. They've made puppets for a show and have a stash of long balloons for making animals and fancy hats. Mum and Dad take the party favors, cake, a couple bottles of breast milk, Oceanna and River to the park, while I stay with Tom. What I really want is to be there for my boy on his third birthday, gathering kids together for a treasure hunt and handing out slices of cake. Mother things. Tom only dies once, so I've opted for wife things. If he could only tell me who he wants bedside, if anyone, I'd at least know I made the right choice by staying and calling in his family.

Mike and Suzanne drive down with Stella. Jessica and Eliza come by with Louise. Monica has been here since morning. Everyone is on flex-mode not knowing if they're showing up to a bedside vigil, a three year-old's party, or a viewing. I've called it as a vigil/birthday and have invited people to rotate between our bedroom and the park, so neither gets neglected. Eight of us squeeze in around Tom on the bed while he lies on his back, hands folded behind his head on a mound of pillows, exposing his atrophied arms. His eyes wander about, occasionally coming to rest on one of our faces with a flicker of recognition and a slight smile before closing off and diving deeply into other realms. The span of silence between each of Tom's raspy breaths lengthens— 30 seconds, 38, 47 and 55. Each break, murmurs of goodbye and streams of tears arise in response to it being his last breath. Each time he gasps, we startle in unison.

I cue up the Ave Maria tape sang by Tom's Auntie Beatrice at a relative's funeral years back. A month or so ago, he mentioned wanting to hear her angelic voice as he neared passing. I'd dug through his desk to no avail at the time. Then, this morning, I found it sitting in plain sight.

As I play it now, it seems to strike a common chord of history among his siblings and mother. Catholic or not, it's impossible not to be moved by the beauty of the song. In fact, I can almost feel myself take flight into spirit with the final crescendo. *This, I think, is the moment of release.*

The song ends, the player clicks and five seconds later, Tom gasps. For the good part of an hour we replay the Ave Maria tape and hover over Tom in muscle-tweaking, bladder-busting positions, while counting silently between his breaths as if they are reverse contractions. The circle breaks at last when Mike uses the bathroom. I run downstairs and grab another box of tissues and some water for Stella. Monica lets her dogs out into the side yard. Our tear wells have drained themselves in the course of the vigil and we begin to get a little chatty, heading quickly to giddy. Even Stella seems to have spent herself for the time being. Meanwhile, Tom retreats inward and the gaps between his breaths are back down to 37 seconds.

"It's not happening," I say. "Maybe we should divi-up and take the pressure off, give him a little time alone." I'm not sure who is waiting for whom anymore: us for him to pass, or him for us to be ready.

Before heading over to River's party, I cup my hand over Tom's ear and whisper: "We're ready when you are, my lovely. You go when you need to."

I'm still trying to clear all barriers for take-off, though it really seems like he's got an internal accounting of whose really ready and whose not, no matter what I say.

As I drive to the park, it feels as if I'm moving into another timeframe—from a still photograph to a movie. I've got butterflies and my hands are trembling. I'm hungry, not for food, though I don't remember eating lunch. Rather, for the sight of my boy playing, his life moving forward in the company of loving friends and family. For a moment, I sit parked in my car, watching River and his three other child-guests jump about holding hands and shrieking with laughter in the bouncy-house. All three children are from our support network. Their parents or grandparents have taken the opportunity to expose them to the human side of life's tragedies. I'd like to think, like me, they'd grow to be better people for it.

Virtually every person at the party knows River's daddy is not there because he's in the process of dying. I've anticipated the big question: "Has he died, passed over, flown onward yet?"

Before I leave the safe haven of my car, I've got a coded response ready: "Status quo on the home front." Soon enough, we'll be talking about Tom's death. For now, we eat cake and watch puppet shows.

Gears shift and I'm back to my children and their needs. Nature forces mamma's to focus on such matters. She's engorged my breasts a size larger than my bra from missing two feedings. Now I've got two large wet circles on my chest. At least my tee shirt is black (guess I assumed I'd be a widow by day's end).

Evan has Oceanna over his knee, rubbing her back, trying to soothe her. He and Vicky have a son the same age at home, so he's got the technique down.

"Hate to break up your roll, Evan," I say, retrieving her. "But I need some de-milking right about now and she's due."

"What a feisty little pumpkin you've got here," he says with affection as he hands her over.

"Yeah, that she is." I lift her to me and walk away. We are like hungry magnets. Her body fits perfectly over the emptiness I feel in my breadbasket and my breast fills her arm-span and then her belly.

People tend to leave nursing mothers to their privacy and I'm freed from socializing while I gather my ground. Oceanna grunts and snorts under my shirt, while I watch the kids congregate around the makeshift puppet theatre. River carries on a full conversation while shaking the hand of a puppet Amy animates from under the table. I marvel at the imagination required to have inanimate objects come to life. It reminds me of how Tom was always able to personify anything at the drop of a hat. *Oh, how he had me in stitches with such antics!*

Had.

Already, he feels past tense. The man lying in bed at home is almost an empty shell. It's difficult to think of that body as Tom when he was so much more than it. Possibly this is the genius of a drawn-out death. He's been morphing into a bundle of vivid memories saturated with emotion that feel quite alive, as if he's here with me—minus the body.

I'm off wondering if this is how it will be after he is completely gone—as in ashes, when Oceanna pulls her head back with my nipple clenched between her gums.

Jennifer Allen

"Ouch!"

Oh yeah, cake and puppet shows, cake and puppet shows.

She's constantly pulling me back to the moment. I tuck all my spare fleshy parts back in, hoist Oceanna over my shoulder for burping and find a seat next to Nick. I'm longing to talk to him about all that's going on inside me because I know he'll understand. I'm tongue-tied and no words come. A lump forms in my throat. Now I'm nervous and on the brink of something too heavy for a child's birthday party.

"How are you doing?" he asks.

"Okay, I guess." I try for a smile, but a frown wins out. Suddenly, I'm painfully self-conscious, questioning my own motives. *What are you thinking, unloading on him? What if he thinks you're coming on to him? Well, are you?*

God, I hate that nagging voice inside. It would have me leave myself, over and over, unless I felt up for a wrestle with it. Right now I don't. Instead of exposing myself, I talk over it in dying spouse lingo. Though he looks a little confused, as if I'm not delivering what he expected, he hangs in there anyway. Words become meaningless without the truth to support them. I feel myself staggering through the conversation, looking for the closest exit so I can return to Tom's bedside where I belong.

Afternoon light descends and guests begin to leave. The bouncy-house guy comes to pack it up and I feel leaden. It's possible I've missed Tom's moment. River is loaded on cake and running around like a wild animal. Oceanna is satiated, burped, and happy as a clam. I leave my babies and the clean up with Mum and Dad and drive home, anxious and guilty.

Just as I turn the knob, I hear Suzanne's hearty laugh and I'm instantly relieved. Everyone chatters among themselves in the living room and Stella sits at the kitchen table eating grapes. Tom is still with us—or rather his body is.

Jennifer Allen

30

Final Passage

November 1997, Day 36

After the party, I put a halt to urging Tom onward until River's *actual* birthday passed. In his unfathomable knowing that the party was held two days early, I hoped he'd also know better not to leave River a lifetime of birthdays marked by his daddy's death anniversary.

Late into the evening, on the same day and about the same time that our son came into the world just three years prior, I slipped under the covers beside Tom and felt him cool against me.

Tracing the outline of his boney face I said, "You've already impressed yourself on River, Tom. He's had the three most crucial years of his life with you. You're in him now. And Oceanna, she has your potency in her scream. What a firecracker of a last seed you've given me . . ." I trailed off falling under the spell of exhaustion and dreams pulling me elsewhere.

Somewhere into the night, Oceanna's howling pulls me back. Before I retrieve her from the crib, I listen for Tom. It's become habit, over the past month, to check numerous times to see if he's still breathing. Each night I've become more vigilant, not wanting to miss his passing. The result is that I'm delirious from sleep deprivation on the very night I think it will matter most. The clock reads 12:47 a.m., which means we're officially past River's birthday and six months from the anniversary date when Tom and I met eight and a half years ago. It's another *perfect* time.

With my hand resting on his ridged chest and our daughter nursing noisily between us, I continue the one-way conversation from earlier this evening—hoping it's true that hearing is the last to go.

"Remember, love has nothing to do with having a body . . . we can still . . . love," I mumble, feeling myself grow hypnotized by the baby's rhythmic sucking.

Below the surface of consciousness, surreal scenes swirl about, mixing up realities under the cover of night. Somewhere deep into the place of dreams, I hear moans. A wild animal is lying wounded in the brush. I move toward it, despite my fear. I'm not sure I want to witness the suffering and I don't know how to stop it or if I should interfere with nature. Still, I'm drawn to find it. The sound grows intense as I search through tumbleweeds and come upon an opening. Startled, my body jolts to waking and I orient. Tom groans with urgency.

"Button, what's wrong?" I ask, even though he hasn't been able to speak for days. The clock reads 2:10. "Shit, did I forget your last dose of morphine?"

I jump out of bed and rub my eyes hard, struggling to read the pink sticky note by candlelight. My writing started out legible. Over the past week, it has begun to look closer to Arabic than English. I can't decipher the latest entry. Nor can I string together the events of the past six hours well enough to connect one of them to giving him pain medicine.

Tom is restless, writhing in place and moaning with each exhalation. I rush around the bed, kneel beside him, and tell him the dilemma: "Okay, I'll give you another dose, Tom; just not too much. I don't want to interfere with nature's course. I promised. God, I wish you could tell me what to do."

Just then his eyes flash into focus momentarily. Even in the dim candlelight I can read them: "Screw all that talk about needing a rite of passage into death after missing it with a C-section birth, just give me the drugs. NOW!"

I pull one dose of morphine, and not a drop more, into the syringe and squirt it under his tongue. In minutes, his moaning notches down to an intermittent growl-snore. Now I doubt both our past insistence on au-natural passages. By the time I have Tom re-tucked and settled, the baby needs a new diaper and another feeding. Pillows prop me up as I hold her and nurse.

For too many nights now, sleep has come last. It slithers in seducing me under, for another dip. Amongst the dreams, part of me remains semi-aware, like a tennis official watching from a high seat. While I'm off swimming around in other realms, my body safely repositions the baby and myself to reclining and tracks Tom's moaning when it picks up again some time later. Still though, sleep wins, just as it has over occasions of crying babies whose needs I'd have otherwise moved mountains to meet.

Oceanna eventually adds her voice to the decibels until the sound sparks a prickle of adrenaline down my spine and I break the surface. Tom is suffering. It's 4:17, too early for another dose. Despite all my time at hospice learning the benefits of morphine in a *good* death—a comfortable death, I can't seem to use it for Tom in that way. The suffering he was willing to take on for a conscious passage, which was once his idea of a good death, seems like undeserved torture. For now, though, I stick to his plan.

Barely touching his shoulder, I tell him just what he said to me in the past with rock climbing, with his razor lesson, and during the crux of Oceanna's birth: "You can do this, Tom. Step by step. Be only with this moment. You'll be somewhere else soon enough."

I'd like to tell him I'd be right here with him throughout, only he's already been on his own most of the night thanks to my nodding off. Ultimately, death is a solo journey. His eyes roll about and he wrings his hands over his head. I can hardly stand to watch.

"It's almost over—you're almost there, Tom," I coach him along with no indication of the magic moment. For all I know, this could drag on for another couple days and he could have been made comfortable for the duration. By 5:14, I can't take it anymore. He needs relief. I boot up another round of morphine and leave it on the bedstand while call the hospice nurse and find out how much I can give him without compromising a natural passage.

"He wants to go as consciously as possible," I tell her.

She's heard this before and so have I. Everything is different from this position. This is his one and only passing and I don't want to screw up his karma. I'm grateful she doesn't lecture me with what I already know to be true: He's going to die very soon and the morphine may or may not make it sooner. Meanwhile, it will settle him.

"Go ahead with the dose you have and keep on dosing as needed, until he gets relief. He sounds like he's getting close. I'll come over if you want, Jennifer," she says.

"Thanks. I just wanted to know I could give him more, without stealing his passage. I'll call later."

The medicine takes hold and his arms relax onto the pillow, his palms facing up in surrender. Purr-like ticking replaces his moans, lulling me into semi-slumber, where I can feel the cold sticky sweat that has absorbed into the sheets from his body.

The sensation weaves easily into dreams of rowing a boat out to sea in fog-drenched clothing. Tom is in a little yellow dinghy well ahead of me when I decide to turn around. The water is too deep and I yearn to feel solid ground under my feet.

As I touch back to shore, I hear someone say, "I'm right here with you, it's okay."

I barely recognized the voice as my own. A death rattle wakes me into the light of morning. Tom is in new place, one that the "Gone From My Sight" book we hand out at hospice describes as the last minutes of life, when breathing sounds as if the lungs are full of liquid. I equate it to the baby's head crowning in labor. I stagger out of bed with our infant in my arms.

"Wait. I'll be right back, Button."

I suppose I'll regret this if he dies in the two minutes it will take me to hand-off Oceanna to my parents downstairs in the garage/guestroom. It just doesn't seem right having her here, if only because I want to be one hundred percent with Tom in these final moments. Swiftly, I make the hand-off and pad back up the stairs, careful not to wake River.

"I'm here," I tell Tom as I move around the room, lighting a stick of sage off the constant flame in the votive candle that sits on his altar. When I open the window, the smoke trails from the bed, up and out, clearing a path for him to fly free. Then, careful not to touch his body, for fear it will pull him back to this world, I sit cross-legged at his torso. His eyes are open and still shiny brown, though they are focused on the heavens and surely nothing in this world. His breath wanes until it sounds more like an echo of his soul separating from flesh. I'm listening carefully for cues of how to be with him. What I get is silence. Somewhere deep in my bones, I know for Tom, it is best not to touch him or talk to him until he's gone—completely out of his skin.

And then he is.

The shallow gurgling ceases and at the same time, his eyes flatten into dull puddles.

He's gone.

Morning sun illuminates a column of sweet sage smoke over his body and I imagine him there, past the point of return. It's time to begin our new language. Closing my eyes, I feel into my heart and let words arise amongst surges of tears.

"Fly away man, you are free at last," I whisper. "Fly home, Tom, fly home."

As I sit with his body, tears give way to hiccup breathes like how I cried when I was little.

Childlike thoughts ride in on the next crying wave: *No you can't go, I want you back now! You can't leave us.*

I'm having a child moment the way others have senior moments. Luckily, they pass almost as abruptly as they came. Hopefully, they don't cause Tom a snafu on his way out.

Thoughts and feelings whirl through me quickly. Relief. Heavy dread. Joy. Longing. Sadness and happiness arise simultaneously with a peppering of ecstasy. Shoulders feel like wings; belly, like tar. There's a tickling sensation in my chest. It feels like the difference between life and death. Tom's skin is lavender-gray and flat. It's lukewarm on the chest, cool at the shoulder, and tacky to the touch. *He's not there.*

Curiosity.

Can I? I ask his permission from my heart.

His reply comes in the form of imagining what he, in all of his Curious George-ness would have said: *Have at it! Don't forget to try the eyelid thing they do in movies, I've always wondered if that worked.*

I smile to myself, gently closing each lid over his vacant stare to no avail. The lids are stubborn and they creep up to half-mast each time I seal them shut.

"Can you believe that? It doesn't really work," I report back to him my findings and move on, running my hand under the sheet to his stomach, where my fingers spiral around his bellybutton. Out of habit, they touch as if the experience is mutual. It's not. The cool firmness building in the places that have always been tender tell me so. Skin suit, not Tom.

Sad. Longing. Tight throat.

Pulling off the covers, I look at his entire body—something I haven't done without the distraction of worry, in a very long time. His rib cage is high as if he should have been a lumberjack type when fleshed out. A diamond shaped bone protrudes out from where the ribs come together. His legs and groin have lost most of the dark hair he treasured, having been a late bloomer. Even his armpits I notice, looking into the deep caverns they form with his arms propped over his head, have only a few sprigs remaining. Though he was athletic, Tom's upper body was never defined. His muscles were smooth, like his skin. As I trace up each arm to where they meet in folded hands behind his head, I feel the cold-hardness taking over. Even with so little mass left, his skin feels like it's stretched tightly over what flesh remains. Even the creases at his elbows are like thick rubber bands. Before he's too rigid, I unclasp his hands and lower them to rest on his chest. His wedding band falls off and drops to the floor.

'Till death do us part.

Guess we aren't married anymore. It doesn't seem right that a marriage can be undone by death. No fair.

Jennifer Allen

I pick up the ring and string it onto my necklace. *It's just different now*, I soothe the child-self inside who stomps her feet in a tantrum of wanting.

Love goes beyond the body. Love. Pure love. The kind that Rumi speaks of in a poem I remember of his about meeting in a field beyond right and wrong. Love—beyond the practical dilemmas of bringing home the bacon and frying it up in a pan, beyond the struggles of personality differences, preferences, child-rearing styles, and relationship dynamics. There are wings on my back as I let this love permeate through me. It feels like dreams I've had of soaring down low over meadows of purple lupine.

Ecstatic peace. My greatest prayer is that this is what it is like for Tom as he orients to spirit.

I sit for a time in this place of flying, until River's footsteps stomping down one stair at a time, land me. I air the sheets over Tom's naked body, sending the cleansing sage smoke into swirls over it. Neatly, I fold the blanket's edge at chest level and gingerly tuck around him.

As I turn and go downstairs to deliver the announcement, I notice the guardian angel votive candle is out. The flame has been transferred to new saint votives along the way, burning a constant vigil since his dying process began over a month ago, until now. To me, it means he's made it into another place, perhaps to be a guardian angel himself. *This is how I'll tell River.*

Downstairs, my children are snuggled in bed with my parents. Mum is reading to them and looks up with an empathetic frown when I enter.

"He's gone," I say. The finality of the words unleashes another round of tears.

"Where? Where's Daddy?" River asks, curious more than alarmed, reminding me I'm parent before I'm a widow.

"Daddy died, River. His body is still in bed, but his spirit is gone. Come up and see."

I carry River upstairs on one hip and my parents follow with Oceanna. We sit on the bed and River edges over to Tom, reaching out to touch him.

"This is just a body now. Daddy has gone to be an angel, River. I think he'll be the guardian kind that protects you and helps you. You can't see angels, though, they're invisible." As I'm explaining, River pets Tom's elbow and stares just above his head in unusual silence.

Pointing into space, he asks, "What's that, Mamma?"

"Where?" I strain to see and make sense of things for him.

"The white thing over Daddy's head," he says. I take his position and squint, trying to blur my eyes in hopes of a glimpse.

"I don't see it, River."

"Right there!" he insists. His little arm is straight as an arrow. Whatever he sees must be beyond my perception.

"Mum? Dad?" I ask and they shake their heads indicating they haven't the vision either.

"See? It's big!" My son's focus falls short of the back wall. Clearly, he is looking at *something*.

"Maybe, that's his spirit you see, Riv. Sometimes grown-ups can't see those things." He stares, mesmerized, until hunger pulls him back into the business of being a kid.

River makes the leap at three that takes most adults days, weeks, and, sometimes, years to get: Tom is no longer his body. He defies the textbooks I've read about children comprehending death. Even hours later as people come by for our in-house viewing. River never asks when Daddy is going to wake up.

The day seems endless. The house flexes with people coming and going. Mostly, it's quiet, with knowing hugs and tearful exchanges. I feel light, as if I've been launched from a familiar planet into space. Ed comes by. He holds me, pressing my head into his chest and rocking slightly.

"It's going to be okay,"

I know this is true, yet I find myself melting. Crying again, when I was sure I was bone dry of tears.

It's been so long already since Tom has held me this way.

Before Ed leaves, we plan the invitation to Tom's memorial. Only hours after Tom dies, I'm back on the fast track of the living. I've got to call and check availability of the hall, send in his obituary, and notify the mortuary. Sometime this afternoon, they'll need to come pick up the body.

The body.

If Tom's done with it, I'm done with it. I decide to call them sooner than later.

Jennifer Allen

By early afternoon, the mortuary guys show up like pizza delivery boys going to the prom. One of them carries the body bag folded into a shape that resembles three pepperoni pizzas stacked in thermal outerwear, while the other parks a gurney in the hallway. A woman about my age, with brown hair pulled up neatly in a business-like bun, follows them in. She must be the PR part of the deal. She asks me how I'd like to dress the body. When I tell her that his birthday suit is perfect, she blinks back her surprise and says, "Sure, whatever you like, Mrs. Sanchez."

I leave them to their work, feeling numb as I listen to them heave the body down the stairs and watching them load it onto a gurney. River looks up from his play and pauses briefly with his railroad sound effects as the black bag containing his daddy rounds the corner and exits the house. And then he continues, "che-che-che-che . . ."

As they leave, the woman shakes my hand and offers her condolences for the third time. I'm not sure how it goes from here, so I ask.

"Guess I'll need to come to your office and make plans?"

"Oh, yes, I'm sorry." She gives me directions only I'm still snagged up on the fourth sorry. It's the word that makes me feel pity—downright sorry for myself. I don't like it, especially from a stranger.

What I want her to say is "Congratulations! You've made it through your husband's illness! The grand prize is living. Get on with it, woman!" She can't read minds, so I tell myself what I most need to hear.

Right now, I want to pack the children into the double stroller and go out for a walk—without worry or guilt. I want to hold Oceanna without the constant interruption of a medical regimen. I want to read every page of Lyle the Crocodile to my son and then later, take him to his new preschool's annual Lantern Walk. I want to march upstairs, change the sheets, and then jump on the bed and sing loudly. Inside, I feel a bit giddy in a manic kind of way, as I consider the possibilities. First though, there is the mortuary visit.

Dizziness sets in. I feel like a whirling dervish dressed in a helium filled foam suit. My hands tremble and I'm nauseous. As much as I still, at thirty-one, try and prove my independence to my father, I need him along for this meeting. He's solid ground when I'm all air. And he does read minds. His offer is out before I ask and we leave abruptly. I'm eager to get this part over with.

The mortuary smells like a florist's bathroom when we enter. A tall man dressed in a black suit (perhaps the father to the pick-up crew) cuts into the vacuumed space, inviting us into his office. I feel like I'm buying my first car with Dad along to coach me, making sure I don't get screwed.

After the initial niceties, the man addresses Dad: "I see here there's an insurance policy that covers cremation."

I can't believe he isn't directing this conversation at me: the one who bought the damn insurance and whose husband—*not* son-in-law—is the customer.

"Now," he says, "it doesn't specify the type of casket and you know, you can always upgrade. We have beautiful selections for your loved one." He opens a thick catalog, turning it toward us. The page is filled with a whole slue of polished cherry caskets that are probably more expensive than any car I've owned to date.

My face is burning now and Dad is wisely silent.

"Don't tell me people actually spend loads of money on a box only to burn it. Got cardboard?" I ask.

"Oh. Certainly, Miss," he says, shifting his eyes to me.

"Mrs.," I correct him.

"I'm sorry, Mrs. Sanchez."

"Actually, it is Mrs. Allen-Sanchez," I say, fully landed.

"Of course, Mrs. Allen-Sanchez. If that is your choice, we can accommodate you; however, let me show you just a few other options that might be more appealing to your budget. Simple wood with nicely cushioned interiors," he says, thumbing back a heap of pages.

"Cardboard is fine," I cut in. "No open casket, no service, no need to burn wood. Anyway, it's not like he's in that body."

I can't believe this guy is trying to sell me cushioned interiors. Dead is dead. He knows that better than anyone. There's clearly some profit to be made from our culture's need to avoid

Jennifer Allen

what dead really is. Honoring Tom will take many forms, though I doubt any will be material.

The man slides the catalog to the side and scrawls "cardboard box" across the bottom of a form. We finish our business with a handshake and on the way out I add, "Three days or more in the fridge, okay? That means no cremation until Monday."

He assures me the protocol I've concocted would be followed. His smile gives way to a confused look as he turns back into the building, as if to say: "Didn't she just say he wasn't in the body? What's up with the waiting?"

Had he said it out loud, I'd have told him it was about me doing what *I* need to do based on the medley of beliefs Tom and I had woven together, whether it's rational, in fashion, or neither.

When we get home, Eliza tells me River has had a hard time while we were away, crying inconsolably to his big sister in my absence. He wanted me and I was gone—to the mortuary, no less. To him, this could only mean I died too. *My poor baby.* And here, after I've been so vigilant to cover all bases with him leading up to his daddy's death, I blow it in haste to freedom. Not only had I forgot to say goodbye and kiss his forehead as I always do when I go anywhere, I had prepped him on mortuaries earlier and then disappeared to one. Just like Daddy.

The first impulse I have is to wake River from the sleep he eventually collapsed into and snug his sinewy little body tightly to mine so he feels my heart beat, strong and constant. Seeing how my last impulse went, I settle for being here when he wakes up and let sleep tend to his grief.

Later in the afternoon, River rustles about in his room. I rush in to give him proof of a living parent. He's only interested in a piggyback downstairs and going to the Lantern Walk tonight. We didn't skip his birthday and we won't miss this, no matter how uncomfortable it might be making my debut as a widow on the same day my husband has died. Too many things have been put on hold for River because his daddy was sick. I already have a chronic sense of owing our son, knowingly bringing him into the world when we knew he'd likely lose a parent before adulthood. So, when River asks, I give him a firm "yes" with an unrestrained gallop around the living room.

We leave the house as a tribe: Mum, Dad, Joyce, the children, and me. They buffer me from a loneliness I can feel closing in on the periphery. Word has made it to the preschool ahead of us, via the support network's phone tree. Even if it hadn't, River searches out Conrad and Kira upon our arrival and announces his daddy's death. The children stop playing momentarily; incomprehensibly—except for Conrad. He exudes a field of knowing empathy. After a millisecond, the children laugh and pull River into a game of tag at the edge of the forest where the families gather to begin the walk around the neighborhood. How I wish it were the same for adults.

After a long run of Indian summer, the weather has shifted. It's cold enough to warrant a sweater but not enough to have teeth constantly chattering the way mine are now. Pools of saliva congregate under my tongue every time I say Tom's name; as if the tears took a wrong turn and ended up mouth-bound, slurring my speech and causing me to swallow repeatedly.

The sun is down and faces grow dim in the dusk. I'm glad for the darkness as preschool parents approach me, making first introductions and condolences simultaneously. Strangely, I feel embarrassed to be the subject of sympathy. It's not the impression I like to make on first meetings. With each exchange, though, there is warmth in this group. It permeates any self-consciousness. These are the families of my new community—post Tom. I couldn't ask for a more graceful reception.

Teacher Dominique moves around the forming circle, lighting each child's lantern as she passes. Her melody is mesmerizing as she sings about the light inside each person that shines most bright in the darkest of seasons. The children instinctually hush to hear her, while I take off with her lyrics in a silent conversation with Tom about how perfect this ritual is at the end of his death-day. How perfect this school is for all of us. Everything makes sense. No doubt, there is a flame inside of me. I'm warming to it with each song, at each doorstep, and with each gracious smile in response.

Jennifer Allen

In the darkness, children and adults are discernable only by voice and body silhouette. My parents and Joyce are at the back of the lantern parade, chatting amongst others. River's curls and tipsy lantern give him away up at the front. Conrad's little man voice places him next to River. With Conrad comes Nick, close behind. My light inside burns a few degrees brighter as I make my way over to him. No surprise there. He *is* the one who has shown me—through his encouragement of finding ways to love Tom in his dying—how such a life circumstance could make the heart fire stronger. And he is the one who helped the whole support network understand the potential of gratitude in what looked like a grim situation. Based on what I've seen from Nick so far with his unassuming genuineness, he probably has no clue of the impact he's had on me, nor any clue of how bright I'm burning right along side him in the dark.

"Hey, Nick." Junior high type nervousness flushes my cheeks, from the inside out.

"Oh, hi, Jennifer," he says, recognizing me by voice. "I heard Tom died this morning. How are you doing?" He turns to me and all I can see of his face is his beard, fire-red in the glow of lanterns.

Before I can answer, we are at another doorstep and the singing begins. Between houses, I squeeze in just a fraction of what I want to share with him. He knows, or at least he has his own version of a similar loss. Common threads are everything right now.

In the commotion of parents gathering up children at the end of the walk, Nick slips an envelope into my hand. On the way to the restaurant, I finger the seal, working a slow rip and then, once we're seated, I open the card under the table and glance down occasionally to read it. Though it isn't an invitation to debrief this long disenfranchised grief as I had hoped, it is an invitation to be touched by the beauty of witnessing a loved one pass through the doors of death. It's a David Whyte poem from the CD he gifted Tom and it brings tears to my eyes.

Mum sees this and responds with a warm sympathetic frown as if to say: "We're right here with you, Jen." She doesn't know my tears are inspired by the secret sweetness in grief. Tom would recognize it if he were here. So would Nick.

Bone Knowing

Oceanna nurses voraciously at the restaurant and then falls asleep in her car seat on the drive home. No sign of colic for the first time in six weeks. Tonight we'll sleep in peace—all of us. Mum reads to River while I change the sheets. The bed is as Tom left it, wrinkles from his frail body still outlining his last mark here. I hesitate briefly, feeling at a crossroads of how I'm going to move on with life. *Preserve the wrinkles or pull off the sheet?* Tom is in me the way I told him he was in River and no physical proof is necessary. I pluck the sheet corners and roll all except his pillow up in a ball and throw them in the washing machine.

Gone.

The new sheets smell of fabric softener and the sage I blew over them before getting into bed. Tom's pillow carries his scent in contrast—an oily, musk smell I've noticed in Oceanna's hair as well. Hugging his pillow, I feel a mix of longing and freedom as I drop into a heavy sleep. No moans to keep me semi-conscious, no urine soaked towels to clean up and no morphine to administer. I have only the cries of children to tend now. Even they are silent tonight.

Jennifer Allen

After Tom

Jennifer Allen

31

Returning to Life

After Tom, Day 1

At four a.m. I'm awake out of habit and nauseous with fear. This
is the first official day of my family's new constellation and I'm
the only grown-up. The bubble of suspended time I've been in with
Tom and all the others witnessing his dying has been pierced by
the concept of survival. Party's over, the guest of honor has
departed. Days of sitting Shiva have already happened before he
died. Now it's time to secure my job, look for a rental before we
get the foreclosure boot, and pay down the stack of bills mounting
on the kitchen counter.

      Thinking of work causes a neon yellow sticky note to
surface from the back files of my memory. It reads: November 6th.
That would be today. The mandatory all-day training at hospice

was announced at work about six months ago, when news went out that we'd be merging with the hospital. Reminder notices circulated regularly: Mark you calendars! November 6th. It's *that* kind of mandatory. Change was heavy in the air when I took my maternity leave just ten weeks ago and missing this meeting might give them reason to change or fill my position.

I'm up early, pumping a day's supply of milk—probably loading it chock-full of the adrenaline panging in my stomach. By seven, River is bright-eyed and bushy-tailed, ready to jump Grampy. My heartstrings pull taught against mother instincts as I tell him I'm going to a meeting today. Gone is another of my fantasies. There will be no of huddling up with my babies at home for at least a week before we re-emerged as a new family unit. Surviving seems out of sync with such notions. The comfort I fall back on is knowing for a few more days, anyway, my children will have loving grandparents around the clock while I get my feet back on the ground.

The conference room at Hospice House is at full capacity with every employee I know and many I don't. I'm late with a new milk stain over my left nipple. What I would give for a vest, or better yet, a cloak of invisibility. Familiar faces register the changes: a baby born and a husband died. The former is obvious, as I've deflated over 40 pounds since I left for maternity leave. The latter they know because Tom's name, like Larissa's and so many others, is now a smudge mark on the dry-erase board under the heading of patients. He's graduated to the deceased list—something I don't want to see. There lies the problem: He was their patient and I am their co-worker. Not a good mix.

Normally, families receive an abundance of support with hospice both before and after the death. I have kept ours bare bones, worrying it would impact relationships at work. Co-workers might not trust that I could do my job. They'd have to watch their death humor, just in case I was in my cubicle. The tension would be unbearable. If only I could skip the awkwardness of being the young widow, so easy to pity.

Jennifer Allen

I'm frozen in the doorway. My legs want to move in reverse, taking me out the door and home to bed. Images of homelessness counter the impulse and win out with a movement deeper into the room. As I scan for an empty chair, I lock into Jill's soft eyes. She's the kind of nurse every patient hopes for: Abounding compassion, warm hands, and a good sense of humor. Moving toward me with her arms wide, she takes me in. The survival armor I wear to get by gives. My breath catches, making a ticking noise at the back of my throat as it disperses into Jill's soft shoulder. She rocks side to side. In this moment, it would be so easy to melt the hard places, surrender, drown, and (hopefully) re-emerge like the phoenix.

Then, through a fat tear, I see the facilitator glance at his watch and whisper something to the co-facilitator. Abruptly, I pull back and smile a thank you, composing my quasi-melted body into a chair. A few minutes into the talk, the co-facilitator sneaks over to me.

"Are you sure you want to stay?" she asks, cupping a hand to my ear. "You really don't have to be here, you know."

"I'm fine," I smile back, now on a tangent of worry about *why* I don't need to be here. Boss-woman Carol isn't at the meeting, so no reassurance to be gained. At lunch I use the phone in the library and call her. No answer. I leave an enthusiastic message about being ready to come back.

After the meeting, I repeat the calls at home from Tom's desk, while Mum and Dad are still out with the kids. I'm careful not to move anything from the positions he left them in. Carol calls back and suggests I take some time with the kids.

"Next week is soon enough. I'll set something up—introduce you to the new *big* boss," she reassures. Her usual wit and mellow tone calm the paranoid tangent I have veered off on.

Return to work: one to-do item checked.

Next item: plan memorial.

I call the Elk's Lodge in Hollister, following through on the reservation for a "function" I had left on the answering machine last week with a guesstimate of next Sunday, the 16th. No one called back because I didn't leave a number. I'd get to it once I had a sure date.

"Yeah?" An older guy with a gruff voice answers on the first ring. I picture a row of Harleys outside and a line of leather vested bikers sitting along the bar inside. My request might be completely out of line.

"Hi, um, I called about a week ago about a function for next Sunday."

Yes, glad you called back, we didn't have a number for you. The hall is available on the 16th. You having a party?"

"Kind of. More like a celebration-of-life, a memorial service . . . for my husband. Is that possible?"

"Hang on Ma'am." The man hesitates and I hear his hand cover the phone, a muffling of voices and then he stumbles through a reply. "Yeah, I guess so. Let me tell you, though, it certainly isn't our usual gig. Mind if I ask why here?"

Somewhere in his reply I get a memory flash. *This is the same place we attended Tom's 30-year class reunion.* I'm not far off with the Harleys. If memory serves correct, the interior is dark and the lodge is in an awkward location out on the periphery of town, by the landing strip. I, too, wonder why Tom picked it.

"Well, he requested it. He was compromising," I say. "Don't get me wrong. He was trying to make it easy for his family to attend, without the Catholic part."

As I explain, the anger I felt when I told Mike of Tom's wishes flares up. He, acting as the spokesman for the family, warned me that without the church, the family might not come.

"I know it sounds crazy," he had said with his best intentions, "but it's a *Catholic* thing. Any chance you'll reconsider?"

It had been all I could do to quip, "No" and get off the line before I dumped a heap of junk that wasn't mine to unload. As I remember this conversation from last week, I begin to understand exactly why it *has* to be at the Elk's Lodge. It is Tom's last way to challenge his family to question the beef behind the rituals they've assumed. He was never interested in converting anyone, only expanding.

"A local family?" the man's voice brings me back.

"Yeah, Sanchez family. Tom Sanchez is . . . I mean was, my husband," I answer.

Jennifer Allen

"Tommy Sanchez? No kidding. God, I'm so sorry. Tommy Sanchez, what a nice kid. Used to work at the grocery store on the corner. His family owned it I think," he says, dating himself as a town elder.

"Yup, that's the guy, only he was 52."

"No kidding. Seems unfair, doesn't it?" he says more to himself than me.

"I guess," I say, not wanting to go where this is headed.

He coughs, returning to the task at hand, "What did you have in mind for the funeral?"

"Oh, not a funeral. It would be a celebration-of-life. I'd make an open invitation for people to come and share memories of Tom," I clarify.

"Would, um, would the *body* be here?" He sounds queasy just considering it.

"Oh, no. Well actually if I get them back in time, I wanted to bring the ashes—in an urn or something. Unless you're not good with that."

"No, no. I'm sure it will be okay." He sounds relieved.

We talk logistics: table setup, T.V. monitor to show videos, cash bar, buffalo wings, and the like. It's a go for next Sunday. By the time we finish the call, old Lance and I are buds.

I'm thanking Tom out loud for a good plan, when I hear my parents drive in with the kids. Returning the pen to the exact angle I found it, I rise and welcome home my two little bundles of living hope.

Jennifer Allen

32

Guardian Angel

After Tom, Days 2–4

Friday is a freebie—permission to enjoy the freedom of unencumbered time before my parents leave and I delve into a busy work schedule. We go out to breakfast at Nancy's Café, then stroll the full length of Del Monte Beach. In the evening, Dad and I hike up to the lookout point with Oceanna bundled in her sling, where we watch the sun melt into the sea. I tell him how grateful I am for all that has happened. Not that Tom died. A while back, I decided his dying wasn't a God-issue. No blame there. Rather, it is how Tom's drawn-out death brought both he and I to life that has me praising the whole experience. Dad doesn't say much. He's a nodder and that works for me.

"It definitely hasn't been all roses," I tell him. "More that it's beyond being sad or happy—bad or good. Someday, I'll weave all of this together. Paintings . . . poetry, who knows?"

Come Saturday I'm homesick dreading Mum and Dad's departure.

"See you soon. Maybe we'll come for Christmas!" I say, hugging each of them with River on my hip. I'm careful not to say goodbye as if the word could break my boy. More likely, it could break me.

The door closes behind them and it feels like a vacuum. No buffer. There is so much to plan—the memorial, the job, the home, and the future I've been pacing in wait for. I'm tempted to fill this naked void with plans except I'm suddenly depleted of all energy. The children and I nestle into bed and I put on 101 Dalmations. All three of us are out cold before it's over. At four a.m., I turn off the T.V. and slip fluidly into dreams until seven, when River wakes me.

"Daddy came to visit, again."

"Really?" I ask, genuinely interested in what he experiences. "What did he say?"

"You're silly, Mamma. He can't talk," he answers, looking at me like I'm some kind of dimwit.

"What do you mean?"

"*Maaammma*," he says exasperated. "Like that!" He points to the ceiling light.

"Oh, I get it. He looks like light. How do you know it's him?" I seriously want to know.

"Because it *is*." He runs out of the room, tired of spelling out simple concepts to a grown-up.

In truth, I'm a little disappointed not to be getting any signs myself as promised. I run through dream scenes of the night. No Tom. Maybe tonight.

Once Oceanna has nursed and we are all dressed, I suggest we walk to the corner market for cinnamon rolls and the Sunday paper. River is ecstatic. It's been over a month since he's been to

Mal's. Skipping ahead down the sidewalk, he announces names of neighbors, orienting me to the ritual being transferred over to me from Tom. At Mal's, River announces to the guy behind the counter that his daddy died.

"Sorry to hear that little guy," the storekeeper consoles, coming around to the front and squatting down at eye level. His hair and eyes are both sandy-brown. With the right haircut, he'd qualify as attractive.

River looks ready to climb up into his lap. I'm mortified.

"We'll take two cinnamon rolls and a paper," I cut in, before one of us does something inappropriate.

"Sure thing." He understands. "Two cinnamon rolls coming up!" He taps the register. I'm relieved he charges me full price.

At home, I set the baby in her swing, make myself some coffee, and River a sippy-cup of rice milk. Pastries in-hand, we settle onto the couch.

"Now you read the funnies, like Daddy," he instructs as he unravels his roll into a long road of pastry.

"Okay," I concur, feeling the importance of this first with River and without Tom.

The paper isn't my gig, so I flounder around the sections, getting distracted in search of the funnies. In my search I find Tom. Not like I didn't know his obituary would be printed, it's just I'd been checking the paper daily since Wednesday and found nothing. I was planning to call tomorrow and see why they hadn't run it after I went to such lengths to get it to them the morning of Tom's death.

As I stare at the handsome picture, taken just after our wedding four years ago, I can't believe it's been just a week since the awkward scene at the photography store where I had it printed.

The clerk had told me the turnaround time would be a week because I didn't have the negative. Uncharacteristically, I had started to cry.

"You don't understand," I had said. "It's for my husband's obituary."

"Oh, I'm so sorry Miss," he had frowned.

"No, he's not dead yet," I had denounced, attempting to defer the pity. It only confused him more.

I remember the clerk called over his supervisor—the fixer of all problems—and he had asked confidently: "What can I help you with Miss?"

Either I looked especially young or my widowhood was showing prematurely. No one had called me Miss since high school.

"Please," I had said. "I need this picture copied by tomorrow—maybe the day after. I can't wait a week. It is for my husband's obituary. He's dying, maybe even dead by the time I get home."

The supervisor's face had turned red and then mine did, sympathetically. "Sure, we can do that for you, Ma'am, no problem. Why don't you get home and we'll see you tomorrow."

"Thanks." I had picked up the picture the next day and sat down to write a customized obituary. Doing so reminded me who I was losing before he was gone. If the obituary didn't capture at least the flavor of his vivacious spirit, the photo would pick up the slack. The envelope had sat by the phone, ready to go, once Tom did. It went out with Wednesday's mail and here he is five days later making his debut in the Sunday paper.

"You sly dog!" I say aloud, remembering back to when Tom told me he'd communicate via the newspaper. By God he has, despite my insistence that it wouldn't be a reliable method.

"What dog, Mamma?" River muffles through a full mouth of cinnamon roll as he pulls the paper aside to see what I'm talking about.

"No dog, River, it's Daddy's picture. Just waiting for us in the Sunday paper. Here's a little story about him."

"Read it Mamma!" he begs. I do, slowly, savoring the one-time deal of an obituary.

"Now funnies," River demands the moment I'm done. We open to the comics. River looks for his favorite.

"Look Mamma guardy angels!"

There, in the one frame comic, was a woman who was waving goodbye to her son and daughter as they went out to play. She was looking up with a confident smile at two angels hovering above the children. Out of her mouth came the words: "Have a good day!" Over her head a thought bubble reads, *All* of you!"

Jennifer Allen

"Hmph. And the name Thomas means twin—two angels," I think out loud. "Looks like Daddy found a way to let us know he's officially you and your sister's guardian angel, River!" I pop off the couch and get a pair of scissors to cut out both his obituary and the comic. I'll frame them together to remind me of the possible connections between the living and the dead, should I ever doubt them.

Returning to the couch, I feel close to Tom, as if he's been sitting with us anticipating the joy we'd feel in this simple ritual. River's delight is contagious and I find myself laughing over silly comics that had never before even lifted the corners of my mouth.

"Thanks," I whisper to the empty side of the couch.

Jennifer Allen

33

Ashes to Ashes

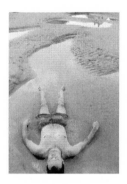

After Tom, Day 7

All morning I clean like a maniac to the tunes of UB40. If it wasn't for the constant interruption of tending children, I might just raise the roof with this swirling energy. The juicer is packed up for storage and Tom's slue of supplements and medications are stashed away on a high shelf for now. I've gone through what's left in his closet after Eliza and Jessica picked out what they wanted, stacking a pile to give away and one to keep. Tom specifically asked me to give his sneakers and a couple outfits to Jerome, a homeless guy who comes by every so often to wash our car windows. I've got them packed and labeled "Jerome" as well as his umpiring gear boxed up for donation to the local officiating association. The mask and strike/ball counter stay, set aside for River. They're reminders of the many games he has watched his daddy officiate and how special he felt when the "blue" came off the diamond between innings and handed him the counter through the fence.

People call and leave kind messages; only I'm too occupied with boxing up the past and making room for what's next, to answer. While I'm in box-mode, I figure I may as well pick up Tom's ashes before my meeting with the new boss. It'll save a trip across town. Monica is scheduled to watch the kids from noon until four, anyway. She's simply a Godsend. I hand off a baggie of milk, kiss my little dumplings goodbye, and drive over to the mortuary. I bounce up the front steps, ring the bell, and the same man—in the same dark suit as a week ago to the hour—answers.

"I'm here to pick up the ashes," I say.

"Oh, yes. Your husband, right?" he asks, tapping his temple, like he's working hard to connect my face with the body he's had in the fridge. And here I thought I was the only person picking up their loved one's ashes.

"I'm sorry, I meant Thomas Sanchez," I say.

He invites me in and then disappears for a few minutes, returning with a white cardboard box, no bigger than a shoebox. In fact, smaller. Way too small to contain my Tom. He hands it to me. I'm fine until I feel the weight of it and read the label: *Thomas Sanchez.*

It's all I can do not to double over. My smile quivers and breaks. I turn away quickly, letting myself out the door and into the street. An oncoming car screeches to a halt, just inches from me, assaulting me with its horn. Hugging the box-o-Tom to my chest, I stumble forward, edging along parked cars until I find a silver Volvo wagon through a haze of tears. Ducking inside, I buckle Tom's box into the passengers seat.

"You're too damn small!" I tell it and start laughing hysterically until my mascara smudges and my abs hurt. *Okay, okay, stop!* But I can't. The meeting begins in fifteen minutes and I'm ready to check into Garden Pavilion. "Job, job, job," I chant incessantly as I drive, leaving no room for anything else. In the

Jennifer Allen

parking lot, I use a baby wipe to clear the black rings from under my eyes and it leaves behind the smell of a new mom—not the best fragrance for perceived professionalism.

Carol meets me in the hall and looks apologetic. "Hi Jennifer, come on in."

How about "welcome back?" Oh no. The lump already lodged in my throat is just one thought away from busting.

We enter the office of the new boss. She leans in and introduces herself from across the desk. Her hand is doughy and her hair over-styled. As a matter of fact, her breath is bad and there isn't a scrap of good I can say about her, knowing what she is about to do.

"I'm so sorry to hear of your recent loss," she begins.

The lump teeters. I swallow it back.

"As you know, many changes have taken place here since you left. One of them is a move away from per-diem in social work. We have full-time employees covering social services now." Pause. "I'm sorry," she says frowning and smiling simultaneously.

Meanwhile, boss-woman Carol is wincing and my throat lump is threatening to explode into wails of laughter or tears. I can't tell which. *Job, job, job* . . . A tedious silence passes before the threat subsides enough to move language around the lump.

"I see. Is there another position available?" I ask, trying not to sound desperate, when I am.

In the minutes that have elapsed since I've learned I no longer have this job, I've already tallied my income from the art therapy job and internship, added estimated social security benefits and come out negative against living expenses and unpaid medical bills. Moving to Maine is the only way I can make it and I'm not ready to move that far from my life with Tom. I need this job.

She looks surprised. "Possibly. There is a position in the outreach program. It would be a 50% pay cut. If you're interested, you're welcome to apply."

"I'll think about it." I stand and shake her hand, squeezing through the dough in search of something of substance. "Thanks."

For the second time today, I turn quickly and let myself out of a building before I explode into public grief. Thank God for cars.

Bone Knowing

On the way home, I pull over and talk to Tom's box. "What a bitch, huh? Can you believe that bullshit?"

He's with me on this one. I can almost see him rise up out of the box like a genie, sit beside me, and shake his head with vigorous empathy.

At home, I enter with box-o-Tom in tow and collapse onto the couch. Residuals of the lump spill forth.

"What is it, Jen?" Monica asks.

River pushes his way to the front lines, "What Mamma, what? Why you crying?" As far as he's concerned, we're past the sad part about Daddy dying.

I want to tell Monica that I lost my job, that I'm already failing as a single parent, and that the body that I've made love to for years and that gave me two children can't possibly be contained in this box. But words snag on new rounds of grief, with every attempt to speak. Instead, I hold out the box. She read her brother's name aloud and it hits her, like it had me—straight in the gut. River grabs at the culprit of all the upset.

"What is it?" he asks.

"These . . . are the ashes . . . from Daddy's . . . body," I tell him between sobs.

"I want to see Daddy!" He booms, trying to pry the top open. Monica and I cry harder at this.

"No, River, Daddy isn't *Daddy* anymore. Just ashes. Here, I'll show you." I'm irritated at my three-year-old's wonder of how his daddy fits in a shoebox. Really, I'm just as confounded as he is.

Inside the cardboard box is a black plastic one. Carefully, I pry open the lid, not sure I really want to know what Tom looks like in ash form. I pull out a clear bag, full of fine white powder mixed with a few shards of bone.

"See?" I hold it up. "That's all that is left of Daddy."

River looks bewildered, like he knows what is left of his Daddy and this bag of stuff has nothing to do with it. No questions follow and I don't think it's because I'd already given him the cremation spiel.

Throughout the evening, he inadvertently pushes matchbox cars up the legs of the coffee table, parks them at the black box, and peeks inside. When he isn't looking, I do the same, only without the cars. Change really floors me sometimes.

34

The Memorial

After Tom, Day 11

Time has cancelled itself out since Tom died. By day I move forward—making plans to return to my part-time medical art therapy job and, reluctantly, set up an interview for the *other* position at hospice. By night I move backward—remembering the history each item in Tom's desk carries as I contemplate what to do with it in an effort to clean out the space for Monica. She'll move in at month's end as a childcare trade. Vacillating from future to past, I'm going nowhere. Perhaps once this memorial is over, time will come unstuck.

      Louise and the girls have been coming by over the past week, dropping off pictures for the memorial collage. The photos are thick with rounded edges and muted colors, just like the ones in my childhood albums. Only I was nine when we converted to the camera of the day and Jessica and Eliza were babies. It dawns on me, yet again, how Tom lived a lifetime before we met. In every photo he's smiling, looking like an adolescent playing house. Playing life, really.

There's one with Tom dressed up as a woman at a Halloween party, looking completely natural among the crowd of females chatting and laughing. In another, he dons seventies garb—a down vest over a western shirt with long pointed collars. His hair scoops to the side—longer, but still fitting like a cap. He's standing in front of the same truck that got stolen and burnt to a crisp in Sacramento. It was probably the envy of his peers; much like his life at the time. Jessica stands on one side of him, her Sanchez eyes squinting from beneath her brown bangs and her freckled nose crunched up in glee. Eliza is on the other. Her cherub features stretch out into a growing girl's face and her blonde curls darker and long. All three hold up fish they've caught and share looks of delight indicative of childhood firsts.

As I'm making final touches on the collage, trying to squeeze in every last picture without cutting them, I feel a mix of intimate familiarity with this part of Tom and sadness; as if too many parts of him went to the grave unknown—at least to me. A voracious appetite is wetted for memories of him from Louise, Jessica, and Eliza. Even his mother could tell me about what kind of baby he was. *What was his first word? What was his favorite dinner growing up?* Maybe I'll take the microphone around to each table today and ask.

I slide the collage into a black garbage bag and load it into the car with care on par with placing my baby into her carseat. The compilation of memories from family back East is already packed. I'll read from it to get things started. That is about the sum of my plan. River is dressed in his favorite play clothes and he's put together a bin of toys to bring along for the celebration. Water droplets begin to spatter against my windshield just as I back out. I catch a glimpse of myself in the rear view mirror and startle. Not only did I forget to dry my hair, I forgot to brush it.

"Shoot!" I turn the ignition off and lock the kids in the car. "I'll be right back, River. I forgot something." I scramble upstairs, force a brush through my heap of tangles and twist my hair into a quick bun. Lipstick can happen en-route and mascara probably isn't the best idea. A quick tag check results in a find on both the sweater and skirt I splurged on for the event. I pull them off and give myself a last check-over in the mirror. Brown is definitely not my color. It was Tom's. He liked earthy colors as a ground for passionate ones, like purple, turquoise and magenta. Today I'm missing the passion-part. It's okay, though, I need all the ground I can get.

As I'm racing out the door, I notice Tom's ashes sitting by the phone. *Whoa, close call.*

The box is still damp from mish-mash of paper maché River and I covered it with a few days ago. Something had to be done with that ugly black box. Ceremoniously, River and I made a concoction of Sunday funnies, water that sat for weeks in Tom's untouched water bottle at the side of the bed, leaves we had collected on our Sunday morning walk to the market, and bunches of Tom's hair stashed in a jewel box from back when it all fell out six months ago. River added some shreds of his favorite colors of paper and squished the mixture between his fingers while I dripped in a hearty dose of glue. Things got exciting when I pulled out the scissors and started cutting snippets of my hair and tossed them in.

"Me too! Me too!" River cried out.

"Okay, stay still." I clipped a few curls from his head and then the baby's. He laughed hysterically at his crazy Mamma. Who'd have known a box of loved one's ashes could be so fun?

River helped plaster the mash onto Tom's box, leaving a window for a photograph. It actually looked nice. Interesting anyway. Certainly better than anything I saw in the mortuary's catalogue. Tom would like having little parts from us holding little parts from him.

And to think I almost forgot this! Small pieces tear off as I carry it to the car, where I wedge a diaper between it and the seatbelt to prevent further damage. Leaving behind a swatch of black rubber, I speed off in hopes of arriving to the memorial ahead of the guests. Oceanna starts screeching ten minutes into the forty-minute drive and River yells for her to stop. In all the hurry to leave, I forgot to nurse her. I'm going out of my skin before I even find the Elk's Lodge. *It's not supposed to be this way,* I think for the hundredth, perhaps even thousandth time this year.

The day is gray like the long stretch of road going out to the tiny airstrip, where the Elk's Lodge sits on the flat cropland outside Hollister. Gray is not a color of Tom's—not at all. I wish Mother Nature would clue into this.

Both children have fallen asleep by the time I get there. There are no Harleys or any guests, for that matter. I worry that it's too far for people from the peninsula to drive and that his family really did boycott a non-religious ceremony. Lance is waiting at the door dressed casually, with navy blue polyester dress pants and a green army coat over a white dress shirt with a bolo at the neck. Tom loved bolos. I made him one out of shells for his forty-fourth birthday. He wore it with silk shirts and vests, creating an eclectic look. Like Lance here. He stamps out his cigarette, comes over to the car and introduces himself.

"Here, let me help you bring things in. Your guests will probably be showing up any minute," he says. I hand him the collage and I take in a crate of Tom's things—a set of teeth he made in the lab, trinkets from our travels, a football from his youth, his umpire mask, the book I compiled of his short stories, photo albums, sport trophies, the golden egg, and whatever else I could come up with to reflect his interests in life.

Inside, a short busty woman with big hair drills me with questions I can't answer: "Do you want me to pre-dress the salad? Are we doing a full bar?"

Honestly, I can't think at all. It'll be a miracle if I get my name right on introductions. "Whatever, just do whatever," I tell her as I hustle about setting up Tom's table, before my children wake and guests arrive. Sweat beads down my sides making wet semi-circles on each side of my skirt. Thankfully my top is long and loose-fitting, good for covering up all sorts of spills and post-baby bulges. A few more deliveries from the car—children and Tom's ashes included—and I'm flooding perspiration. Oceanna cries when I set her down, and milk joins the flow of liquids spewing out of me. If I don't sit down now and nurse her, not only will I look like I've just run a marathon, I'll be caught up in this frenzied whirlwind when people arrive.

From a chair, I direct River in the setup of a small play area for kids, should any come, while simultaneously lifting my cover-all sweater, opening the barndoor on my bra, and bringing

Jennifer Allen

Oceanna's head to the general vicinity. She is like a crazy drunk, wobbling her head frantically and latching onto any skin that could mean drink. Two misses and then, bingo! She's on and I'm forced to sit still.

At quarter after and just as it's starting to sink in that this memorial is for Tom—Button, my lovely sweetheart—people arrive. Louise and the girls stand in the doorway and I wave them over and close up the dairy. Eliza offers to burp the baby while I greet the steady stream of arrivals. People from all parts of our lives show up: the support network, our satellite family made up mostly of buddies from art school, friends from the many chapters of Tom's life, Monica, Joyce, Amy, and even Martha, my best friend from high school who I've only seen a handful of times since graduation. Through the crowd, I spot Mike with Stella on his arm and a wave of Sanchez family behind him.

They came.

I'm so relieved. Had they not, I'd have held a grudge, though more about religious doctrines than any of them individually. Tom wouldn't have wanted me to hold any personal grudges. "Not worth it," he'd have said. His final design challenged the older generation. They've had to push past previously held thresholds just to show up today. For this, I'm grateful to tears.

Stella cries when we hug. "My Tommy . . ." is all she can say. Mike and Suzanne guide her to a table, giving the altar with Tom's ashes on it a wide girth. Tom's aunts, uncles, nephews, and cousins file past with warm greetings and condolences. Everyone knows Tommy was the trendsetting livewire of the family, so when I see pity on their faces for me, I know beneath it somewhere is a wink of recognition that I've been one lucky woman for having been in close proximity to such vitality. Many of them I've met, though it's been a while since I've seen them. Many I've only heard about. Louise knows them all by name and it's a homecoming of sorts for her, having left the family with the divorce. They all move, like a giant herd, over to the tables Mike has deemed for the Sanchez clan. Monica, Louise, and the girls have already hunkered down at the "other" family table in the front. As the large room fills to capacity, I can't help but feel proud of Tom.

Well, look at that, your umpiring bud showed up. And there's cousin Rita. I'm keeping an internal conversation going with Tom, when I notice the silhouette of a figure standing in the entry.

It's Nick. He's scanning for a seat.

I've endured enough awkward moments these days, not to wish them on anyone else, so I go to him. He meets me halfway and we hug.

"Thanks for coming," I muffle into his shoulder. When we part, it feels like we are in a spotlight. I've got either a bad case of stage fright or heavy paranoia going on. Because I can't seem to say anything, I signal him to follow and seat him next to me. The room is a hush. Francisco and Ian are set up and taping. Louise has her hands full with Oceanna. Someone needs to get this party started and it looks like that someone is me.

Not good planning to be the emcee at a husband's memorial, I note.

From up on the platform, I invite guests to come up and share memories, readings, whatever they want. My voice sounds unfamiliar, almost like a game-show host. Mike saves me, coming up to the stage before I'm finished. He covers the family angle, welcoming them and acknowledging with a joke how the Ave Maria may not sound as good in the Elk's Lodge as it does in the church, but the wine is better. He shares a few memories growing up with Tom as a little brother and shows a video he's compiled of family gatherings and vacations. There is a scene of Tom at about fifteen, walking down a sidewalk. His gangly body somehow maneuvers into suave movements. He turns his head and gives that one-sided smile of his to the camera and the video freezes on a zoom. At least half the room breaks into tears. I follow the video with some clips from Tom's last year and the other half joins in. Everyone, it seems, but me. I don't feel sad when I see them. In fact, I feel happy, like Tom is in the room with us.

Things are rolling now. People are lining up to share. My attention moves to the ceiling, where I take the position Tom always envied: that of a fly. From above I look down on our table and I see Louise and I sitting side-by-side, passing Oceanna back and forth, as we each tire from bouncing her. I see Eliza and Jessica sitting, for the first time ever, at the same table as their

310   Jennifer Allen

mother and me. I see Nick, beside me, his full attention on the memories being shared in an attempt to get to know Tom retroactively. I see Joyce and Amy on either side of Monica—all sisters from Tom's different families. And I see River weaving among all of us and popping up from under the table between Nick and I to tug on my arm. It all looks natural, as if these relationships have always been in place. Perhaps, on some level, we all knew we would become a new family, spun together by Tom.

There's no shortage of sharing and then, no shortage of eating the precarious buffet items. We easily max out the three hours I rented the hall. Lance says it's no problem and helps me load up my car once everyone is gone an hour later.

"That was a real nice memorial, Ma'am," Lance says, holding the car door open for me.

"Fitting for a real nice man," I reply, buckling each of my exhausted babies in.

"He sure was," Lance says.

"Thanks for everything!" I holler to him through an open window as I roll out the gravel lot.

The box o' Tom is, once again, buckled into the passenger's seat. All the way home, I talk to them—him, reviewing the day's events while the children sleep. When I get to the part about Nick, my mind short-circuits, replaying those moments over and over again. I tuck a coat over the box, shielding Tom from such invasive thoughts.

It's not until I'm home and the kids are fed, bathed, read to, and put to bed that the bottom drops out. The vacuum of space in our bedroom almost takes my breath away as I slip into the holes of longing and loneliness. Too many times I've walked around those holes and said: "No, not today." A much easier stunt to pull off when Tom's body was here to tend, no matter that his mind was off elsewhere. Now, the holes have grown gaping and hungry. They easily engulf me the moment I run out of items on my must-get-through list.

All night I'm churned deep in the bellies of longing loneliness. My chest is tight and it feels like I have no skin. I hug Tom's pillow with no relief. There is just no getting comfortable with these places, unless I want to go downstairs and chug a few beers. Believe me, if I didn't have two little gems to raise, I might just go there. Anyhow, I know the grief path is through, not around. It's time to walk my talk.

Jennifer Allen

35

Giving Thanks

After Tom, Days 17–20

Dark places have been my staple every night for almost a week. I'm getting impatient. If gratitude weren't culminating in my heart by day, I'd have bailed on the nightshift with grief via some kind of sleep-aid. Only somewhere inside I remember dark makes light perceptible. They are two sides of the same coin. Avoiding one dulls the other, making it shallow.

It must be the reason I feel thankful from my very toenails when the sun shines: To Tom for letting me be part of both his living and dying, for all the people who stepped outside their comfort zones to help us along the way, to grace for showing me beauty in what I thought to be ugly things, for relationships mending along the way, and for these two children Tom gave me. The list ranges from esoteric to the daily concrete.

River loves preschool and has deemed Conrad his best pal. Nick and I manage play-date schedules between them. We're both on the widow side now, only he's coming up on the first year anniversary since Wendy died and I've just begun that road. Already, I want to give back. Just as he did, when he joined a stranger's support network. For now, I write a thank-you letter to friends and family and call up those living locally to join the kids and me for hearty soups and fresh bread on Sunday evenings. It is my way of nurturing the bonds created through Tom's dying. They'll live on, just as he had wanted; just as I need them to now.

11/22/1997
Dear Friends and Family,

Tom's timing makes more sense to me now, in retrospect. Just as I am settling into the reality of life without him, Thanksgiving approaches. We began a ritual of giving thanks at mealtime with River just last Thanksgiving. It was a real change of perspective to take as Tom's health was deteriorating. I'm reminded of this perspective during this time of "thanks" and "giving" as I think about the immense generosity and demonstrations of love sent our way over this past year. The manifestations of these gifts came in many ways: Taking River to the park, dropping off meals, juicing those endless bags of carrots, bouncing Oceanna through that nasty colic, doing laundry, throwing a baby shower—the list goes on. Tom took great relief knowing all of this support existed for his family.

While I grieve losing Tom, I simultaneously celebrate having him in my life for as long as I did. Of course I yearned for more time—time to share delight in our children as they grow and time to ripen into old age together. It wasn't to be. In accepting the inevitability of Tom's death and keeping hope (in it's fluctuating definitions), we were able to begin the mutual process of letting go. Tom shared his dying experience generously, allowing those of us around him to witness glimpses into the great mystery and release any fears we had attached to dying. I have come away knowing in the marrow of my bones that love goes beyond the boundaries of

Jennifer Allen

this life. The whole experience has been utterly exhausting, overwhelming at times, heart-wrenching and, yet, beautifully rich.

As Tom's body gradually faded, his spirit grew strong preparing for the journey ahead. So much led up to his last breath. He took that breath at 7:36 a.m. on November 5th. With the sun beaming down on him from the open window over our bed, he flew free from his house to his home.

It will take time to integrate all I've learned from Tom and life in the last month and over the last years. What I'm clear on right now is the importance of patience and surrendering control.

Somewhere out there, Tom's spirit is smiling widely and sighing: Yes!

Thank you for your support throughout. Enjoy your holidays.

Love,
Jennifer

In sync with gratitude pulsing through my veins, Thanksgiving marks the first holiday without Tom. Things have been *lasts* for so long, I'm actually a bit excited to have a predictable first. Blank slate. No expectations. Joyce invited the kids and me to her place up in Capitola, which means no cooking pressure either. She's the catch-all for Thanksgiving stragglers. This year, we qualify.

Excessive amounts of saliva continue to pool under my tongue when I talk about Tom, causing me to lisp and swallow. I'm already pretty good at telling people my husband died recently without breaking down, though a public breakdown would probably be the best medicine. With a worst fear faced, I'd no longer be held captive by it. *Maybe Christmas.*

Today, I'm a newbie in the world of widowhood with surprising jubilance. Over the course of the meal and the long walk that follows, I've done nothing but talk—about my plans to rent the house two doors down, about new job possibilities, about Oceanna's latest developmental milestones, and about River's regressions.

From across the crowded living room, I've noticed Stella doing the same. Talking. She has stepped out of her element, driving over from Hollister to be among a bunch of unfamiliar faces, to be in it—telling stories about Tom and the past. Her arms and eyebrows fly up in animation just like Tom's used to. Nobody is rolling eyes in passing. In fact, they excuse themselves to the bathroom or to get a drink and return for more of the same. If they're only being polite, they've got me fooled. Stella deserves kudos for doing grief the way she needs to.

It's not for me, though, this going back into time. I'm full-bore into what is right now and on the cusp of the future. The air is salty, a flock of birds take off overhead leaving white splotches all over the roof of my car and I'm walking among friends—light as a feather. Thankful.

Jennifer Allen

36

Winter Solstice

After Tom, Day 46

The Sunday meal-deal has caught on and my kitchen table is predictably crowded once a week. Darkness comes early now. We eat by candlelight, just like Tom and I always have. Amy, Joyce, Louise and the girls, Nick and Conrad, Ed, and Roxanne, Ingrid—whoever shows up, in whatever combination, are the Sunday guests. We break bread together. It's as holy as any communion I've ever experienced. Better yet, laughing is encouraged.

This, I think, *is God. And we are that. No separation.*

Today will be a different routine. We'll bring our church to the beach for the sacred spreading of half Tom's ashes. It's Winter Solstice—the longest night of the year, after which each day gains light. I've chosen this particular day to commemorate both my passage through dark places and Tom's, as his spirit travels through the Bardo.

Tom chose how and where—out to sea from the rocks where we got married. From a box labeled: *Wedding,* I unpack a bunch of seashells that had decorated our wedding cake. As I spread them across the table, River picks them over and gleans the best ones for the task. Carefully, he polishes each one before handing it to me. I pull a scoop of ashes from the mish-mash box and fill each shell, losing most of the ash to the kitchen table. It's not long before River wants part of the action. Sandbox skills come in handy here. He immediately reverses the order: dip shell into box, then polish. No ashes lost.

So here we are, my three-year-old son and I, our hands white with his daddy's ashes, working with intense focus to fill every shell to the brim. I have to wonder if there is any connection between such ventures and his return to diapers. Doubt. Guilt. I've caught them red-handed interfering with me again and I turn them away. From the marrow of my bones, I know this is right. Forget convention. Kids and ashes go together like peanut butter and jelly; like the beginning and the end.

River is proud of his efficient packing job.

"All done!" he exclaims, holding up a basket full of shells. Half the ashes stay behind for another release in the Sierras sometime after the snows melt, just as Tom prescribed. We pack the basket carefully into the car, drive to the beach early and sit on the bench built with the money from condolence cards.

Back when I first called, the Parks Department said there weren't any places available for benches at the beach we where we were married. A day later I got a call saying they could allot one more space, just below the giant cross on the hilltop overlooking the ocean where the river flows into it.

"Perfect!" I said. And it was, especially for a man who named two of his children after bodies of water.

Now, as we sit on the thick slab of redwood still musky with pulp, I tell River the story of his daddy and my wedding down below on the rocks—how he and his sister were gifts from that marriage. Should he ever forget where he came from, he can always come to this bench and remember. Being three, he's more interested in how many rolley-polley bugs he can find than

Jennifer Allen

anything I have to say. I'll have to tell the story again at five, eleven, and seventeen. Oceanna is cooing from the sling on my chest. The same goes for her: A retelling of the story as she grows.

We walk back to the car and gather up the basket of shells. Ed, my sisters, Louise and the girls arrive, and we set off together down the dusty trail. The sun flashes diamonds off waves made choppy by the wind, blinding us as we parade out to the wedding/ashes site. Though our vows weren't traditional, the phrase 'till death do us part runs over and over in my mind as we walk. With the ashes, I'll release our marriage. Not our love though. Death can't take that.

At the tower of sandstone rocks, we stand in silence, looking out from the edge of the Western Hemisphere over the open horizon of the Pacific Ocean. This is where Tom wanted the remains of his earth-self dispersed into currents that span the planet. Grit of his bones will eventually settle deeply into the silent sandy floor. And we landlubbers will wonder from shore about the many places they came to rest.

One at a time we visit the basket, gathering a shell or two and then climb down onto the rocky ledges. In silent prayers of release, we begin sending the shells flying. Mine are thrown in the first wave with others, fast and far, trailing white clouds of dust behind them. Others are coveted close to the heart before release finds its way; ashes mucked into a paste from tears passing between the fingers of clutched hands.

River insists on throwing his own shell and it lands on a rock just below him, where the ashes catch in the wind and blow back into our faces. Instinctually, I inhale them, as if doing so can merge Tom permanently into me. River immediately begins scrambling over the first ledge, intent on a successful release. Ed intercepts him, lifting him onto his hip and down-climbing to the rock below. Ed hands River the half-full shell and holds him out over the water for a fail-safe launch. River shrieks with success and then clings tightly to Ed on the climb up. Though Ed isn't all that into young children, he holds River close until we all finish and return to the cars.

That's when I notice Jessica still has her shell.

"I couldn't," she says pressing it into the hollow of her neck, unready to go fatherless. He'd understand.

Jennifer Allen

37

Faith Tested

After Tom, Days 48–56

A couple weeks before Christmas I got word the hospice
outreach job was mine if I wanted it. Need it, yes. Want it, no.
Which is why I declined. Desperation is not a good place for me to
operate from. Besides, I don't want to be away from the kids that
much. Something will work out. It always has.

Faith is building momentum. So much so that I booked a
flight back to Maine for Christmas and I haven't lost sleep over
how I'm going to pay for it. I'll leave in the morning and return on
New Years' Eve. Just in time to ring in 1998 from the place I've
decided will be home for my children. Here, among the community
woven together by Tom's illness.

The sun is low, shooting orange light over the suitcase that lie open on the bed. A heap of Tom's clothes are spread out on the floor. I paw through them trying to select choice items to bring back East for each family member. Funny thing is, no one I know dresses like Tom did. *Who's going to wear polka-dot shorts or silk suspenders?*

He hears me from wherever his spirit flies and answers: *Oh, those are clearly Sam shorts. They'll prompt a little attitude in his wardrobe. And that sweater? Your dad. He may not wear it, but it will remind him of me. He needs a token.*

We go on like this in unspoken dialog until I've got everyone covered with very little room left for the kids' and my clothes for the trip. Poking through River's closet in search of the winter coat Janice handed down from her son, I find nothing but stuffed animals and retired baby toys.

"River, sweetie," I call over the back deck into our tiny fenced yard, where he's been building a woodchip pile with his toy bulldozer all afternoon, "Do you have your coat on?" It's unlikely, as I practically have to bribe him with cash or candy to wear one. He doesn't answer; probably thinks he's getting the no-coat wrath again.

"Answer me River-kadiver," I holler. "I need to pack it for Maine."

Nothing. I run downstairs and look around. There aren't many places to be in an 800-square-foot home. Adrenaline starts up and I talk myself down remembering the last time, when he was out in the doghouse. I check there. No dog, no boy. As I turn to come inside, I see the gate is swung open.

"River! Riiiiiiiiiiiver!" I'm screaming as I run out into the driveway. Neither boy nor dog is in sight. "River! Kizma!" I take off down the street and realize I can't leave the baby *and* I don't know which direction they went.

"Help! Somebody help!" I yell, not really knowing what else to do. The same neighbors I fought to hold off their demo project are out in their yard setting up forms for a concrete pour. They drop their tools and run over.

"My son, River—he's gone!" I point to the open gate and start bawling. The guy runs off in one direction, his girlfriend takes the other. She stops at her mom's house, two doors down and

Jennifer Allen

delegates door-knocking to her. Meanwhile, I'm frozen. One minute passes, then two. Oceanna's cries catalyze me into motion. I go back in through the gate, upstairs, bundle her into a sling and run out between houses calling for River. Kizma comes trotti,ng up to me alone, wagging her tail as if it's everyday she goes out for a stroll around the 'hood and loses my son.

"Bad girl! Go home Kizma!" I yell. That bee-bop tail of hers sweeps right between her legs. For all I know, she was going to guide me to him, Lassie-style. Now, I've upped and ruined the best lead I have. Kizma creeps away, belly to the grass, looking at me as if I'm a monster. She can bet I will be if I lose a child.

I'm five blocks from home when I hear my neighbor call for me. Clutching Oceanna to me I run toward the voice. She starts to cry and I slow to a race walk. *Do I really need shaken baby syndrome on top of a missing child?* On the corner, I see my neighbor in front of a robust African American man, who looks like he's talking on a portable phone. As I close in, I can see the man is holding something like a grocery bag with a white thing on top. No, it's a child.

"River!" I start running and crying again. "Oh, baby boy!" I rush over to retrieve him and the man pulls away.

"Give me my son!" I demand.

"Back off, Ma'am!" he yells, covering the phone. "Look, I don't know who you are, but this kid's name is Mathew, not River. And if you think I'm handing him over just 'cause you got a face full of tears, forget it. Besides, what kind of mamma lets their baby out in the streets. He was walking right through the middle of this intersection, for Chri'sake. I'm calling C.P.S."

I'm dumbstruck that this could happen to me. I'm a good mother, or at least I was. And it's *my* job to call Child Protective Serevices on parents who are *really* bad.

"Tell the man your name, River," I say with maximum composure for the situation. He stares blankly, completely checked out. Okay, I'm a bad mother, *really* bad.

My neighbor vouches for me: "Look, man. The kid is hers. They live next door. The little guy slipped out the back gate with the dog."

Big Man turns his back to us and continues his phone conversation.

Bone Knowing   323

"Cut her a break, man. Her husband just died." my neighbor says, trying not to look at me.

Big Man turns to us, with River still in tow. He looks at him and then at me as if that tidbit explained everything.

"Okay, Ma'am," he says, tucking the phone into his back pocket. "You take this boy home and watch him close. He needs you. If I see him out here again, I'll finish that call." He lowers River and I snap him up awkwardly, wedging him on a hip under the baby carrier.

"Everything is okay, baby boy. It's all okay," I whisper into his soft curls.

I look back at Big Man and don't know whether to flip him off or thank him, so I nod. The neighbor I've been cursing for the past six months has instantly made rank: St. Neighbor Guy who finds lost children. I thank him profusely as we part ways at my driveway, still not remembering his name.

Inside, all three of us plunk down on the couch and start wailing. River is first, finally checked back in once on safe turf. I'm right behind him, feeling another layer of his three-year-old innocence peeled away. Oceanna starts in sympathetically; too little to know why and little enough for it not to matter. River instinctually nuzzles into a breast, trying to suckle through my shirt. Nursing is his comfort—not his food. In this moment, all the time I've put into weaning him is moot. I can't bear to deny him this. Both children latch on as soon as my shirt is raised and my skin meets their cheeks. They calm, breathing staggered inhales through their noses until their breath matches rhythm with their bobbing chins. The three of us rock in unison until it's dark. They sleep rock-solid, while I lie awake most of the night racking my brain for fail-safe ways to keep from losing anyone, ever again.

The alarm goes off too early. Our morning is hectic with last-minute packing and getting luggage and two little ones on an airplane without putting out my back or losing patience.

Once we are in Maine, a fresh blanket of snow falls. With it, my worries and grief go dormant, in favor of the blinding white landscape and Christmas spirit. Mum has the tree and house decorated with endless lights and a counter full of fudge, shortbread cookies, and fruitcakes she's been gifted on her mail route. The fridge is stocked with prepped meals and eggnog, so she

Jennifer Allen

can invite over anyone on whim to meet her latest grandchild. Nothing better than a new baby to soften the awkward reunion of seeing people for the first time without Tom. They focus on life, rather than death and, somehow, the whole thing seems like a miracle rather than a tragedy. Right now, that works for me.

River has been off with Grampy all morning, traveling the school bus route like a big kid. He returns with bright pink cheeks, snot running down over his chin, and happy as a clam. Later, when he hears us remembering Tom, he stops his play momentarily and adds his own two-cents in present tense.

"My daddy likes those kind of cookies."

Julie gets teary, while the rest of us search for a funny tag-on episode that links into River's line. In no time, we're off and running with more Tom stories. Bittersweet.

On Christmas morning, River opens a large box from Santa and it's a kid-sized guitar.

"Just like Daddy's!" he exclaims, holding it high for everyone to see. Immediately he begins strumming. His enthusiasm, the way he hunches over the guitar, and the way his long fingers curl over the frets—all remind me of Tom. I watch, amazed at how a father lives on through his son via genetics, gestures, and personality.

The void Tom left is partially filled by the children; both in their likeness of him and in the occupation of caring for them. What's left is a giant hole-punch right through my solar plexus. It's not even something I can name—like the absence of someone to parent with, make love to, or talk to about mundane events like the price of gas, or the latest episode of N.Y.P.D. Blue. It's none of these and all of these. In fact, I can't put my finger on the gaping space that transcends my best fantasies of a partner down the line. It seems unfillable.

Nick talked about something like this awhile back in a conversation we had about him starting to date once he made it through the one-year anniversary of Wendy's death. God, I wish I could call him now only he's down in Palm Springs for Christmas with his mother, brother, and kids.

The phone rings. I startle. Mum answers and hands it to me.

"A man, don't know who it is," she says, one eyebrow flared and half a smile. Like she's not sure she should be condoning this. Whatever *this* is.

"I'll take it upstairs," I answer, hoping against the odds that Nick has telepathic powers and knew I needed to talk to him.

"Hello?"

"Hey, Jennifer. It's Nick."

We talk for a while, mostly about family. In usual form, I lose my nerve to ask him about the void-hole-thing. By the time I hang up, it has shrunk to the diameter of a quarter rather than a pie-plate. I can't wipe the grin off my face. Mum looks questioning.

"Oh, it was that guy, Nick. Remember him? With the cute little boy, Conrad?"

Mum nods, smiling to herself. "Yeah, nice guy. I remember him from River's birthday party."

I feel as if an explanation is in order to anyone in earshot. "We were just confirming plans for New Year's Eve. Thought we'd get some kids together from the preschool for First Night," I say, looking away so she can't see this perma-grin I have going on. I'm a hair away from bursting into laughter, like I've been known to do at communions and funerals. It's a compulsion I've never had a handle on.

"Sounds fun. I'm glad you have someone to do things with." She's giving me generic approval in code. Though I don't need it, I'm glad to have it for someday when the time is right.

"He's a good *friend*, Mum."

Once landed back in California, my good *friend* Nick and I meet up for New Year's Eve as planned. River jumps Conrad on sight. With the animation of his daddy, River tells him about the snow he's been playing in all week. Nick greets me with a hug. As we pull apart, my hand runs down his arm. It's full and firm, alive and well. Not like Tom's body I've felt atrophy over the past year. The touch sends a yearning through me to be held by a healthy man— any man who can promise not to die (for at least twenty years).

The boys are off racing to where they have spotted balloons. Nick and I have no time to talk, we are off chasing

Jennifer Allen

behind them—me with the baby stroller and he with his backpack of snacks, wipes, extra underwear, and a jacket for Conrad. He's more organized than most moms I know, including myself. The kids are at the craft table, making puppets for all of five minutes before they hand off their creations to us, turning their attention to a clown making festive hats from balloons.

They eventually slow as the evening darkens and the crowd builds momentum. At eight o'clock we decide to call it a night. As we head to our cars, we come upon a warm glow of candlelight on the lawn of the town hall. I recognize the winding path, doubling back on itself in the shape of a circle. It's a labyrinth. At the center there is a pad of paper, pens and a box where each person pauses in silence and then deposits a resolution for the New Year.

"Let's do it," I suggest.

"Sure," Nick says and we enter. The boys are somber, not even attempting to fire-jump the votive-lined path. Candles equate to something extraordinary to them, something to quiet for. As I move inward to the center, a resolution begins to take form, only coming to language once I'm there.

Dive into life, deep and without regret. I whisper it back to myself and then drop it into the box. On the way out it's me who wants to jump across rows of candles. Better yet, fly over them and soar into the rest of my life. It's the best way I can honor Tom, myself, and God—as I know it.

At the end of the labyrinth journey, Nick and I part ways, heading to our respective homes to tuck children into bed and do whatever it is single parents do on New Year's Eve. Though I'd like to be dancing, sleep is in long order. I'll need it for all the living I have ahead.

Jennifer Allen

Epilogue

August 1998

Nine months have passed since Tom's death. It's the same amount of time it takes to gestate a child, only the seed I've been growing is one of relationship. It will birth into a marriage next month, provided I make it through this impasse. I cannot dive fully into the next chapter of my life until I have completely released Tom.

The second half of his ashes has sat on an altar in the bedroom I've converted into a shrine. They have waited until the snow in the High Sierras has melted. More importantly, they have waited until I could let them go.

Now is that time.

Mike gives me leads on finding the lakes and Louise and Nick agree to stay with the children at base camp while I make the three-day quest with Joyce, Amy, and her partner, Brett. I've arranged for the immediate family to meet us on pack mules at

Lake Marie on the second evening for the final distribution of ashes. It has been nearly impossible finding a date that meets everyone's schedules, including mule availability. As it is, Mike and Suzanne can't make it. And, I'm worried my milk supply might dry up being away from the baby for three days straight. She can take a bottle, but neither of us is ready to wean. Snags like these have me resenting Tom's wishes—feeling pulled backward at a time when I'm moving full-steam ahead.

Our ash-scattering caravan finally hits the road in early August. As we head east toward the Sierras, I reminisce about the many road trips Tom and I made to Mono Hot Springs, Yosemite, Tahoe, and back and forth to Sacramento. The very first time I saw this reservoir was from the backseat of Roxanne's Volvo where bone knowing had paved the way for Tom's charisma to pull me into a life with him. It could only have happened outside the daily grind and familiar places, where I couldn't simply defer to rational thought.

Pacheco Pass is a bridge to another place and time. It even looks surreal: like the soft-haired backs of elephants drinking from the massive body of water that used to be a town. As I swoop at highway speed among the herd of hills, the dream I've had repeatedly over the last nine months since Tom's death surfaces, playing out in silent conversation.

In the dream, Tom walks up from behind me in perfect form, no illness, and puts his hands on my shoulders, kissing the back of my head. I turn in startled shock.

"I thought you were dead!" I say, not comprehending.

Tom smiles not saying anything, though I hear him ask about the children. That should have been a cue it was a dream the first time it happened or even the second. Every time I have had this dream, I've been certain it's real. And every time, I can't bring myself to tell Tom his babies are beginning to bond with a new daddy and I have fallen in love.

"I didn't know you were still alive," is all I can say, while my memory races over his final hours in confirmation that he really did stop breathing. His body went hard in rigor. *It did*

Jennifer Allen

happen. No amount of reality checking keeps me from waking up heavy with guilt.

In the waking-driving dream, I continue where I can't in the sleep version.

You know if you were still here, I'd be with you, right? Tom's face takes up the screen in my mind just as the windshield takes up my eyesight. Not a very safe combination.

There is nothing I wanted more than for you to heal and live. Nothing, I tell him.

Still, he smiles, full-screen. No words.

I'll always love you, Tom. That never changes.

But you aren't here.

He winces for a millisecond and returns to an even smile.

I love someone who is here, Tom—someone who I can share a life with, who can raise these babies with a father. You know love isn't bound to one person in a lifetime. Louise is proof you understand. The love between you, even now—it's palpable. It's what keeps she and I in each other's lives.

Even in my imagination, he doesn't respond. He simply grins in comprehension.

Okay, then. If you aren't going to say anything, give me a sign, huh? My lips move to the internal monolog.

The smile that moves to one side just before he laughs, takes over his expression. Then he disappears with the register of a red light up ahead.

From Los Banos to Fresno I'm occupied with stoplights, directions, and children's story tapes. It's broiling in Fresno. I signal our caravan to pull off the exit. The kids need cold drinks and I need to fill up the gas tank. Wrong exit. There are no stations, only new track housing. As we make a turnabout, I notice the green street sign. It reads: Louise Drive. I wave my hand out the window and point to it. Now I'm paying attention. The next road on the grid reads: Jennifer Street. Honking and pointing, I glance back into my rearview mirror and see Louise nodding and smiling. For miles, I break into laughter, shaking my head in absolute belief. *Funny guy. Yes, I get your "sign." Think you could be any more literal?*

Once we arrive and unload into the base-camp cabins, Louise, Eliza, Jessica, and I muse over the signs, though I dare not

Bone Knowing   331

tell them they were Tom's response to a conversation I was having with him in my mind about the possibility of loving more than one person. Maybe someday we'll share these kinds of things.

In the morning, I feed Oceanna and reassure her I'll be back with full "nursies" in a few days. Amy, Brett, Joyce, and I set out for the two-day trek up to the lakes. The others will load the mules tomorrow morning and meet up with us for the scattering of ashes and a mountaintop feast as the full moon rises. We walk without break all day, hoping to make it past the halfway point by dark. Chatter among us dies down as the sun passes over into afternoon. Fatigue renders us speechless. Collectively, we retreat into ourselves.

The conversation with Tom continues: *You walked this same trail so many times as a boy and then as a man, didn't you?* Instead of being the face on a screen, he is walking beside me this time, nodding.

This is beautiful. Why didn't we ever hike here?
We're here right now, he replies.

I can almost feel his enveloping hand holding mine. When I wander off to wedding logistics, he leaves. Then I am with myself, noticing the backpack digging into my hips and the corns on my pinky toes pining for more space. Discomfort, yes—guilt, no. In the miles left before we set up camp for the night, my body strains past its customary energy output, while the rest of me sheds any self-imposed restraints on possibilities. By the time the moon is up and my head hits the pillow, anything—even maintaining a loving relationship with Tom—is possible (though I can count on conversation being heavily weighted to one side).

When I wake, both breasts are engorged and look like the California landscape from the air. Neither sister will lend a suckle simply to keep our adventure free of an exploding breast.

"Sorry, too weird," they say. If either of them had babies, they'd know what I'm asking is no different than changing a diaper. Brett is out of the question. Asking him to make the jump from sex object to food source is too much. I'm left to my own devices. Hand expressing hasn't ever worked. I end up bruised over a couple drops of milk. Seeing as this is probably the only time in my life my breasts will be big enough to reach my own mouth, I give it a try. It requires major contortions for each

Jennifer Allen

mouthful of fluid that tastes like soap. I spit and go back for more, until I'm back to a size C and the roof of my mouth has a hickey. It's the perfect way to realize the resources of my own body. If anyone starves on this quest, it won't be me.

I'm achy and tight on the outside as we begin the ascent. On the inside, I'm soaring open skies. Tears streak my dusty cheeks spontaneously throughout the day. The ecstatic realization that love really has no limits overtakes me. No memories from the past or plans of the future pull me from this. All day, I climb and feel love.

By afternoon, the steep rocky trail littered with branches of redwood extends beyond tree line, expanding into an open path toward snow-tipped mountains in the distance. Brett checks the map and declares our successful arrival at Lakes Rose and Marie. As we crest the next incline, white cirrus clouds overhead are perfectly mirrored back in the still waters of Lake Marie. The path ends in an expansive spray of lush grasses reminiscent of a postcard from Switzerland with the contrast of snow-capped peaks as backdrop. We come to an unspoken consensus on a common camping area and drop our packs. We'll part ways until late afternoon when the mules carrying the remainder of our clan and our dinner are due to arrive.

No thoughts pervade me, leaving my body to do as it sees fit. My hands grasp the bag of ashes. My legs carry me to a private inlet at the water's edge. No plan. I'm bending, setting the bag down on a slab of granite. And then rising slowly, I inhale the bouquet of stone, warmed to scent by the sun—and grass, rooted deeply into the moist earth. At standing, my eyes sweep over the full circle of beauty around me: a green-yellow rise of meadow to the southwest, a row of overlapping purple and white mountains to the north, a sparse forest of gnarled pines to the south, and a bird's-eye view of the valley below to the west. My gaze blurs with wetness as I lower it to the ashes at my feet. The bag is barely discernable from the rock on which it sits. The dark waters blend with green-purple landscape and blue-white sky, creating a fluid kaleidoscope of color.

From deep in my belly, a powerful surge arises. A low, throaty moan surfaces, growing louder and pulling my insides up with it. Clothes are a cumbersome restraint to this force. I peel them off and feel naked beyond the skin. Finally, there are no barriers between me and the world or even me and myself. I sprawl out over the downy grass and place the bag on my belly.

"Finally, Tom. No barriers between us," I whisper between sobs, feeling closer to him now, than in life. I long to imprint his being into mine.

A vague hunger comes through my solar plexus. I spread my arms, arching my chest in surrender. I've felt this before and tried satiating it with lovemaking, though it never lasted. This hunger wants more—a permanent merger. It has me opening the bag and scooping Tom's ashes out onto my stomach, where I work them into a paste with the breast milk that leaks out freely and pools at my navel. Rising, I smear the life-death substance over my entire body. With my face and hands turned skyward, I let the sun dry Tom into every pore.

The hunger subsides. As I step out onto a granite overhang and look into the dark water, beyond the reflection of my chalky white body, time disappears. No thought. Without warning, my body leaps forward, piercing the white blur head-ward into icy blackness. Every nerve knows full well I'm alive. And what isn't alive comes free of me, swirling to the bottom like snowfall. The silence under the surface is intimately familiar and I feel as if I've met Tom halfway. Part of me wants to swim deeper, settling with his ashes to the bottom in absolute stillness until one day we are swept up in a current and delivered by rivers to the ocean, where we'll join other specks of him in the constant undulation of tides.

Dependence on air returns me to the world of the living. Slowly, I lift myself onto a rock. What was not mine to keep is gone and what will always be mine has already become part of me. From a high mountain place, I can clearly see all the pieces that led to now coming together in perfection. With palms pressed in prayer at heart-level, I bow deeply to Tom's spirit, to the mountain peaks, to the ashes swirling below the silver surface, and to the knowing in my bones. All are God speaking.

Jennifer Allen

Acknowledgments

Gratitude, like I'd never experienced before, was one of the most unexpected gifts that came out of living with Tom's dying. For this, I thank him.

As I reflect on how this book came to be, I feel a surge of gratitude for those who lived out the story with me and for those who have supported it coming to print. It is with heartfelt appreciation I give thanks to the following people:

To Joyce Lyke, Jessica Britt, and the Medicine Wheel family they formed. After four years in our circle, the culminating vision quest sparked a clear knowing that I was to write. The ongoing encouragement of our tribe supported its manifestation.

To Amy Schwartz for showing up in my life and helping both of us get the ball rolling—me with writing the story and she with continuing to live hers out.

To Barbara Tam for confirming Tom's blessing.

To Anne Marie Hagn for her support both during Tom's decline and the many years after via the women's group she formed. For eight years on every Tuesday, these women inspired me with truth-telling.

To the Endeavor group: Judd Miller, Cindy Gum, and (especially) Judy Tatelbaum, for their ongoing faith in this book.

To Kedron Bryson and Eric Elfman for bringing me along the steep learning curve of writing with their keen editing skills; to Scott Brearton for clean-up proofreading; to Lisa Gebo for her enthusiasm in the project; and to Fred Lakin, a kindred writer on the path, for his technical generosity.

To my children, Conrad, River, and Oceanna for being my anchors to the present and for being so very patient with all of the time I've spent glued to the computer screen in uninterruptible concentration.

To my sisters and parents who are a backbone in my life with their inherent support.

To the many good listeners who lent their ears and feedback to readings of this work as it progressed.

And finally, to my sweet husband for reminding me to love well and for respecting the knowing in my bones.